Robert Garran has produced the most comprehensive history of the intellectual, political and economic trends which set the stage for the East Asia financial crisis.

David Hale

The first attempt to document the story of East Asia in crisis comprehensively—the economics, the politics, the response in each of the troubled economies and their major partners in the region . . . an intelligent guide to the most important questions that have been raised by the crisis.

Peter Drysdale

Tigers Tamed
The end of the Asian miracle

ROBERT GARRAN

UNIVERSITY OF HAWAI'I PRESS
HONOLULU

To Julie and Eleanor

Copyright © 1998 Robert Garran

All rights reserved. No part of this book may be reproduced or transmitted in any form or by any means, electronic or mechanical, including photocopying, recording or by any information storage and retrieval system, without prior permission in writing from the publisher.

First published in 1998 by
Allen & Unwin
9 Atchison Street, St Leonards 1590 Australia

Published in North America by
University of Hawai'i Press
2840 Kolowalu Street
Honolulu, Hawai'i 96822

Library of Congress Cataloging-in-Publication Data

Garran, Robert, 1957– .
  Tigers tamed: the end of the Asian miracle/Robert Garran.
    p.   cm.
  Includes bibliographical references and index.
  ISBN 0-8248-2160-2 (alk. paper)
  1. East Asia—Economic conditions. 2. Asia, Southeastern—Economic conditions. I. Title.
  HC460.5.G374 1998
  330.95—dc21   98-38572
                                                           CIP

Set in 10/11.5 pt Arrus by DOCUPRO, Sydney
Printed and bound by Griffin Press Pty Ltd, Adelaide

10 9 8 7 6 5 4 3 2 1

Contents

Acknowledgments vi
Note on terms vii
Introduction 1

1 The end of the Asian miracle 6
2 Japan rises 22
3 Flying geese and tigers 45
4 Japan stumbles 71
5 Meltdown 94
6 Korea crashes 119
7 Indonesia implodes 137
8 Taming global capital 159
9 The economic consequences of the crash 180
10 After the miracle 193

Appendix: The crash by numbers 208
Endnotes 215
Bibliography and sources 221
Index 224

Acknowledgments

I am very grateful to all who helped with this book, with interviews and in many other ways. They include Narongchai Akrasanee, Heinz Arndt, Richard Cookson, Ken Courtis, Harold Crouch, Peter Drysdale, Patrick Gallagher, Ross Garnaut, Don Greenlees, David Hale, Hal Hill, Kim Byung-kook, Alex Kinmont, Jesper Koll, C.H. Kwan, Moon Chung-in, Masayoshi Morita, Ross McLeod, Gaby Naher, David Nellor, Padmaja Padman, Hiroshi Osedo, Richard Samuelson, Dennis Shanahan, Arthur Stockwin, Peter Tasker and Nick Valery. Thanks to Paul Kelly, who as editor-in-chief of the *Australian* sent me to Tokyo, and to David Armstrong, his successor, for their support; to Peter Alford, James Cotton, Win Garran, Luke Gower, Richard McGregor, Peter Tasker, Patrick Walters and Alan Wood, who read drafts and provided invaluable feedback; and to Julie Garran, Eleanor Garran and Tim Wood for their patience and support during the gestation. A few portions of this book have appeared in different form in the *Australian*, and I am grateful for permission to reprint them.

Robert Garran
Canberra, July 1998

Note on terms

The geographic scope of this book is East Asia, that is North-East Asia—China, Hong Kong, Taiwan, Korea and Japan—and South-East Asia. The Association of South East Asian Nations (ASEAN) includes all the countries of South East Asia except Cambodia. It comprises Brunei, Indonesia, Laos, Malaysia, Myanmar (Burma), the Philippines, Singapore, Thailand and Vietnam. The four largest ASEAN economies are Indonesia, Thailand, Malaysia and Singapore. The book's main focus is on the more 'miraculous' eight among those fifteen—Japan, the four tigers (Korea, Taiwan, Hong Kong and Singapore) as well as Indonesia, Thailand and Malaysia. References to Korea mean South Korea. North Korea is named explicitly when relevant.

Asian names are given according to local custom, usually family name first, although Japanese family names are given last in accordance with western practice. Many Indonesians have no given name. Currencies are expressed at the exchange rate prevailing at the relevant time. Dollars are US dollars.

Introduction

In many ways 'miracle' seemed a justly deserved appellation for the dazzling economic performance of East Asia in the half century since World War II. A remarkable number of countries in the region achieved extraordinarily high levels of growth that transformed them from impoverished backwaters to industrial dynamos. Since 1960 the region's top performers—Japan, Hong Kong, South Korea, Singapore, Taiwan, Indonesia, Malaysia and Thailand—grew more than twice as fast as the rest of East Asia, three times as fast as Latin America and South Asia, and five times faster than sub-Saharan Africa. Average real income per person quadrupled in the five North-East Asian countries and doubled in the three South-East Asians.[1]

But the idea that this was a miracle is a myth. And in 1997 the myth was shattered by a financial crisis that began in Thailand and spread quickly to the Philippines, Malaysia, Singapore and Indonesia. By October Thailand and Indonesia, small players on the world stage, had both agreed to IMF (International Monetary Fund) rescue packages aimed at stabilising their battered financial systems. When in that same month the Hong Kong share market was mauled and in November South Korea's banking system almost seized up, it became clear that the rest of the world would not be immune. The storm reached Japan in mid-November. When a large sharebroker and several smaller banks collapsed, the world's second largest economy and its largest provider of credit narrowly avoided a financial catastrophe that would have had global reverberations. By early 1998 emerging market economies throughout the world had been hit by the combined effects of intense competition from South-East Asia and increasingly

1

nervous investors. The issue then was how far the crisis would affect the large western economies, the United States, Europe, and the rest of the rich world.

The 1997 financial crisis punctured the myth of a distinctive East Asian model of economic development, the idea that the region had discovered a blueprint for faster economic growth. In important ways it was the myth of the Asian miracle that created the East Asian boom in the late 1980s and early 1990s. When investors realised that the miracle was built on sand, the boom was punctured. The myth ended with an abrupt collapse in confidence that sent East Asian currencies, share markets and real estate prices tumbling and delivered to those countries a severe recession.

In what sense was the miracle a myth? Not because East Asian countries did not have substantial and impressive achievements—they did—but because the exaggerated claims for those achievements inspired hubris, a false sense of invincibility. Like most myths, this one contained elements of truth. A surprisingly large number of East Asian economies achieved remarkable rates of economic growth in the years after World War II. Some of them did so with the use of interventionist policies aimed deliberately at 'beating the market'. Clearly some elements of the Asian model were highly successful. What was mythical about the model was the belief that it showed the way to a new kind of policy for economic development, a distinctive and superior road to prosperity. The 1997 crisis should kill off the nostrum that industry policy and Asian values are the keys to high growth.

Economics does not tell the whole story of the Asian crisis, but it is the most important ingredient. The main elements of the economic story are clear: the crisis stemmed from excessive short-term borrowing that led to economic overheating; problems were made worse by fixed exchange rates, inadequate financial systems, cronyism, corruption and inadequate political responses. But within the economics debate there are several key disputes. One question is whether the economies of Asia suffered from a cyclical boom and bust but still remain fundamentally sound and will eventually recover, or whether their problems are more deep-seated. Another question is whether the bust was made worse than necessary by the irrational response of financial markets, and by the actions of the IMF.

The argument here is that while there were cyclical elements to the collapse, there were more deep-seated problems too that will take more to repair than simply awaiting the next upturn in the cycle. The poorly managed financial systems and the cronyism and corruption were fundamental to the crisis; their roots lie deep in the much-vaunted Asian model of economic growth. On the second question, the crisis was made worse by the response of investors in financial markets, in a word, by panic. But panics are a ubiquitous feature of economic life, a factor that points to an important qualification of rational economic behaviour. It was undue faith in the verities of rational economics that led to the overbearing prescriptions of the IMF, imposing remedies that in the long run were correct and would have helped the suffering economies, but in the short run, especially in Indonesia, compounded the problems.

The Asian model encompasses many ideas. Some aspects of the model conform with free-market economic principles; some aim to augment them; other elements, sometimes called Asian values, have more to do with politics and culture than with economics. The argument here is not that every element of the Asian model was mistaken, but that the loose collection of ideas that made up the model took on a life of its own. The whole became greater than the sum of its parts, creating the myth of the miracle. Investors came to believe, in their hearts if not their heads, that East Asia could do no wrong. The rush to invest in Asia became a speculative mania in which mass investor psychology took over from cold, rational assessment. When the mania was deflated, the miracle ended.

The proponents of the Asian model have several goals. One is to describe and explain the unusual success of East Asian economies. Another is to offer a guide to policy in other countries. If the elements that contributed to East Asia's success could be identified and if the model were robust enough, it would provide a powerful tool for policy-makers throughout the developing world. But these aspirations suffer the fate of much social science: the systems they describe and explain are so complex that although some regularities can be identified, they are often not uniform and predictable enough to provide reliable prescriptions or predictions. That does not mean that the effort should not be made, but that the conclusions reached should be treated with humility. It is a postmodern dilemma: the tension between the contingency of knowledge and the desire to find consistent patterns and rigorous explanations.

The East Asia miracle debate has become polarised between those who argue for and against the idea that interventionist industry policy is the key to higher growth. The pro-industry policy school, the revisionists, have merit in pointing to the importance of politics, political institutions, culture and history in explaining any country's development. This is a useful antidote to the more extreme and austere market approaches to economic development. But the revisionist view cannot sustain its claim to offer a useful guide to future policy, in East Asia or elsewhere.

The Asian model was only ever useful for countries behind the frontier of technology and industrialisation. Once Japan, Korea, Singapore, Hong Kong and Taiwan caught up with the rich world's level of technology the model had little to offer. And even if the Asian model once held a useful development formula, the 1997 crash shows that economic conditions have changed in fundamental ways, especially as a result of increasingly rapid global movements of capital.

Asia's leaders, and their boosters in the West, made the mistake of believing their own mythology about the rise of Asia and ignored the dangers this posed. They applauded the strengths of the Asian model—and their success shows its virtues were considerable—without recognising its weaknesses.

The weakness varied from country to country. Many countries in East Asia suffered the dual economy syndrome that afflicted Japan throughout the 1990s: an efficient, competitive export sector, increasingly dragged down by an inefficient, corrupt and costly domestic sector. The crisis of 1997 began in foreign exchange markets, but the trauma of the massive currency sell-offs exposed deeper weaknesses. Countries with sounder financial systems and more efficient domestic economies, such as Singapore and Taiwan, escaped relatively unscathed.

The region's future need not be bleak in the long run. But recovery from the meltdown in the countries worst affected could take half a decade or more. East Asia will have to wait until worldwide demand for the products it excelled at making catches up with its bloated capacity. It will have to repair its seriously flawed financial and economic systems—moves that in some cases will exact a high political and social price. When East Asia does recover there will be no repeat of the rapidity of economic expansion of the miracle years, although once they rebuild there is no reason they can't return to a more measured prosperity.

The 1997 crisis has undermined claims that a distinctive set of Asian values will produce superior economic outcomes. Some so-called Asian values are shared with the West; others, used to defend authoritarian political systems, contributed to the severity of the crisis. The notion of Asian values is recent and self-serving, but its influence has been strong. Yet while the crisis has undermined the potency of Asian values, it has also weakened the authority of another influential prescription for economic success: the more extreme versions of the free-market model espoused by the IMF and others.

The effects of the crisis go beyond economics. The stories Asians and others use to explain East Asia's successes and failures and its place in the world will change radically as a result of the 1997 crisis. The crisis will bring changes in social and cultural attitudes, and in the balance of power within the region. In responding to the crisis Japan was ineffectual and the United States heavy-handed and overbearing. China, by contrast, did everything asked of it by other Asian countries and the United States, and its influence and prestige have grown accordingly. The gradual shift in the region's balance of power towards China accelerated as a result of the crisis, an outcome that will not be welcome to the West and that will add to uncertainty within the region.

Chapter 1
The end of the Asian miracle

The annual meeting of the International Monetary Fund is usually a staid affair. But the gathering in Hong Kong in September 1997 was different. The choice of venue was meant to symbolise the transfer of the quintessentially capitalist state, Hong Kong, to the still nominally Communist China—a sign of the quiet revolution in the global economic order. But instead of the afterglow of the Hong Kong handover, conversation was dominated by the financial storm raging to the south. The crisis had begun with the collapse of the Thai currency on 2 July and quickly spread to the other largest nations in South-East Asia: Malaysia, Indonesia and the Philippines. Within months of the IMF meeting the turmoil had spread to Hong Kong, South Korea and Japan, and was threatening economic prospects throughout the world.

Two men were the focus of attention at the Hong Kong meeting: Malaysian Prime Minister Mahathir Mohamad and American billionaire financier and philanthropist George Soros. Mahathir believed he and other Asian leaders had learned to beat capitalism at its own game. His Look East policy, first enunciated in 1981 and still his exemplar, held Japan's postwar 'developmental state' as a model for Malaysia, a model superior, he said, to that offered by the West.

'After World War II we saw Japan's phenomenal progress and concluded it has the formula for rapid development', Mahathir wrote in 1994. 'East Asia, with Japan leading the way, will continue to drive the world economy and play an increasingly important global role in the coming century.'[1]

Soros is said to have made $1.6 billion in 1992 when he sold sterling ahead of the United Kingdom's decision to pull out of the European Exchange Rate Mechanism and Mahathir blamed him for the Asian meltdown. Soros had made billions from his market speculations and spent more than another $1 billion in aid to former communist states of Eastern Europe. His philanthropic Open Society Institute has been highly critical of the military regime in Burma, another cause of annoyance to Mahathir. Mahathir and Soros had diametrically opposed views of what had gone wrong in Asian financial markets, differences that crystallise the debate on the factors behind Asia's economic miracle, and its downfall.

In September 1997, as the heavies of the financial world descended on Hong Kong, the problems, though serious, seemed to be local. For several months before the IMF meeting, Mahathir had been attacking speculators in general and Soros in particular, branding him the leader among the rapacious speculators he said had set out to ruin his country and the region. 'We have definite information that he [Soros] is involved. Of course, he is not the only one. Others followed suit. But he started it', Dr Mahathir said just before the IMF meeting.[2]

Soros had been attacking ASEAN currencies to punish them for accepting military-ruled Burma into the organisation, Mahathir said. 'All these countries have spent 40 years trying to build up their economy and a moron like Mr Soros comes along with a lot of money.'[3] All through the turmoil Mahathir, the quintessential East Asian chauvinist, had insisted that Malaysia's economy was fundamentally sound and that the financial troubles were the fault of speculators. He hinted at a Jewish conspiracy behind the crisis, pointing out that Soros was a Jew.

Soros was a quirky representative of global finance and an ironic choice of target for Mahathir's venom. Although one of the most successful exploiters of the capitalist system, Soros had an abiding wariness of some of its key features—especially the consequences of unbridled laissez-faire capitalism and the 'excessive individualism' of the West. Soros is one of the most astute critics of the consequences of the growing spread of financial markets and of the kinds of dangers exposed by the East Asian financial turmoil.

By September, South-East Asia's financial turmoil was showing no sign of abating and Mahathir's attacks on Soros were becoming increasingly strident. There was great anticipation over what the two men would say when they appeared, separately, at the IMF meeting. When he addressed hundreds of financiers on 20 September, Mahathir did not disappoint. 'I know I am taking a big risk to suggest it, but I am saying that currency trading is unnecessary, unproductive and immoral. It should be made illegal. We don't need currency trading. We need to buy money only when we want to finance real trade', he railed.[4] 'The traders apparently make billions with each transaction . . . Their profits come from impoverishing others, including very poor countries and poor people', Mahathir said.

Soros replied the next day. 'Dr Mahathir's suggestion to ban currency trading is so inappropriate that it does not deserve serious consideration. Interfering with the convertibility of capital at a moment like this is a recipe for disaster. Dr Mahathir is a menace to his own country', Soros said. 'He is using me as a scapegoat to cover up his own failure. He is playing to a domestic audience and he couldn't get away with it if he and his ideas were subject to the discipline of an independent media in Malaysia.' Soros denied that he had been a big player in the crisis. His huge investment funds had not sold any Malaysian ringgit or other ASEAN currencies for two months before the crisis hit, or during it.

If Soros was not impressed with Mahathir's comments, neither were global and Malaysian investors. On Monday, when the markets next opened, the ringgit fell another 2 per cent and the Kuala Lumpur share index fell 3.4 per cent.

The irony of the spat between Mahathir and Soros is that the forces that undermined Mahathir's Asian model are in some respects equally vehemently opposed by Soros—though for different reasons. Mahathir might even agree with Soros that capitalism has to strike a balance between the needs of the community and the individual. Where they would differ is on where that balance should lie.

Even in a narrow sense, their spat at the Hong Kong IMF meeting was important enough in that it raised two important questions: what were the reasons for the financial meltdown that began with the collapse of the Thai baht in July 1997? Who was to blame? But the Mahathir–Soros dispute goes further, to the heart of a key debate: if Asia really had discovered a better way of running capitalism the lessons could help not just the rich world become richer, but the poor world too. Was Mahathir right, that the otherwise good work of the East Asian miracle had been undone by capricious and wicked speculators? Or was Soros right, that Mahathir was using him as a scapegoat to cover up his own failings—and by extension, the failings of the East Asian miracle model?

This book seeks to answer those questions, in the light of events that have radically altered perceptions of East Asia's prospects and undermined shibboleths in both Asia and the West about the region's dynamism.

Mahathir and the markets

Mahathir has long made a virtue of basing his nation's economic development on the Japanese model. He likes to contrast Asian virtues of frugality, hard work and loyalty with western decadence. Another of Mahathir's themes is that the West, especially America, fears the rise of Asia. The West sees the East as a threat to its own global dominance, Mahathir says. The message resonates well in a region where, aside from Japan and Australia, there is at best only grudging acceptance of America's dominating economic and military presence.

American politicians, academics and journalists provide plenty of fuel for Mahathir's case. Two decades ago the message from the West about Asia was upbeat. In the early 1980s American scholars—notably Chalmers Johnson in *MITI and the Japanese Miracle*—popularised the notion of a distinctive Japanese economic 'miracle'. The miracle moniker was soon applied more broadly throughout the region as other countries imitated Japan's success.

Particularly striking was their view that Japan had demonstrated an alternative model of economic development that improved upon laissez-faire capitalism. This challenged the traditional 'neoclassical' or 'modernisation' view that Asian economies were in a transitional stage of economic development and would in due course come to resemble more fully developed economies, epitomised by the United States. The most influential proponent of the modernisation view was Edwin Reischauer, an American ambassador to Japan and historian. In his book, *Japan: A Reinterpretation*, Patrick Smith argues that Reischauer and his circle, known as the Chrysanthemum Club, were uncritical apologists for Japan who created a highly misleading picture of its inevitable progress towards a western model. Parts of Reischauer's work 'can fairly be called propaganda passed off as history', Smith argues. In the late 1980s the Chrysanthemum Club was challenged by a loose group of journalists and scholars known as the revisionists— a moniker bestowed by journalist Bob Neff in a *Business Week* cover story entitled 'Rethinking Japan' on 7 August 1989. They were bound, as Smith says, by the assumption that the modernisation paradigm is false, and that the West should reassess the way it looks at Japan. The revisionists argued that Japan had assumed only the outward trappings of democracy, that its institutions did not function as westerners expected, that the government was an advocate as well as a regulator, and played an active role in the economy with defined social and economic goals. The revisionists drew another important conclusion: here was a model for economic development that could lift nations from poverty.

But it did not take long for a negative message to emerge in response to the revisionists' insights: Japan was not playing fair, and was exploiting the free-trade system championed since the war by the United States without reciprocating by opening to the West their increasingly wealthy markets. The popular view in America was that Japan was cheating, that Japan was stealing American jobs.

Mahathir knew of the hostility towards Asia spawned in the United States by the revisionist stance, a view that had had a strong influence on the administrations of both Republican George Bush and Democrat Bill Clinton. A consummate politician, Mahathir exploited the ambiguity in western attitudes towards Asia and the unsavoury social consequences of western capitalism. Mahathir wanted to choose selectively from the benefits offered by the West. He wanted its technology and its capital, but not its social problems or the democratic values that could weaken his hold on power. He championed the notion of Asian values, a view that encapsulated his idea that Asia could take a different path.

But the rules of the economic game were changing behind Mahathir's back. There were always some risks in the Asian model, but for half a century they had mostly been avoided. Only Japan, the vanguard of the new model, had suffered in recent years from its shortcomings.

How Japan paved the way

Japan played a bigger role in fomenting the 1997 crisis than any other country. Japan was the inspiration for the idea of a distinctive Asian model of development. And it was the rise in the yen until mid-1995 that created both a flood of capital and an export boom in East Asia. When the yen fell the conditions that created the boom were reversed. The flow of capital slowed, and the region's exporters lost some of their competitive edge.

Japan, the original miracle economy, was the largest source of the capital that created the 1990s East Asian boom. The Japanese economy is biased towards very high levels of investment in manufacturing. This was the basis of its success; this was the way Japan beat western capitalism at its own game. To fuel that investment Japan's financial system evolved in ways that encouraged households and corporations to save and invest at high levels. The system worked well as long as the Japanese economy itself was growing rapidly, or there was strong growth in demand for its products from offshore. Japan was lucky that for a decade after its growth slowed to the rate of the mature, western nations, there were other sources of demand for the surplus capital it produced. In the early 1980s it was the massive budget deficits of the United States under President Ronald Reagan that did the trick; in the late 1980s it was Japan's own speculative bubble; in the 1990s it was East Asia.

The tendency towards high investment was both a fundamental cause of the original Japanese miracle and that of many of its imitators, and the source of its recent weakness. The increasing value of the Japanese yen from 1985 until 1995, a phenomenon the Japanese call *endaka*, gradually undermined Japan's advantage as an exporter. Yet against the expectations of western economists Japan continued to save more than it consumed and invested at home. Japan has a dual economy, a highly efficient export manufacturing sector, and a cosseted, closeted, sclerotic high-cost domestic sector that performs poorly by world standards and restricts the opportunities for domestic investment. With the end of its own speculative bubble in 1990, Japan's surplus savings had to go somewhere, so they went offshore, with an ever-increasing proportion flowing to the rest of East Asia. The other large sources of capital that fuelled the East Asian boom were the swelling pension funds of North America and Europe. But by far the largest proportion came from Japan.

The upsurge in investment in North-East and South-East Asia gave these countries their big break in world markets. By setting up factories outside Japan where labour was cheaper and costs lower, Japanese companies could keep a hold on the world markets for cars and consumer goods they had come to dominate. Exports boomed from South-East Asia, and from Taiwan, Hong Kong, South Korea and China, and increasingly from the newest member of the miracle economy club, Vietnam.

Flaws in the model

A surge of capital investment, much of it from Japan, fuelled an East Asian boom. In the euphoria of the boom lenders and borrowers grew greedy and careless. Investment poured into export sectors, leaving the problems of the domestic economy untreated. East Asia's economic institutions were too weak to cope with the flood of capital. Cronyism and corruption added to the weaknesses. In 1997 confidence in the miracle evaporated and the boom busted.

But there is another important dimension to the story: the belief in a unique and distinctive Asian model of economic development. Mahathir in Malaysia, Soeharto and Habibie in Indonesia, Lee Kwan Yew in Singapore, among others, believed that East Asia's mix of authoritarianism and market intervention had created an Asian miracle that would be immune from problems that afflicted western economies.

The first exponent of the Asian model was the original miracle economy. Japan had a powerful influence on virtually every other country in East Asia as a model of economic development. Theorists have tried to impose order on the lessons East Asia drew from Japan, but in practice the process was *ad hoc* and flexible, with features that worked retained and those that did not work sometimes discarded. There has never been a clearly designed Asian model template that can be applied neatly onto any country that wants to try it. There is a great diversity of features behind the successes and failures of individual East Asian countries, in their paths to economic development, in their systems of government, in their cultures and in their histories.

Attempts to create a theoretical underpinning came after the event. But even without a coherent theory there are important common elements in different examples of the Asian model that appealed to policy-makers throughout East Asia. The most valuable was an outward, export orientation, an effort to create industries that could compete on world markets.

For decades the results of the Asian model were impressive. But the events of 1997 have exposed the weaknesses of the model. Elements of the model that may once have been effective became key factors behind the crisis. One was the effort to beat the market by force-feeding manufacturing investment. Another was the attempt to manage credit to encourage investment into chosen industries. The Asian model suppressed the true cost of money, fuelling unproductive and unprofitable investments. It took a world where capital has become highly mobile and its effects highly volatile—the new high-tech global financial system—to bring the message home. This was a key factor behind the speculative booms that occurred throughout East Asia, and in the flood of mostly Japanese capital that financed them.

The Asian model was not simply economic, but encompassed a broader world view which held that Asian culture and Asian values were a key to Asia's distinctive and superior economic performance—frugality and hard work, commitment to the family, the claimed absence of 'western' hedonism. The moral and economic elements became intertwined in a story Asian leaders used to create a sense of common purpose and ambition. Asian values became, for some Asian leaders, a political tool to engender local pride by positing a positive Asian identity superior to that of the West.

Asian economics had other faults that deserve to be described as part of the Asian model as much as the positive features: cronyism and corruption that often led to bad investments; financial markets with poor accounting standards and opaque accounts that make it harder to assess the cost of money and the worth of investments; the bank guarantees that create a moral hazard and lead to rash investments.

The Asian model is flawed because dysfunctional features were not always discarded. One of the most damaging features of the model, reinforced by the 1997 crisis, was excessive confidence in the ability of governments to guide and control economic development. Excessive confidence in the efficacy of the model led to failure to tackle other deep-seated problems: poor infrastructure, lack of transparency in decision-making, poor governance, weakness of financial institutions, insufficient accountability, the absence of the rule of law. The smog that regularly envelops much of South-East Asia is a potent sign of the failure to deal with a serious problem that has very clear causes: the rapacious practices of Indonesian landowners with close links to the ruling regime.

The systematic failure to recognise the limits of the model, the hubris of some of the main actors, their belief that they could beat the market and play by different rules, were key factors in the 1997 crisis. Too many Asian leaders thought they had discovered a better method of economic management and were unwilling and unprepared to acknowledge and respond to their failures.

Jean-Pierre Lehmann, a Swiss professor of political economy, argues that all capitalist economies assume a rogue character in their early stages. 'What happened, however, was that following the early stages of their rogue existence, the capitalist economies of the West became more democratic, more liberal and more honest! Governance and the qualities of good governance—especially those of transparency and accountability—improved very significantly.' The challenge for Asia, after the 1997 crisis, will be to adopt, uphold and implement good governance. 'If . . . cronies are to remain a feature of the economic landscape, then, yes, the Asian "miracle" will evolve into a "mirage"', he says.[5]

Lehmann argues that Asia in general, and Japan in particular, have suffered from a lack of leadership during the 1990s. 'Japan is still very, very rich, but that is all. There is no leadership, no vision, no courage, no spark, no strategy . . . The Asian crisis of the late nineties is, in many respects, a crisis of Japanese leadership.' As a result, Asia needs a new leader, and the only candidate is China. But China will not fulfil its promise unless it, too, meets the challenge of good corporate governance and respect for the rule of law.

But while the Asian crisis has undermined key aspects of the Asian model, it has also raised questions about some of the fundamental tenets of the western liberal economic model. The initial response of the IMF, in Thailand, Korea and Indonesia, was a mixture of necessary reform and damaging economic repression. The crisis has sparked a reassessment of whether it is desirable to allow capital to flow freely across national borders, particularly in developing countries, a goal pressed hard on developing countries by the IMF and the United States. The 1997 crisis exposed the weakness in that approach. Open capital markets are desirable in principle, but they increase the vulnerability of an economy which is still suffering from other structural flaws. Those vulnerabilities were disguised in East Asia during the boom years of the 1980s and 1990s, but have now been exposed. The IMF has come under widespread attack for its handling of the crisis, making conditions much worse than they need have been, especially in Indonesia, where IMF demands to close down weak banks sparked an exodus of funds that undermined confidence in the banking system and the currency. The crisis has undermined assumptions that liberalising movements of capital will have the same benefits that have flowed from liberalising trade in goods and services.

The events of 1997 also revealed the downside to a high level of foreign debt—it makes the system highly vulnerable to anything that disturbs the flow of cash to service the debt. To prevent such upsets, East Asian financial systems require a high degree of cooperation between banks and firms and considerable government support. The system also relied on exchange rates remaining fixed to the US dollar, and assumed that the state would carry the ultimate risk of default. Neither of these assumptions was sustained.

Asia's response

Big inflows of foreign capital, much of it from Japan, sparked strong growth in almost every Asian country in the early and mid-1990s, much for projects that were unlikely to turn a profit. As always, the folly was not confined to borrowers but was shared by lenders. The problem, as in any boom, was a failure to recognise that the good days would not last forever.

Bankers 'ignored their own prudential limits on lending to companies with high debt to equity ratios, because everyone else was ignoring the limits and they each wanted to win business', argue UK scholars Robert Wade and Frank Veneroso.[6] At the same time, encouraged by the IMF and the governments, banks and firms of the West, Asian governments loosened controls on companies' foreign borrowings, without any improvement in the supervision of bank lending. While details varied, there were two common links between all these countries—indeed throughout East Asia from South-East Asia to Japan, South Korea, Taiwan, Hong Kong and China. First was the excess capacity that resulted from the flood of foreign capital. This cycle of over-investment leading to excess capacity and then a crash was a repeat of the Japanese pattern. Second was poor supervision of the financial system.

The strong yen had been a major factor behind the flood of capital from Japan to East Asia. But with the Japanese economy under increasing stress, a Japan–United States deal in mid-1995 reversed the decade-long rise in the yen, and knocked the stuffing out of the East Asian boom. The yen peaked in April 1995 at 80 yen to the US dollar. But the yen declined rapidly, and by mid-1998 had fallen below 140 yen to the dollar. The end of *endaka* meant the end of the boom.

It was two years before the rest of Asia felt the effects of the turnaround in the yen. The results, when they eventually appeared, were catastrophic, and exposed the flimsy foundations of the boom. The reversal of the yen brought a slowdown of

Japanese investment in the region, restored some of the competitive edge to Japanese producers and removed some of the advantages enjoyed by their competitors.

New technology had brought rapid changes in the global financial system that ultimately exposed the region to risks that had previously been manageable, but had now become insupportable. The 1997 crisis revealed that with information and capital moving around the world more rapidly than ever before the world's financial system had changed in fundamental, yet little-noticed, ways. As a result of the new system 'errant government policy behaviour' was now being punished far more profoundly than in the past, the chairman of the US Federal Reserve Board, Alan Greenspan, argued in testimony before the US Congress in January 1998. Vicious cycles were emerging more frequently, and once they had been triggered, damage control was increasingly difficult.

The reversal in the yen and the slowdown in the flow of capital to East Asia changed the Asian climate from sunny to stormy. The new high-tech global financial system meant the problems were transmitted much more swiftly and painfully.

The impact of the storm was compounded by other factors. The countries worst affected by the crisis had serious domestic political and economic problems. 'In Thailand they had six finance ministers in 24 months', said investment strategist Ken Courtis of Deutsche Morgan Grenfell in Tokyo.[7] The meltdown revealed that authoritarian governments often lack flexibility in a crisis. Cronyism, corruption and a lack of democratic pressures all inhibited the response to the problems. These countries all had long-term structural economic problems that had not been addressed, including the poor management of their banking systems. Their gravest mistake was that many of them had tied their currencies to the US dollar.

Latent weaknesses in all these areas had been glossed over and ignored during the boom years of the late 1980s and early to mid-1990s. But with hindsight it can be seen that the whole edifice was built on shaky foundations. When the structure began to totter, the system's failings were exposed.

As well as the classic mistake of assuming that growth rates four times those of the rich world would continue indefinitely, investors in the South-East Asian boom assumed that the system of fixed exchange rates used by most countries would remain in place. A key cause of the turmoil in Thailand, Malaysia, the Philippines and Indonesia was that they failed to adjust their currency regimes to take account of the reversal in the yen after mid-1995. Most South-East Asian countries had pegged their exchange rates to the US dollar. With the increasing velocity and volatility of capital flows, the fashion for pegged exchange rates now looks to have been misplaced.

Fallout

The implications of the crisis will be most severe in East Asia, with repercussions in the rest of the world that would have been unthinkable even a decade ago. Rioting over food shortages and steeply rising prices sound an ominous warning of the dangers in Indonesia, which in early 1998 stole from South Korea the ignominious mantle of the 'country worst affected' by the crisis. The economic problems in Korea and Thailand are also profound. Their financial systems are rotten, their businesses heavily indebted. As a result of the crisis bankruptcies escalated and their economies slumped.

Forced by the severity of their own crises to abandon the Asian model abruptly and painfully, Korea and Thailand will reinvigorate their economies more quickly than Indonesia but the process will still be slow and difficult. The structural problems elsewhere in East Asia are not as great as in Indonesia, Korea and Thailand; yet all have been hurt by the economic slowdown and loss of confidence brought by the crash. Growth has been punctured throughout the region, creating a refugee crisis of enormous proportions as governments crack down on millions of illegal workers and force them back to their home countries—sometimes, like the Burmese guest workers in Thailand, to face political repression when they return.

In coming years, if the crisis spreads to Japan and China, the depressing impact around the world could be unmatched by any financial trauma since the 1930s. The first and most likely danger is that the slowdown in growth in East Asia will drag down economic performance in other emerging economies. By early 1998 this process was well under way. A second danger—which could take several years to emerge—is that the deflationary forces at work in East Asia could spread to the West, spiking world economic growth.

Resolving the problems will require tough decisions within the economies most affected. But the fallout will be much greater if Japan and China do not respond effectively with a prompt and substantial economic stimulus to offset the depressing effects of the developing countries' traumas.

As there is after every crash, there will eventually be a recovery, and East Asia has every chance of regaining some of the optimism of the late 1980s and early 1990s. But the recovery could be half a decade coming, and will require a substantial and frank reassessment of the shortcomings of the Asian model and the rebuilding of its key institutions, many of which have been found wanting, and overcoming the corruption and inflexibility that is endemic in economic sectors that are not exposed to international competition. The most obvious problems are in financial systems, but the notions of Asian values and of a distinctive Asian approach to government and democracy have also lost their lustre. How much worse Indonesia's problems were made in late 1997 and early 1998 by the apparent lack of a clear successor to President Soeharto, let alone of a succession process. How poor the debate on the problems in Malaysia, where critics feared the wrath of Mahathir. Yet in South Korea and Thailand, against most expectations, a change of government made enormous differences to the prospects of recovery. The appointment in Thailand in October of the new government of Chuan Leekpai, and in Korea in December the election as president of Kim Dae-jung, gave legitimacy to the painful policies needed to tackle the crisis.

Two of the gravest dangers arising from the crisis are two different kinds of deflation. The first, narrower deflation is an ongoing fall in the prices only of assets such as shares and real estate, which can affect real economic activity by undermining the financial standing of lenders and of their banks. The second deflation is a general fall in prices of goods and services. Because nominal interest rates cannot be lower than zero, general price deflation could push real interest rates to damaging levels. And because, similarly, it is difficult to cut money wages, deflation could increase both real wage levels and unemployment.

Debt plays such an important part in modern economies that the risks of deflation are magnified. Most loans are made against some kind of collateral, which the lender hopes will provide security if the borrower defaults. But in times of falling asset prices the value of the collateral falls while the value of loans used remains fixed. If the problem is serious enough the result will be increasing default on loans and banks unwilling to lend for new investment. The greatest risk is not in deflation itself, but in its effect on the banking system. The problem is familiar in Japan, which has been suffering both asset and general price deflation throughout the 1990s, and has on several occasions in that time come close to a serious financial meltdown. Since the Asian crisis began in 1997 the problem has also become acute in Indonesia and Korea.

The unbridled optimism of those lending money to East Asia during the boom years led to a massive over-investment and to over-capacity in the region's key export industries, from computer chips to ships, from cars to clothing. This over-capacity led to falls in the prices of these products. The risk is that this price deflation will deepen as a result of a downward spiral of competitive devaluations throughout the region. Almost every country is trying to outdo the other with price cuts achieved by lowering their currencies.

The main exceptions are Hong Kong and China. Hong Kong will pay for its determination to defend the Hong Kong dollar's peg to the greenback with a sharp recession, caused by the high interest rates needed to keep investors from deserting the territory at the current exchange rate. China will pay with sharply reduced export earnings as the prices of its East Asian competitors' products are cut substantially by their falling currencies.

Deflation can lead to recession, but to a sort of recession different from those of the previous sixty years. Recent recessions were caused by jacking up interest rates to clamp down on excess demand; the new sort was caused by the phenomenon of excess supply.

Economist David Hale has argued that floating exchange rate regimes, which didn't exist in the 1930s, would allow western countries to cope with the effects of price deflation much better than in the Great Depression. Countries that suffer falling income because of falling world prices can offset the dampening effect by lowering interest rates and using stimulatory budgets. How effectively the key players—the USA, China and Japan—do so will be critical to managing the crisis.

China was protected from the immediate effects of the Asian crisis. With rigid controls on flows of money across its borders, it was not a full player in the new high-tech global financial system. But that will only delay the consequences, not prevent them. The rapidly growing export sector generated most of China's economic growth ever since Deng Xiaoping began the move towards a market economy in 1978. China is suffering its own deflation as a result of the increasing competition, and falling demand for its exports.

China's controls on importing and exporting capital, its fixed exchange rate and its substantial foreign reserves give it some insulation against financial collapse. But its massive and increasing level of bad loans—by some estimates as high as 70 per cent of national output—carry a huge cost. Papering over the bad debts will simply worsen the problem, as Japan has demonstrated. China may succeed in avoiding a devaluation of the yuan, but if it does not the costs of the Asian crisis and its impact on the West will be greatly magnified.

Japan has contributed more than any other country both to the rise of Asia and to its fall, and will be a key player in determining how serious the problem becomes. As the largest economy in the region, Japan can do more than any other country to reduce the pain of the crash by adopting budget and interest rate policies that stimulate spending. But stronger economic stimulus pressed on Japan by the West in early 1998 will not solve Japan's more fundamental problems: the rigidities in its own economy. Unless it tackles these, Japan is unlikely to become the engine for growth in the region. Until it tackles its deeper problems, Japan—the birthplace of the model—will remain part of the problem, not the solution.

In June 1998, after news that Japan's economy had shrunk in the year to March for the first time in 23 years, the currency took a tumble, falling briefly to 146.75 yen to the dollar. This sparked fresh fears of a financial meltdown in Japan, a prospect averted by heavy intervention by US and Japanese authorities in foreign exchange markets to prevent the yen falling further. The currency recovered above 140 yen, but the episode reinforced fears that Japan was unable or unwilling to repair its financial system and resuscitate its economy.

There are two great challenges for the United States in the Asian crisis. The first is to make sure that like Japan it provides enough economic stimulus to offset the dampening effects of any sharp slowdown in demand. The second will be to guard against a protectionist backlash. A round of competitive devaluations could fuel a surge of Asian exports to the West and inspire America's incipient protectionism. Both because of its status as the world's largest economy and because of its latent protectionism and isolationism, the risks are greatest in the United States. So far the United States has benefited from Asia's troubles. Asia can take some of the credit for the remarkable eight-year economic expansion in the United States and the surge in American share markets. Amid the preoccupation with a supposed new economic paradigm, the Asian deflation has been a critical and overlooked factor in the American economy's strength. America has effectively imported Asia's low prices and excess capacity through imports of Asian consumer products, cars and textiles, delaying the day when the US reaches its own capacity limits. The risk is that the American producers competing with Asia will eventually be hit by the same over-capacity and consequent squeeze on profits. This would propel an American slowdown close on the heels of the more severe crunch in Asia. The United States also faces another danger in responding to the crisis: the likely end of the long 1990s economic boom and of the bull market on Wall Street. The US economy will inevitably turn downwards regardless of events in Asia, as the economic cycle turns and the long boom ends. Although deflationary forces have prolonged the boom by restraining inflationary pressures, they will worsen the downturn, when it comes, by subtracting from demand.

Asia will recover, not because of its special miracle model but by doing well those things it did well in the past and rectifying what have now proved to be mistakes. It has often been said that East Asia will recover because its 'fundamentals' are sound. This misses the point: some of East Asia's fundamentals played a big part in its success. But others dragged it down, and will have to be repaired or abandoned. The East Asian countries worst hit by the crisis are suffering a broader version of the dual economy malaise afflicting Japan: their efficient export sectors can no longer carry the burden of increasingly costly, corrupt and inefficient domestic sectors.

Chapter 2
Japan rises

In Kyushu, the southernmost of Japan's four main islands, Japan's famous Ministry of International Trade and Industry (MITI) is spending billions of yen trying to attract new industries to revive the region's economy. In the city of Kitakyushu MITI has won funds for a new cargo airport, for a deeper harbour, for construction of a 'trade mart' aimed at attracting foreign companies exporting to Japan, and to build a new container terminal.

In May 1997, MITI's then director-general for Kyushu and one of its top mandarins, Ida Satoshi, maintained that the ministry's job had not changed substantially since the glory days of the 1960s.

> Our role is to set out a perspective for the future of Japan, for example in 10 years from now, to set out what should Japan be and how should it be acting. Our role is to create guidelines for the Japanese economy. We have played the same role, I believe, in the 60s as in the 90s, we have tried various methods, but basically I do not believe our role has changed a great deal.

Yet the projects MITI is backing in Kyushu are white elephants. The Japanese taxpayer is paying billions of yen (tens of millions of dollars) to invest in public infrastructure that is already in abundant supply, in a region whose heavy industry and need for new port facilities have declined sharply in recent years.

MITI played no role in the region's recent success stories, a boom in investment in semiconductors and automobile manufacturers spurred on by the island's lower wages and land prices compared with the rest of Japan. MITI is just as busy as it ever was, though less influential, and judging from Japan's recent economic performance, decidedly less triumphant. Has MITI changed? Or is it doing what it always did, but with less success? Is this the same MITI that Chalmers Johnson reckons is the body most responsible for Japan's postwar miracle?

The legacy of war

After its defeat in World War II Japan was an industrial wasteland. The war left seven million unemployed in a nation of 76 million people, wiped out a quarter of its industrial capacity and devastated almost every major city. From this dismal foundation Japan emerged as one of the world's great economic powerhouses, second only to the United States.

There were advantages in the grim wartime legacy: a large pool of skilled labour, a technologically advanced industrial structure with high capacity in heavy industries, and a network of financial controls. During the war those financial controls were used to ensure maximum production of bullets and bombs. Afterwards they were kept to help build an industrial superstate. Large American orders of supplies for the Korean War of 1950-53 gave a huge stimulus to Japanese production, as the Vietnam War was to do two decades later for the South Korean and South-East Asian economies.

Japan's economic growth from 1950 to 1973 averaged an extraordinary 10 per cent a year, 'probably the highest sustained rate of increase that the world has ever seen', says economist Ed Lincoln. The conventional explanation is that this growth flowed from Japan's exceptionally rapid increases in the mobilisation of labour, capital and technology, as well as the shift in resources away from agriculture. Whether these factors fully explain Japan's success is the main cause of dispute between the neoclassical and revisionist schools. In the early 1970s many respectable analysts believed this breakneck growth would be sustained indefinitely. In *The Emerging Japanese Superstate* in 1970 Herman Kahn predicted growth was likely to continue at 10 per cent a year 'for the next two or three decades'. The Japan Economic Research Center tipped 9.2 per cent growth from 1970 to 1985. Japan's Economic Planning Agency was a little more modest. In 1973 it predicted growth of 9 per cent for the next five years. The oil shock of 1973 meant these rosy projections ended abruptly, with simultaneous high inflation and recession, but the oil shock was not the prime cause of the slowdown. The economy was already overheated, inflation was rising, and long-term growth potential was falling. In 1974 Japan suffered negative growth for the first time since World War II, a feat it did not repeat even during the slump of the early 1990s, although it was achieved in 1998. Annual growth between 1974 and 1991 averaged 4.4 per cent, less than half the rate of the previous twenty years, and from 1992 to 1997 the average fell to 1.2 per cent.

The sobering conclusion is that having caught up with the West technologically, Japan's growth rate first slowed down to and then slipped behind that of the West. OECD growth from 1992 to 1997 was 2.1 per cent. For the Group of Seven largest economies, including Japan, it was 1.7 per cent. A 1998 research paper from the Bank of Japan implies that the country's long-term growth rate could be zero. Even without its deep structural problems, economic growth in Japan will be much lower in the years ahead than in the half century since World War II. The process of technological catch-up has run its course and Japan's population has stopped growing. Early in the twenty-first century Japan's population will begin to fall unless it reverses its deep-seated aversion to immigration. The cooperation and tightly knit corporate structures that provided stability in the growth burst have turned to inflexibility and become a drag on innovation. Japan is and will remain a rich country. But the days of miraculous growth are long past.

Japan's years of strongest growth were from 1955 to 1969. Between 1948 and 1955 industrial production more than tripled. Industrial production was multiplied almost eightfold by 1960, in which year the Japanese economy grew at a rate of 13.2 per cent. The economy kept up that pace for the next decade. In 1961 Prime Minister Ikeda Hayato set the goal of doubling national income within ten years, a target that was easily achieved. A feature of the Japanese economy during this rapid growth phase was its dominance by a small number of large-scale manufacturers, some favoured by MITI and others outside that privileged circle. All benefited from the opportunity to exploit Japan's domestic market as a result of MITI's restrictions on foreign trade. A second feature, notes historian W.G. Beasley, was the emphasis on products that used advanced technology and heavy capital investments, such as steel and petrochemical industries and manufacturing consumer goods including cameras, televisions, motorcycles and later automobiles.

The rapid pace of growth was already slowing when Japan was hit by the quadrupling of oil prices of the first oil shock in

1973, bringing a massive hike in costs of oil and other inputs into Japanese industry, a trauma compounded by the second oil shock in 1979. The oil shocks gave a new lease of life to MITI, which by then was coming under fire from industries growing resentful of its influence and interference. In response to the crisis and the shortages that it created the ministry was given broad powers to demand industrial information, set prices, make plans for supplying consumer products and fine those who deviated from them.[1] But MITI's heyday was past. Japan's growth trajectory had slowed, although it would still remain above those of the other rich world countries for another decade.

The world's largest creditor

For the first decades of its postwar growth Japan had the benefits of both a low and a stable currency, with the rate fixed since 23 April 1949 at 360 yen to the US dollar. A low exchange rate meant a better price for exporters; a fixed exchange rate meant certainty about costs and returns. This benign environment ended in 1971, when the postwar Bretton Woods system of fixed exchange rates collapsed, and was replaced in the largest economies, after a period of confusion and improvisation, with a system of floating exchange rates. One of the key certainties of the postwar economic order had gone, bringing increased economic volatility and new problems for Japan and the rest of the world.

At the same time that the Bretton Woods system fell apart Japan achieved one of the main aims of postwar economic policy: full employment. The large pool of surplus labour left when the army was dismantled at the end of the war had finally been fully mobilised. Achieving full employment meant the end of the most obvious part of the growth formula. But with an economy still skewed towards unusually high levels of savings and investment, Japan continued to generate high levels of exports, which came to exceed imports by an increasing margin. Japan was producing more than it consumed, and earning more than it spent. The difference Japan lent to borrowers overseas, and in around 1980 it became the largest creditor (or lending) nation in the world.

With its labour force now fully mobilised and its industry having reached the technological levels of the West, Japan's growth rate slowed in the 1970s, with added jolts from the oil shocks of 1974 and 1979 when Arab oil-producing states sent world oil prices rocketing. But although its economy was maturing, Japan kept its unusual economic structure, with its inefficient high-cost domestic industries a growing contrast to the dynamic export sector.

Japanese perfidy or American paranoia?

Japan's current account surplus continued to grow. The growing surplus was both a strength and a weakness—most obviously a strength, because of the massive capital surpluses it generated, which enabled it to invest increasing amounts in assets overseas. But the surpluses had big downsides—real and imagined, political and economic.

The rising Japanese trade surplus had its counterpoint in the growing trade deficit in the United States, and became the focal point of an increasingly acrimonious relationship between the two countries. The slowdown in US growth in the 1980s fuelled a sense that America was in decline, reflected in books such as Paul Kennedy's *The Rise and Fall of the Great Powers*. During the Bush administration, and continuing with Bill Clinton's election in 1992, this anxiety found a focus in America's rising trade deficit with Japan. The trade deficit was seen as a source of national weakness. Japan became the scapegoat for home-grown problems. American politicians wrongly blamed their trade deficit for the loss of American jobs. The rising influence of the revisionists gave intellectual respectability to a scapegoating of Japan, a debate in which the trade gap became the touchstone. Japan supporters dubbed their critics 'Japan-bashers'.

Disentangling the threads of the debate is a useful exercise. Among the questions to be answered are: why was the trade imbalance growing? What were the consequences for Japan and the United States? What was the appropriate response from both sides? Economics, which should be at the heart of the issue, is largely swamped in the debate by the political dimensions.

The revisionists provided important insights in illuminating distinctive aspects of the Japanese political and economic system. But the conclusions for trade policy drawn from these views were mistaken and damaging. One error was the claim that trade deficits are necessarily a bad thing and that they cause a loss of jobs in the country with the deficit.

It is true that Japan has many barriers to the entry of imports, that individual firms in other countries would benefit if those barriers were lowered or removed, and that in spite of moves to lower formal trade barriers such as import tariffs, substantial informal barriers to imports remain in Japan. Where the critics are wrong is in arguing that these barriers are anything more than a marginal factor in the trade imbalance, or have more than a marginal impact on jobs in the deficit country.

The overwhelming influences on trade balances are the level of savings and investment in each country. Japan has a trade surplus because it saves more than it invests. The United States itself had trade surpluses until the 1980s, but then became a deficit country—not because of anything happening in Japan, but because of changes in its own spending and investment habits, due in part to the misguided nostrums of Reaganomics. There is nothing instrinsically wrong with either a trade surplus or deficit, although a large imbalance can point to other problems within the economy.

There is merit in the argument that trade barriers in Japan can be damaging to individual exporters, and it is legitimate, indeed responsible, for other countries to urge their removal. But the magnitude of the American response has been out of proportion to the damage caused. The causes of America's economic problems (and its strengths) lie largely in America, not Japan.

American critics also seem to forget that Japan is a sovereign country. According to values Americans profess to uphold, sovereign countries are entitled to make their own decisions for their own reasons. This gets closer to the nub of the problem: the colonial relationship between America and Japan. Japan after World War II ceded its security to the United States in return for its promise of support for American security and economic interests in the region. But Americans have become resentful of what they perceive as Japanese economic skulduggery, and their response has been exaggerated and sometimes hostile. One folly in the American argument is that the United States in the 1980s needed the Japanese surplus to pay for its growing trade deficits, which were fuelled by the supply side economics and big spending of the Reagan presidency. Japan's surplus saved the United States from the consequences of its own profligacy. The irony is that in saving America's bacon, Japan delayed by a decade the reckoning for its own misshapen and dysfunctional economic system.

Where Japan is culpable, and where American criticism came increasingly to be directed during the Asia crisis of late 1997 and 1998, was in its failure to play a role as the region's market and lender of last resort. By running its own economy at a snail's pace Japan was doing little to provide a market for the surge of exports being produced by increasingly desperate East Asian neighbours—a role which since the 1940s has been taken by the United States (and which in the 1930s America failed to play, to its own and the world's immense cost).

It was Japan that supplied much of the capital that created the 1990s investment boom that in turn led to the crisis of 1997. Japanese money was the main factor behind the surge of lending in the first half of the 1990s, much of it in direct investment in subsidiaries of Japanese companies. As the flow of Japanese money to Asia slowed after the yen began to weaken in 1995, the slack was taken up by Taiwan, Hong Kong and Singapore. Japanese investors appear not to have been the main players behind the withdrawal of funds from East Asia that punctured the boom in 1997, but the boom would not have been nearly so great without Japanese capital.

Lending within Japan is often made on projects with little regard to return, and some analysts argue the same lack of scrutiny is applied to lending offshore. Loans and investments were made with the goal of increasing productive capacity, but with little regard for return or risk. Some of the money was well spent. It was the badly spent money on the margin that caused the problems, and for which borrowers and lenders and the institutions that failed to manage them are culpable.

Figures from the Institute of International Finance show that private capital flows to Korea, Indonesia, Malaysia, Thailand and the Philippines climbed rapidly in the mid-1990s from $40.5 billion in 1994 to $92.8 billion in 1996, but were sharply reversed in 1997 to an outflow of $12.1 billion. Private and bank lending increased far more rapidly than equity investment, making up four-fifths of the net capital inflow in 1996, up from two-thirds in 1994.

Figures breaking down the source of total capital flows by country are scarce, except for bank lending, which in 1996 made up 63 per cent of net private capital flows to the five Asian countries. Bank for International Settlements figures show that Japan is by far the biggest single lender, as would be expected given that it has the largest current account surplus. At the end of 1995 Japan accounted for $87.7 billion or 41.8 per cent of loans outstanding to the five, of a total of $209.9 billion. A year later Japan's share was $93.6 billion, or 35.8 per cent of $261.2 billion, and in mid-1997 its share was $97.2 billion, or 35.4 per cent of $274.4 billion.

During the late 1980s Japan experienced the greatest speculative boom in world history. Share and property prices reached dizzying and unsustainable heights. At the share market's peak on the last day of 1989, the value of shares on Japanese markets was two-fifths of the combined total of every market in the world. Japan's real estate was valued at four times all the property in the United States; the grounds of the Imperial Palace in Tokyo were worth more than all the land in Australia. This frenzied speculation was fuelled by heavy lending from Japan's banks, which kidded themselves that their loans were safe because Japanese land prices had never before fallen, and their loans were all backed by property.

When the bubble burst in 1990 the banks were in serious trouble. Dozens were technically bankrupt, with liabilities well in excess of their assets. But the banks were allowed to keep their doors open in the hope they would gradually earn enough money to cover their bad debts.

It might have worked, but the end of the boom also meant an end to the huge demand for construction and other investment. The failure to write off the debt quickly and to overcome other bottlenecks in the domestic economy delivered Japan a prolonged recession that ran through most of the 1990s.

Was it a miracle?

Japan's economic performance until 1973 was brilliant, and until 1992 was still respectably bright. But why? Since the early 1960s there has been endless debate over how Japan achieved its economic 'miracle', whether by following or ignoring the prescriptions of mainstream economics, or through some mix of the two.

In his highly influential account of Japan's success, Chalmers Johnson tells the story that the Japanese themselves only became aware of the extent of their achievement in September 1962 when the *Economist* of London published a long two-part essay entitled 'Consider Japan'. Where other critics had complained of Japan's spendthrift budgets and its unsustainable boom, the *Economist* saw rising demand, high productivity and savings and a quiescent labour force. 'Thus began the praise, domestic and foreign, of the postwar Japanese economy—and the search for the cause of the "miracle"', Johnson wrote. In the early postwar years, the usual answer to the miracle question was simply that Japan had applied the methods of conventional economics in a particularly effective way. Johnson provided a highly influential rejoinder to that view with his 1982 book, *MITI and the Japanese Miracle*. Johnson is an American political scientist who had first visited Japan as a US Navy officer in the 1950's. His book provided the first comprehensive argument that Japan's success had unorthodox roots.

By the 1990s Japan's example was being copied extensively in various ways in neighbouring countries. Practical leaders didn't especially need a theoretical underpinning for what they were doing, but Johnson gave the idea intellectual legitimacy. He coined the term 'developmental state' to describe Japan's approach. *MITI and the Japanese Miracle* had a cathartic effect on the debate about Asia's economic success. It became the benchmark in an argument over the reasons and lessons for Japan's success that remains as fierce as when it began. Johnson's work provided the arguments for a generation of academics and policy-makers seeking a rationale for an activist industrial policy.

Johnson's book contains important insights into Japan's success, especially on the importance of MITI and other institutions, notably the Ministry of Finance. But Johnson puts too much weight on the importance of these institutions and too little weight on other factors. He overstates Japan's uniqueness and overestimates its virility. Johnson argues that the key issue is not that the state intervened in the economy at all—every state does—but the way it did so. The dominant feature of this 'developmental state' approach is the priority it gives to industrial policy. Such a state will set substantive social and economic goals, and must take a 'strategic, goal-oriented approach to the economy'. This contrasts with a market-oriented state, whose domestic and foreign policies will stress rules and reciprocal concessions, but which may have broad, non-industry-specific goals such as price stability and full employment.[2]

Though many bureaucratic centres contended for power in the Japanese system, the body that exerts the greatest positive influence, Johnson argues, is that which executes industrial policy: MITI. Johnson argues that the most unusual part of the Japanese approach was the cooperation between government and business. He lists the chief mechanisms of the relationship:

> selective access to governmental or government-guaranteed financing, targeted tax breaks, government-supervised investment coordination in order to keep all participants profitable, the equitable allocation by the state of burdens during times of adversity . . . governmental assistance in the commercialization and sale of products, and governmental assistance when an industry as a whole begins to decline.[3]

These practices aren't uniquely Japanese; although the Japanese have worked harder at perfecting them, Johnson argues.

Was Johnson right?

But does his analysis stand up to scrutiny? There are several key questions. One is whether that growth was as exceptional as Johnson says. A second is whether Johnson's developmental state model provides a good explanation for Japan's economic growth. A third is whether the developmental state model is a good guide for economic policy.

For all the extensive debate on these questions, the conclusions are highly equivocal. Even the most sympathetic of the mainstream economic assessments of these questions, the World Bank's *The East Asian Miracle*, is cautious about whether developmental state interventions can be used to boost economic growth in any systematic way.

The strongest conclusion in the World Bank report is that market-friendly policies are the surest guide to success. Next most important are interventions that aim to encourage exports, a goal which of itself imposes the competitive discipline of selling into world markets. 'More interventionist policies have the potential to contribute to growth in cases where they address economic coordination problems, but to succeed they must combine the benefits of cooperation with competitive discipline by creating contests', the report argues.[4]

Even this limited endorsement of intervention has been highly controversial, seized on by proponents of industrial policy to justify widespread interventions, and attacked as a result by the pro-market school in spite of its cautions and heavy qualifications.

Kent Calder's study *Strategic Capitalism* is among the most thoughtful and comprehensive response to Johnson's argument. Calder is respectful of Johnson's work, which he regards as a groundbreaking analysis of Japan's institutional structures. But Calder is also critical, and concludes that by focusing on one particularly powerful ministry, MITI, Johnson overstates the cohesiveness and effectiveness of Japan's industrial policy.

Japanese policy-making, Calder argues, has had many central actors, whose goals often conflict. Key actors have included many private firms and groups as well as those in government. 'Sometimes state strategists, centred at the Ministry of International Trade and Industry . . . have brilliantly formulated and pursued national objectives in strategic, developmental fashion. In important instances, such as in helping to stimulate the mechatronics [industrial robots] revolution, they have triumphed.' But against Johnson, Calder argues that the political world and the private sector have both at times constrained and supplanted the state's strategic efforts. 'Only in relatively unusual circumstances have the industrial strategists of MITI displayed enough vision, and been able to centralize enough political influence, to achieve industrial transformation in dirigiste, developmental fashion', Calder argues.

> A strong developmental orientation has often prevailed at MITI, but other ministries, such as MOF [the Ministry of Finance] and the Bank of Japan, have often held a perspective closer to the American regulatory orientation than to MITI's developmental stance. Their preeminent orientation—and intermittently that of MITI bureaucrats as well—has been toward stability rather than strategy . . . Government has been especially slow to get into emerging industries in Japan, and slow in getting out of declining sectors . . . In successful industries as diverse as consumer electronics, textiles, and petrochemicals, it has been the private sector, in the main, that has defined strategic long-term goals, and market competition that has generated the structural transformation essential to competitive success.[5]

The most crucial aspect of developmental state industrial policy, its influence on the allocation of credit, was unambiguously successful only in the unusual circumstances that existed most clearly between 1946 and 1954. In these years four unusual conditions prevailed simultaneously: state power was relatively centralised, the private sector in question was disorganised, domestic political intervention and transnational linkages were limited, and demand for credit was sharply greater than supply. But the state in Japan has also been plagued by its hesitancy and obligation to particular clients. 'The state has been remarkably cautious—and reactive—in supporting new industries, waiting for dramatic international developments to force its hand', for example in computers during the 1960s. And the government has poured large amounts of money into declining sectors without much success, for example in shipping and coal mining. Japanese bureaucrats had more difficulty attaining their objectives than is commonly thought, Calder argues, and except for the provision of infrastructure, the course of Japanese capitalism was set primarily by the private sector.

Calder's argument is that Japan's success stems not from the developmental state, but from a hybrid public–private system 'driven preeminently by market-orientated private-sector calculations, but with active public sector involvement to encourage public spiritedness and long-range vision', a notion he calls 'strategic capitalism'. By the 1990s, Calder argues, the days of this corporatist Bankers' Kingdom was drawing to a close, as the highly segmented and heavily regulated financial system made way to one with greater scope for market forces and which gave correspondingly less leverage to the state.

Calder shows that the success of the developmental state model was limited. But that did not stop the *idea* of the developmental state, the Japan model, from providing a powerful example for other countries in the region. It was a positive force in showing that a late-developing country could achieve strong economic growth. But the 1997 financial crisis offers further evidence that the developmental state model is deeply flawed.

Academic research on the reasons for Japan's growth is extensive and has identified so many varying explanations that it might seem rash to try and attribute the Japanese miracle to one or even a handful of factors. Yet, in spite of the variety of influences and the lack of academic backing, Johnson's solution has become immensely popular in the non-economists' community. Johnson's explanation for the discrepancy between economists' and others' views of Japan is simple: the economists are wrong; they are wedded to an ideology that blinds them to the reality that the Japanese achieved their miracle deliberately. This is an appealing view because of its simplicity, and because it meets a deep-seated desire to set the world to rights.

Less appealing but more likely true, however, are the economists' orthodox explanations. The *ad hominem* charge that Johnson frequently lays against economists—their ideological blindness— does not answer their substantive arguments.

One simple fact undermines the Johnson 'miracle' hypothesis: Japan is no longer miraculous and it is no longer growing at miraculous rates. Japan has not thrown away the gains of the postwar years: that would require truly astounding incompetence from a country that has achieved such great success. But the Japanese economy, once predicted to grow at 10 per cent or more each year well into the twenty-first century, has throughout the 1990s been struggling to record an average growth rate of 1 per cent a year. For much of that time it was possible to argue that the stalled economy would soon burst back to life. But that hope was demolished convincingly by the Asian crisis.

One variant of the attack against the economists' views of Japan's decline is that they are looking at the wrong indicators.

Author Eamonn Fingleton is the most vociferous exponent of this view. He argues that Japan's massive trade surpluses have created a massive pool of capital that gives Japan the ability to project its economic power throughout the region. Clearly Japan's trade and capital surpluses give it enormous influence, but Fingleton has to perform contortions to defend his thesis in the face of other evidence that Japan's strength is waning: its stagnant growth, rising unemployment and fragile financial system. Fingleton's variant of the revisionist view is that Japan's unique economic structure has given it extraordinary strength that is both unfair and damaging to the rest of the world. The claims of unfairness and of the risk posed by Japan are exaggerated. The problems posed for the region and the world by Japan's unusual economic structure reflect not its strength but its weakness: its inability to transform its rigid domestic economy now that it has caught up with the rich world.[6]

Johnson and the revisionists are right about one thing: Japan differs in many ways from other rich economies, all of them western, more than they differ among themselves. But isolating which of those differences helped and which are now hindering Japan is more difficult than it once seemed. The developmental state approach may have been useful, with hindsight, for explaining some features of countries in the catch-up stage of economic development, but even for them it is now less useful than in the past because of the increasing globalisation of world finance, and because of the disciplines imposed by the potential for rapid withdrawal of capital.

Japan's economic stagnation in the 1990s upset many of the more optimistic views of Japan's prospects, both the traditionalist view of its convergence with the West and the revisionist view of its uniqueness. The crisis forced considerable change on the Japanese economy. The institutional features highlighted by Johnson, and which until the end of the 1960s were a virtue, later became a drag on Japan's prosperity. The revisionists' mistake is in contending that Japan's institutional structure is still optimal. It may have been, but it ceased to be so long ago—arguably as far back as 1969 when Japan achieved full mobilisation of the labour displaced by the war. The 1997 crisis simply reinforces the point.

The benefits of the model also turned out, eventually, to be costs for Japan's imitators. All the East Asian miracle economies have benefited from Japanese capital, the fruits of Japan's own 'non-capitalist' capital market. But they have also been harmed by the non-market allocation of the capital. The lack of proper scrutiny of risk fuelled the 1990s boom—and the crash that followed.

This is not to argue that markets are always right, or that intervention always fails. It's a matter of experience as much as abstract principle. We may like the idea that clever bureaucrats can design a better world, but experience shows they can do so only in limited ways. Just where and when they can and cannot will be a matter of experience, and will involve applying the lessons of the past.

One of those lessons is that market solutions are generally the best; that markets are generally the best way of allocating resources. There are exceptions, which will be discovered by trial and error as much as by economic principle, and they can be significant. Economics is a valuable tool for analysing the costs and benefits of these decisions. Attacks on market economics, or in Australia on 'economic rationalism', frequently confuse the decisions made on the basis of an economic model with the model itself. There are elements of the model that are disputed, but in most cases where the model is attacked the real target should instead be the way it was applied. Attacks on 'free-market economics' or 'economic rationalism' usually obscure more than they clarify; the attack is often not an argument about the merits or demerits of a decision, but an accusation about the political motives.

Supporters of the revisionist view of Japan frequently deride 'ivory tower' or 'liberal' economists for their misunderstandings, and then proceed to dismiss their arguments. Undoubtedly ivory tower and liberal economists have made serious misjudgments about Japan and East Asia—as has just about everyone. But it is more fruitful to identify where they made their mistakes than reject their theories outright.

For many years it seemed that the Japanese, and then the East Asian, interventionist model would produce results superior to those of a more market-based model. The 1997 meltdown has shown that there were limits to those strong results. Indeed the market model gives very good explanations—with hindsight—as to why that is so, even if part of the answer is that in some respects Japan does not function as a market economy.

Tokyo sharebroker Alexander Kinmont argues that Japan's interventionist approach was not nearly as distinctive as the revisionists contend.

Right up until about 1964, when Japan really did believe in an industrial policy of a rather old-fashioned type, so did the rest of the world. The interesting point is not whether the Japanese were unique in following this policy, it is why the Japanese policy appears to have delivered higher growth rates than other places.

Peter Tasker, a Tokyo sharebroker and author, concurs.

Coming from the United Kingdom, we have a slightly different perspective from the Americans. We had a very interventionist industry policy all through the 50s and 60s. In fact by the mid-70s the government practically owned the whole economy, including the entire automobile sector, steel sector and coal sector. Everything was owned by the government directly. There wasn't any question about industrial policy. There wasn't any debate about it. We had it.

One explanation for Japan's higher-than-normal growth, Kinmont says, was its large pool of labour.

If you draw the trend line of pre-war growth through the post-war period, it takes until 1967 for Japan to get back where it would have been if the war hadn't intervened. Japan ended the war with idle labour of 7 million people. It took until 1969 for all the excess labour in the economy to be soaked up. That's why you had a high growth rate, it was mobilisation of more labour.

In explaining how Japan was able to mobilise that labour so effectively the revisionists offer an important insight, pointing to the institutional structures built in the 1930s. These still exist today and have fostered the high level of saving that has force-fed Japan's investment.

Another factor behind Japan's unusually strong growth was identified by Iwao Nakatani in a 1984 paper 'The economic role of financial corporate grouping'. Nakatani shows that Japan's industrial structure, with most firms taking part in inter-market business groups or *keiretsu*, has had a significant effect on the nation's economic performance. It is true, as western theories of monopoly maintain, that the formation of such groups increases the monopoly power of its members. But curiously, from a western perspective, this monopoly power is not necessarily used for raising the rate of profit. 'Rather, I take the view that the firm in any of the corporate groups maximises the joint utility of its corporate constituents—employees, financial institutions, stockholders and management', Nakatani argues. 'More specifically, monopoly power is utilized in the pursuit of a desired mode of distribution of output, as well as in stabilizing corporate performance over time.' The benefit of this structure is that risks are shared among members of the group, and with its bankers.

Far from producing monopoly rents—the unearned extra profit achieved because of the inability of others to enter the market—this arrangement has actually delivered lower rates of growth for its participants. The trade-off is that members of the group suffer less variability than independent firms. Another important feature of *keiretsu*, Nakatani shows, is that they tend to have much higher levels of debt compared to their equity base than independent companies.

At the time of Nakatani's paper, the point was to show how this structure contributed to Japan's economic success. It helped, for example, to minimise the damage from the oil price shocks of the 1970s. But now this structure can be seen as a factor in the Japanese slowdown. The *keiretsu* structure encouraged intensive capital investment that fuelled the postwar miracle. Once the benefits of that process had been won, the inflexibility, unresponsiveness and high levels of debt became a burden that retarded growth.

Success that soured

Economic journalist Richard Katz argues that Japan's problem is that it is still stuck in the structures, policies and mental habits of the 1950s and 1960s.[7]

> Four decades ago the developmental state policies that gave rise to the nickname 'Japan Inc' made a lot of sense. But that was only because the country was in the 'catch-up' phase of its economic evolution. Applying such policies at that point fostered an industrial takeoff the likes of which the world had never seen. But, by the 1970s and '80s, when Japan had become a more mature economy, catch-up economics had become passé, even counterproductive. Developmental state policies make sense only for an economy still in the state of development.[8]

Katz points out the stark contrast between the two sides of Japan's 'dual economy', its world-beating export sector and its sclerotic domestic industries. 'The bright side of Japan's economy is its export sector—industries like autos, consumer electronics, semiconductors, and machinery . . . In almost every case, these export stars owe their initial take-off to the developmental state policies applied in the 1950s and '60s.' Japan's starring export industries stand in contrast to those parts of the economy not exposed to international competition, its service industries, utilities and highly protected agricultural sector. Although in every country the industries exposed to international competition are more efficient than those that are not, in no country is the gap between the two as great as it is in Japan.[9] During Japan's years of strong growth, Japan could afford to let its export sectors subsidise its domestic industries. But as Japan's growth has slowed that subsidy has become increasingly difficult to sustain, and the pressure will increase in coming years as the average age of Japan's population rises and fewer workers are obliged to support more retirees.

A non-capitalist economy

The most crucial aspect of the Japanese system, the area where it diverges most from a market model, is in the way capital is allocated. The key to economic growth is to maximise productive investment in people and in plant and equipment—in human and physical capital. To invest, investors need money. So if governments can fiddle with the system to increase the flow of money to productive investment they will have achieved the Holy Grail of faster economic growth and happier citizens. The organisation of the financial system in pursuit of this goal is a key part of the Japanese story. (It is vital that this investment be productive, that it actually generate more wealth than the amount of money invested in the first place. This goal is not always acknowledged or achieved, and in Japan it was eventually thwarted by the weaknesses of its own peculiar financial system.)

Superficially the Japanese banking system is not so distinct from that in the West. But at its core the system is vastly different—although it has recently begun to change. The most important difference is in the way lending decisions are made. Western bankers have established rules for deciding whether to make a loan. They boil down to assessing the likely profit from an investment and how great is the risk that the borrower won't repay the money. But neither of these two fundamental rules is important in Japan. Instead, the key factors are the amount of collateral standing behind a loan and the question of personal contacts and the relationships of mutual obligation, in which the Ministry of Finance plays a central role.

The design of the Japanese banking system greatly diminishes the need for bankers and investors to assess risk and return on a loan. One reason for this is that the banks are effectively protected from any mistakes by the guarantees and safety nets in the system. Another is that banks are not, in practice, accountable to shareholders but to the bureaucracy, in the shape of the Ministry of Finance.[10]

Accountability to shareholders in Japan is much weaker than in the West, in part because of the tight networks of obligation and cross-shareholdings. Companies that are members of the same *keiretsu* or industrial group have imprecise but almost limitless obligations to help each other out, based not on western notions of contractual liability but on personal connections and networks. As a result of these arrangements the Ministry of Finance has a pervasive influence on lending decisions, decisions in which western notions of credit assessment play little part. The lack of concern with risk delivered an enormous benefit to Japanese businesses: it made the cost of their capital much lower than that of their western counterparts.

Because they were in effect guaranteed by the Ministry of Finance and its implicit promise of support, Japanese banks could effectively ignore the need to hold the 'cushion' of reserves that is required of western banks to enable them to cope with bad loans. This meant that for any given level of deposits they could make a greater proportion of loans. And the lack of pressure to deliver profits to shareholders meant that typically these loans didn't earn what in the West would be considered a fair rate of return.

The government's investment criteria, argues author Taggart Murphy, were to pick industries with global growth potential, or that had strategic significance for other industries, or industries like automobiles and consumer electronics with a large number of industrial spin-offs. Other considerations were whether Japan could secure the necessary technology and whether it could undercut western prices to maximise production runs.

The bias of the Japanese economy towards high levels of investment fuelled a transfer of wealth from households to companies that continued until the mid-1990s. This massive force-feeding of credit to areas selected by the MITI, in a process overseen by the MOF, delivered impressive results in the postwar years. But it had some inbuilt weaknesses. Murphy argues,

> If Japanese banks had applied conventional credit standards to their lending, the economic miracle of the 1950s and 1960s would never have happened . . . The banks went into and out of businesses not

because of sober assessments of the profits to be made but on the basis of cues from the MOF.

Following Calder, Kinmont maintains that Japan's credit allocation mechanism is the key to understanding why its economy is so distinctive.

> Japan has no market for capital; therefore it is essentially a non-market economy. Japan not only need not earn a return on capital, it has no idea it costs anything at all. However, abolishing the mechanism by which the cost of capital is easily discovered (the cause of Japan's 'success') does not abolish the cost of capital (the origin of Japan's current difficulties). The whole system rests on a pretense.
>
> Turned another way around, the Japanese system finances everything indiscriminately (or more precisely according to criteria unconnected with financial efficiency) and by accident therefore will happen to finance 'winning' industries and companies ... Moreover, because managements are not responsible to the capital providers, they are essentially indistinguishable from bureaucrats. The public/private distinction we (Anglo-Saxons) are so used to is quite useless in Japan.[11]

The result of this structure is that the Japanese economy has a built-in bias towards investments whose overall profitability is poor. But this skewing of investment can survive only as long as present generations of savers are prepared to forgo a fair return on their investments in favour of the present generation of borrowers, and in favour of the workers whose jobs rely on their investments. This trade-off can work as long as the population is growing rapidly, when there are more workers benefiting from investment than there are retirees losing out from a poor return on their investments. It is a trade-off that will very soon become untenable in Japan, whose declining birthrates and improving health early next century will give it a larger proportion of retirees than any other country on earth.

Saving

Japan's high level of investment is helped by its high level of savings. Until the 1980s households had little choice in where to borrow, and consumer credit was stifled precisely to encourage saving. Japanese also have little choice about where to invest. 'Japanese keep so much of their money in banks because there are really only two sorts of financial assets in Japan: first, risk-free ones that yield next to nothing, and second, highly risky ones that also yield next to nothing. The choice is not difficult', commented Richard Cookson in the *Economist*.[12]

A 1989 study by Charles Horioka identified no fewer than 30 different explanations for Japan's high savings rate and analysed each of them to assess its importance. His first point, even before getting to the reasons for Japan's high savings, is to argue that the figures are actually exaggerated due to variations in the way data is collected. This is one of the four factors that Horioka finally considers were significant, but it only accounts for part of the difference. The others are Japan's low proportion of aged in the population (from the 1950s to the 1980s), the system of twice-yearly salary bonuses, which made saving much easier, and the rapid rate of economic growth. The important thing about all these factors is that none is immutable. As has been previously noted, early next century Japan will have the highest proportion of aged people in the world, and this will place a significant drag on its level of savings. Horioka's conclusion almost a decade ago has been borne out, that Japan's household saving rate will decline, but only gradually.[13]

Until the 1990s saving by Japanese households was supplemented by a high level of saving by the government, which was in the habit of running budget surpluses. But efforts to kick-start the stagnant economy have seen a reversal of that habit. At the start of the 1990s Japan was running a government surplus better than any other developed nation, amounting to 4 per cent of the nation's annual output. By 1998 the surplus had become a 2 per cent deficit, a massive turnaround.

Social and cultural landscape

Less tangible but equally important elements in the Japanese miracle were its social and cultural landscape. The island nation had radically embraced western technology and ideas since the Meiji Restoration of 1868. But Japan's long isolation and the habits developed over millennia of social life focused on rice cultivation had created a highly cohesive people with a strong sense of their uniqueness and their abilities. The most important characteristic, from a western point of view, was a highly developed sense of social obligation that made a person's commitment to the broader community—whether the family, the village, the firm, the army or the nation—much more important than their individual needs.

Other manifestations of Japan's group orientation are its social homogeneity and its people's respect for authority—qualities, to put it more bluntly, that make its work force both docile and hard-working.

This same emphasis on the group rather than on the individual makes Japan's political system anaemic. The Japanese political system is notionally democratic in that it allows for a peaceful change of government based on a popular vote, but the strength of other centres of power in bureaucracy and business and the high value placed on consensus leaves politicians weak.

The individual and the group

The priority given to the group over the individual is one of the defining differences in attitudes in Japan compared with the West. This is most extreme in Japan, but also features strongly in the other Confucian cultures of East Asia with their strong emphasis on hierarchy and family: China, Taiwan, Hong Kong, South Korea, Singapore; and in the influential Chinese communities elsewhere in South-East Asia, such as Indonesia and Malaysia. The priority of the group is also one of the qualities hardest for a westerner to grasp, as it is so different from our own way of thinking, which takes individual fulfilment as a self-evident and obvious goal.

This difference, though powerful, is not absolute, and really amounts to a difference in emphasis. Westerners still place a high value on some of the same groups that are so important in Japan, and Japanese are not immune from wanting to satisfy their individual needs and desires. But the two cultures strike a different balance between these two demands, with important consequences for social, political and economic life. Indeed, the shifting balance between these two forces—away from the group towards the individual—is one of the key features of change in Japanese society, a shift likely to be followed elsewhere in East Asia as the modernising process continues.

The process of modernising—adopting the latest industrial techniques, along with the corresponding but less tangible changes in social attitudes—is not the same as westernising. But the two are intertwined, as western fashions and habits are often the most desired manifestations of the affluence that comes with modernisation.

It is in this process, this move towards individualism, that Japan and East Asia are becoming more western. Even as they maintain and adapt many of their cultural traditions, this is a powerful change. It is a force that will undermine the insistence of some of East Asia's present leaders on distinctive 'Asian values' that underpin their economic success and social cohesion—an ideology that has more to do with providing a rationale for authoritarian political systems than with providing a useful explanation of Asian culture. At the same time, argues Jim Rohwer in his book, *Asia Rising*, the absence of another western trait, its welfarism, may remain a potent advantage for East Asia.

The different emphases in the East and West on the individual and the group reflect values that go right to the core of their philosophical world views. This means that the pressure of the West on Asian society and culture is more than economic: it threatens some fundamental beliefs about the way the world works. These differences are important in explaining the strains between the two world views at many levels, economic, social and cultural.

In spite of their differences of culture and history, Confucian East Asian societies share similar attitudes with regard to authority and group obligations. These attitudes are the result of their common Confucian heritage and of the strong historical influence all have felt from China. It may be that it is not the Confucian group orientation that is unusual historically, but western individualism.

Japanese political scientist Masao Maruyama, the Eastern thinker who has come closest to reconciling the two traditions, has had a profound impact on modern Japanese political thought. But it is notable that he has had no influential intellectual heir. Western traditions of philosophical inquiry do not seem to resonate deeply in Japan, or elsewhere in the East, yet intriguingly, Eastern philosophical traditions have had a considerable impact in the West over the past century. Rationalism, in the sense of logical, scientific thinking, has been a central feature of western thinking—to varying degrees—since the time of the Ancient Greeks. The rationalist tradition runs so deep in western culture that it is a taken-for-granted aspect of the western world view, even in the postmodernist reaction against it. Many Japanese intellectuals have studied and embraced western intellectual traditions, including its philosophy, since Japan opened its doors to western thought after the 1868 Meiji Restoration. But while intellectuals such as Maruyama have become engaged deeply with these traditions, they have not penetrated deeply into everyday Japanese attitudes. In contrast to western rationalism, the philosophical underpinnings of Confucianism are anti-rational.

Maruyama regarded the social immobility imposed by Confucianism, the deference to Confucian norms as the source of all authority and the Confucian hierarchy of values as an archaic intellectual framework that modern Japan had to overcome.[14] But Maruyama's efforts to build a new intellectual framework for modern Japanese have not taken root. Modern Japanese retain a deeply pragmatic and instrumentalist view of the world. They have brilliantly adopted and adapted as much of western technological knowledge as is needed for their technical needs, but without embracing its deeper, rationalist roots.

The exceptions are invariably the people who have had long exposure to the West by going overseas to school or university. Many of this increasingly large group take a deeply western approach to these issues. But they remain a small minority in the community as a whole.

Economic change, however, is beginning to modify attitudes. Notwithstanding the economic stagnation of the 1990s, Japan's considerable wealth has created the opportunity for greater leisure and increased the means for satisfying individual wants. Western, especially American, popular culture is the clearest manifestation of those aspirations, in Japan and East Asia, just as much as in America and the rest of the West.

The increasing individualism spawned by this growing affluence will increasingly affect underlying attitudes and beliefs—a process that is most obvious in Japan, but which can also be seen in more recently affluent East Asian countries.

Chapter 3
Flying geese and tigers

Mahathir Mohamad's attack on George Soros was typical of his ambivalence towards international capital. Mahathir has been a longstanding critic of the damage wrought by western speculators on defenceless developing countries like Malaysia. But he has also trumpeted the virtues of capitalism as the vehicle for Malaysian development. Mahathir reconciles these two opposing threads with his appeal to Malaysians to 'look east' for their economic models and inspiration—away from what he considers the decaying West, towards the brilliant success of Japan and the Asian tigers.

Soros was the symbol of unbridled speculation, of the bullying and corrupting West that had deliberately set out to undermine and weaken developing countries because it feared that their success in East Asia had become a threat to western dominance. Mahathir's criticisms of Soros were an affirmation of his belief in Asian values and the way they had helped create a superior Asian economic system.

The World Bank and others have argued that the economic successes of Malaysia and East Asia stemmed from their adherence to free-market principles, but this is not the view held by Mahathir. Mahathir's career gives an instructive insight into the forces that drive economic decision-making in one East Asian miracle economy—forces that often have more to do with politics and history than with economic theory. There are several consistent themes that run through Mahathir's career, notwithstanding the tensions, contradictions, paradoxes, changes of mind and modifications to his stance, argues Malaysian academic Khoo Boo Teik. As the 'foremost Malay nationalist of his time', Mahathir has from his earliest days in politics in the 1960s pursued the goals of promoting Malay interests ahead of Malaysia's economically powerful Chinese community, Khoo argues in his penetrating biography, *Paradoxes of Mahathirism*. In the first and most famous exposition of his views, in *The Malay Dilemma* in 1970, Mahathir contrasted the economic backwardness of Malays with the 'economic hegemony' of the Chinese community. Khoo shows that by 1976, in Mahathir's book, *The Challenge*, the target of his enmity had shifted from the Chinese to the West. Here Mahathir argued that defence of Malaysia's Islamic values demanded resistance to the corrupting influence of the West, where the collapse of moral values was leading to economic decline.

Mahathir refined this stance further after he became prime minister in 1981, holding up the successful Asian tigers as models for economic development. The tigers showed that Asian countries, with their superior moral values, could beat the West at its own game. At the heart of Mahathir's view, Khoo argues, is his resentment at the rich western nations' reluctance to share technological know-how, capital, management and marketing skills and their huge markets, along with his anger at the readiness of western countries to change the rules of free trade to suit their own interests.[1]

> There was more than incidental resemblance between Mahathir's earlier perception of the 'Chinese economic hegemony' and later perception of 'Western economic dominance'. He thought racial barriers and racial ground rules maintained the former, while 'big power' restrictions and changes in rules effected the latter. In either case, he chafed at the threat of economic exclusion.[2]

Some of Mahathir's praise for Japan 'bordered on idolization', Khoo argues. Where Mahathir was scathing about western protectionism, he applauded protectionism in Japan, which he thought could be usefully emulated in Malaysia. Like other East Asian leaders, Mahathir is ambivalent about the free market and enthusiastic about the benefits of interventionist industrial policy. In 1980, as Minister for Trade and Industry, Mahathir established the Heavy Industries Corporation of Malaysia, and as prime minister made it a central plank of his economic policy. The corporation was a fundamentally 'developmental state' project, aimed explicitly at kick-starting the development of Malaysian industry.

Mahathir also negotiated several large manufacturing joint ventures with Japanese and South Korean multinational companies, including a national car project, a steel complex, two cement plants and three motorcycle engine factories. Mahathir overruled objections from within his own government and elsewhere that the car project would fail because the domestic market was too small and export potential was minimal. He acknowledged the industry's profits might be slight, but argued it would bring profit to the nation. When in 1984 he announced a policy of privatising many state enterprises he claimed inspiration not from the United Kingdom Prime Minister, Margaret Thatcher, or the United States President, Ronald Reagan, but from Japan, the Asian tiger economies and especially Deng Xiaoping's China.[3]

Mahathir's authoritarianism is another feature of his style common to many East Asian leaders. Mahathir holds a dim view of democracy, which he considers a threat to newly independent countries because pressure groups and lobbies make heavy demands on government while local and foreign criticism undermine its authority.[4] In 1987, in a climate of rising ethnic tension and with his political standing under threat, Mahathir arrested dozens of opposition figures and teachers, and suspended four newspapers. In the same year he launched an assault on the judiciary, which had delivered unfavourable verdicts that he considered infringed on the government's prerogatives.

Mahathir's greatest political skill is his populism, his ability to appeal to Malay nationalist sentiment and to redefine it for his own purposes. Mahathir's attack on George Soros at the Hong Kong IMF meeting in September 1997 encompassed many of these strands: his populism, his aggression, his nationalism, his anti-westernism and his alternative pro-Asian model of economic development.

Geese and tigers

Japan provided an important model for all the East Asian miracle economies except Hong Kong. It was the Japan model more than the prescriptions of orthodox economists which provided the inspiration for East Asian leaders. Western theorists argued that the process of economic development would inevitably lead to democratisation even if it did not start there. But to the East Asian leaders economic success was more important. The keys to economic success were seen in values as much as in economic doctrines. Mahathir, for example, saw as virtues in Japan those very qualities that in the West he abhorred.

What was it about Japan that appealed to Asian leaders? It was not a precise detailed blueprint, but a broader, amorphously defined style of development, of which government intervention and soft financial policies (either tax breaks or forced-credit policies or both) were important tools, and in which boosting exports was the primary vehicle for promoting growth.

The detailed economic analyses of the model came later, as an *ex post facto* justification, although they in turn became useful rationalisations for those seeking interventionist policies, for example the establishment by B.J. Habibie, when he was Indonesian Trade and Industry Minister, of an Indonesian Ministry of International Trade and Industry—clearly inspired by the MITI of Johnson's *MITI and the Japanese Miracle*.

Eight years after Japan started picking up the pieces left after World War II, Korea lay devastated by civil war, a clash that many feared would turn the Cold War hot. Taiwan and Singapore were backwaters. Even in the 1960s, after Japan and Korea had begun their 'miraculous' economic take-offs, analysts held little optimism for Thailand, Indonesia and Malaysia. Indonesia was described in 1968 by one respected analyst as a 'chronic dropout'.[5]

The East Asians' reputations improved rapidly. By the 1990s three South-East Asian countries—Indonesia, Malaysia and Thailand—had become the new tigers. Japanese economist Kaname Akamatsu argued that economic development in Asia could follow the pattern of a formation of flying geese, with Japan in the lead and the others following according to their level of technological and economic sophistication. The idea was popularised in the 1980s by Saburo Okita, described by one analyst as 'Japan's most revered developmental mandarin'. Okita said in a 1985 speech:

> Because there is such great variety in the Asian nations' stages of development, natural resource endowments, and cultural, religious and historical heritage, economic integration on the European Economic Community model is clearly out of the question. Yet, it is precisely this diversity which works to facilitate the flying-geese pattern of shared development as each is able to take advantage of its distinctiveness to develop.[6]

The flying geese theory was the first explicit exposition of a Japanese model. Japan was the goose that laid the golden egg. The idea is that a country starts with technically simple industries, then as it builds up expertise it works up to the next level of complexity. Japan set the pattern, starting in the immediate postwar years with textiles, moving on in the 1950s to chemicals, then onto iron and steel, then to automobiles, and most recently to electronics and electrical equipment.

The flying geese pattern is repeated in another dimension. The same flying geese pattern appears in the succession of countries concentrating on each industry at a given time. For the textile industry, the pattern starts with Japan, moves on to the four tigers (the 'newly industrialising economies'), then to the South-East Asians, then to China, and most recently to Vietnam and India.[7]

In spite of two oil shocks and a weak world economy in the early 80s and the early '90s, economic growth averaged 8 per cent a year for three decades in the four original tigers. In the mid-1990s growth picked up in South-East Asia as a result of a rapid increase in foreign investment. Growth in China accelerated from the late 1970s to around 10 per cent a year as the government encouraged foreign investment and exports.

Seen from a distance the miracle Asian economies may have looked like flying geese, but imitating Japan's sequence of industry development is only part of the story, and alone doesn't explain how the geese became tigers—or dragons, in some accounts. Edith Terry argues that the resurrection of the 'flying geese' metaphor is part of an effort by Japanese officials to promote the view that Japan's economic system is one of a plurality of possible capitalist systems, an argument intended to fend off American efforts to open up the Japanese economy and overcome its inflexible market and regulatory structures. The World Bank report *The East Asian Miracle*, Terry argues, was produced at the sponsorship and urging of Japan as an effort to bolster this argument. It was an attempt by Japan 'to deflect international criticism of its cartelized, highly protected domestic market and recent expansion of its industrial system to Southeast Asia'. Even though they paid $1.2 million for it to be conducted, Japanese officials were annoyed at the outcome of the World Bank report, Terry argues, particularly its rejection of the North-East Asian, Japanese model, in favour of the South-East Asian, more market-friendly version. In Japanese eyes the Japanese model is the basis for the Asian model, both through imitation of Japan's development path according to the flying geese metaphor, but also through direct Japanese investment in the region, Terry argues.[8]

What was distinctive about East Asia's development that made it so successful? And did that success come from following or breaking the rules of orthodox economics? This is a vexed question and the subject of great debate. But the lines of the argument have become clearer with the crisis of 1997. The tigers' paths can be divided in various ways. Alice Amsden makes a distinction between a 'market-conforming' approach to development—the orthodox model—and a 'market-augmenting' approach—the developmental state model. Under the second approach markets are still important, but for late-developing countries behind the technological frontier there is an important role for government to improve on the market result, Amsden argues.

The nature of intervention has varied widely among the tiger economies. The old and new tigers differ markedly in how closely they followed the most interventionist aspects of Japanese 'developmental state' model, particularly policies aimed at directing credit to force-feed export industries.

But they share one feature: an orientation towards exports. This was a key feature of Amsden's 'market-augmenting' approach. Higher exports of themselves are not necessarily beneficial. But for the East Asian tigers the focus on exports has had great benefits. Most importantly it brought the discipline of world markets to their economies by forcing new industries to compete with the best in the rest of the world.

Some analyses, like the World Bank's 1993 study, *The East Asian Miracle*, deal mainly with the economic aspects of the debate, but also argue that some of the success is due to market-augmenting policies—meaning that the state improved on a pure free-market outcome. The conclusions of the World Bank study were heavily qualified, but that did not stop them becoming a much-heralded vindication of those seeking to justify industrial policies of all sorts, a factor which economist Helen Hughes argues has undermined serious analysis of the region's development ever since.

Economic explanations are central to understanding the East Asian miracles. Korea and Taiwan both benefited early in the process from large amounts of capital freed up by land reform. Landlords stripped of their holdings needed somewhere to invest the money they were paid in compensation. Governments of both countries spent heavily on infrastructure and education, and little on consumption. Governments in both countries influenced investment decisions, though in different ways. In Taiwan there was heavy government ownership of industry, in Korea industry was privately owned, but decisions were guided by government policies that favoured designated industries. Taiwan and Korea pursued very different financial policies. Taiwan left interest rate decisions to the market; Korea intervened heavily. In both countries the costs of interventions and protectionist policies were offset by export incentives.

Development paths were different again in Hong Kong and Singapore, the smaller two of the four tigers. Hong Kong did not follow the interventionist aspects of the Asian model but adopted its export orientation. Singapore enforced saving through pension contributions to the Central Provident Fund and joint public–private ownership of many businesses. Three of the four tigers—the exception was Hong Kong—have had authoritarian, autocratic governments, whose suppression of individual liberties gave them more room to follow aggressive economic strategies. Singapore and Korea are notable for their levels of 'cronyism', the potentially corrupt links between government and business.

The South-East Asian tigers did not follow the 'developmental state' model as closely as Korea and Taiwan, although there were still some similarities. Again, the most important common element was an export orientation. Indonesia experimented with and then abandoned protectionist and interventionist industry policies; Malaysia still favours grand government-inspired 'megaprojects'; Thailand has recently been the most laissez-faire of the group. All three have taken more pro-market policies in recent years, although with heavy constraints on personal liberties and with strong preferences given to their rulers' cronies.

The World Bank's study, *The East Asian Miracle*, points to two critical aspects of the export push created by the successful players in the region. The first was to avoid imposing general restrictions on imports. Import restrictions raise the costs of goods used by manufacturers, especially exporters. The second tack was their effective use of exchange rates—at the very least, keeping currencies stable, or in some cases deliberately undervaluing their currencies so as to help exporters. It was only later that fixed exchange rates were seen as a problem and as a key factor behind the 1997 crisis.

The community as a whole often does not gain from lower exchange rates—households cannot buy as many foreign goods with their baht or rupiah—but exporters benefit. A lower exchange rate means exporters earn more in their local currency for every US dollar they are paid.

All the miracle economies made sure they at least kept exchange rates stable, and sometimes lowered them, to offset the adverse effects of lower trade barriers on local producers of import-competing goods. In every one of the miracle economies there is a clear link between times of low exchange rates and increased exports.

The economic arguments capture part of the reason for East Asia's success, but leave out other important parts of the picture. Only one of the eight East Asian success stories comes close to a pure 'economic model' of success—Hong Kong—and its performance arguably owes just as much to its good fortune in being next to China (and now part of it).

The emphasis placed on institutions by Japan revisionists like Chalmers Johnson adds to the story. But in their zeal to add an extra dimension some revisionists discount the economics too heavily. It is clear that state institutions played a key role in guiding the development of East Asian countries. What is more debatable is whether their success was due to 'market-conforming' or to the 'market-augmenting' elements of their policies—and they all had a mix of both.

One lesson from the 1997 East Asian crisis is that institutions cannot escape the consequences of markets. It may be, as Amsden argues, that part of the explanation for the economic miracle comes from policies that were 'market-augmenting'. The failure of the East Asian miracle came from pushing the process too far, from ignoring or misjudging the potency of market forces and the costs of intervention.

There are fundamental problems with using the idea of 'market-augmenting' policies as a policy prescription. These policies have been identified—in Japan by Johnson, in Korea by Amsden, in Taiwan by Robert Wade—only after the event, and their conditions are so specific and limited that they are of little or no use as general rules for policy. There is no reason in principle why interventions will not *sometimes* work, that governments will not occasionally succeed in picking winners. But in between, and on average, they are likely to pick a lot of losers. Also, many of the conditions for successful intervention in North-East Asia no longer exist because of the increasingly harsh and rapid judgments of globalised capital, a lesson reinforced by the 1997 crisis.

In their 1996 book, *Asia in Japan's Embrace*, Walter Hatch and Kozo Yamamura offer an illuminating variation of the flying geese theory. According to the theory, they note, the following geese should eventually catch up with the lead goose, turning the V-formation into a horizontal line. But what is really happening is the opposite, that Japan is flying further and further ahead of the regional flock.

Using vertically integrated production networks, Japanese MNCs [multinational corporations] have jealously guarded their technology, the source of their competitive advantage . . . By locating discrete pieces of the production process at different sites throughout the region, high-tech manufacturers controlling such networks can thwart the ability of potential Asian competitors to master and appropriate the entire package of technology.[9]

Hatch and Yamamura argue that Japan has embraced the Asia-Pacific region with a network of production alliances like those that exist within the business groups, or *keiretsu*, in Japan. In Thailand, Japanese affiliates in 1990 and 1991 accounted for 40 per cent of total start-up investments. In Malaysia one Japanese firm, Matsushita, in 1993 accounted for almost 4 per cent of national output, they report. Japanese parts drive Asia's machine industries. The flow of investment into Asia stems from the maturing and hence declining investment opportunities within the Japanese economy, and was accelerated by the early 1990s recession in Japan and the phenomenon of *endaka*, the strong yen, which forced Japanese business to find new sources of profit.

The economies of Asia embraced by Japanese multinationals are like the small and medium-sized Japanese firms within the *keiretsu*. They benefit enormously from their part in the group, which guarantees markets and gives them access to capital and technology. But Hatch and Yamamura warn that this could become a 'captive' style of development, in which the benefits of cooperation are no longer shared so evenly. One example was the squeeze on suppliers' profits in the early 1990s, when Japanese multinationals found their profits shrinking. The same squeeze is likely to have occurred in the 1997 crash as Japanese multinationals tried to offset falling sales by squeezing their Asian suppliers as much as possible. The squeeze has been exacerbated by the fall in the value of the Japanese yen, which has improved the competitiveness of Japanese-based suppliers. Japanese producers had scaled down production during the *endaka* period, but brought it back on stream as the yen weakened.

Japan's investment in Asia has been driven not by forces of comparative advantage, but of strategic advantage, Hatch and Yamamura argue. As Japanese multinationals seek to overcome the growing costs of the policies that created such rapid growth in the 1950s and 1960s, they are applying the same developmentalist techniques in Asia. 'Japanese developmentalism consists of a dense web of mutually reinforcing ties—between government and business, between business and business, and between management and labor.'[10] The benefit is seen in the increased employment and the gains from supplying inputs to these new factories. At first, the downside was that many of the inputs were sourced from Japan, although rising prices in Japan led to increased use of local materials. The problem with this approach is that the technological spin-offs in the supplier countries are limited by the practice of retaining the most highly skilled aspects of design and manufacture back in Japan. Until or unless this practice breaks down, the advantages to developing Asian countries of Japanese investment are not as great as the raw figures suggest.

Hatch and Yamamura make the point that 'Asian nations, then, are not lifting off under their own power. Rather, they are being pulled forward in part by Japanese capital and technology or, in other words, by membership in a Japanese production alliance.'[11] The benefits of this process have been considerable, but it also carries risks. The obligation of Japanese corporations lies first at home, and any withdrawal or diminution of investment is likely to occur first in its offshore businesses. And the absence of a strong indigenous technological base makes it difficult to set up industries or firms to compete with the Japanese subsidiaries.

Political explanations

Jamie Mackie, in a pioneering work comparing the political factors behind the successes of the original and latter-day tigers, points to the substantial differences between the two groups. Because they have been in the 'miracle' category for so much longer, the original tigers have been the targets of considerably more attention. Their success, it is widely held, stems from their style of government and their economic policies. Key elements include stable government focused on economic development, strong government prepared to make difficult decisions, flexible planning, and general acceptance of the price mechanism for allocating resources. Most fundamental is support for exports of manufactures, from textiles to ships to computer chips.

Mackie takes the argument further. The economic views do not have much to say about the political and social circumstances that have made export-oriented policies possible, he says. They barely mention 'the authoritarian, repressive aspects of the political structures of the NICs [Newly Industrialising Countries], which were particularly important in the early stages of their industrial development'. In spite of the importance analysts give to their pro-market policies, in all these countries there is distrust of pure markets on the grounds that they do not pay due regard to the welfare of the community, Mackie argues. This view stems in part from Confucian ideas about the relationship of governments to private individuals. The economic successes of these regimes have come from, according to Mackie,

> their ability to combine a high degree of government control over economic life—and substantial public sector activity in certain fields, with strong encouragement to the private sector. It has been their success in finding the right mix of public and private sector activities, appropriate to their circumstances and institutions, that has been crucial; and that is a matter of political judgement.[12]

Mackie points out that none of the four key ingredients cited by Johnson to account for the success of the original tigers applies to their successful successors in South-East Asia: a heavy and consistent investment in education, separation between reigning politicians and ruling bureaucrats, a strong commitment to market-conforming methods of intervention, and the existence of a pilot planning agency.

Mackie prefers another explanation. One common element among the original tigers is that all four had strongly authoritarian governments insulated from popular pressures. The latter-day tigers had authoritarian governments too, but they had to be more responsive to popular pressures in much of the postwar era. All benefited from growth coalitions of interest groups which favoured the development of export industries. These coalitions were able to contain, suppress or outmanoeuvre groups who opposed this approach.

Both the original and the newer tigers were lucky in their timing, benefiting from the 'pull' effects of Japan's rapid growth and the outflow of Japanese capital after 1970. American purchases during the Vietnam War gave a substantial boost to Thailand and Singapore, just as the Korean War had been a big benefit to Japan. Indonesia and Malaysia were also helped by the late 1970s oil boom.

The original tigers

Korea

Korea's development path over the past 36 years has been closely modelled on Japan's economic success. The state played a key role in guiding investment towards export industries. It succeeded where other statist models have failed because the emphasis on exports forced its industries to be competitive in world markets—with the help of heavy implicit and explicit subsidies.

Alice Amsden argues that state intervention was crucial in allowing Korea to 'catch up' with the industrialised world, essentially by 'distorting' the market so as to force a massive level of investment instead of consumption. The sternest discipline was the constant pressure on all firms to export. It was enforced through the government's ownership and control of the commercial banks, through protection and subsidies in new export industries, through price controls, and through controls on sending capital offshore. Discipline was applied by penalising poor performers and rewarding only good ones. Industries weakened by over-expansion were subject to government-directed rationalisation. Part of the discipline was that large, badly managed firms were allowed to fail—although the government's friends always seemed to perform well—and most were bailed out at least once.

In 1953, at the end of the Korean War, South Korea did not have a large enough population to consider using protection to promote domestic industry. Instead it relied on a strategy of 'forced growth' that makes it the quintessential imitator of the Japanese model. After the war most heavy industry was in the Soviet-controlled North Korea. South Korea at first was heavily dependent on American aid, but gradually restored its transportation and communication networks. Aggressive promotion of exports began under the regime of President Park Chung-hee, who came to power in a 1961 coup. Park maintained protection against imports, and officials closely controlled trade, foreign exchange and financial policies with one very clear goal: to promote exports. Park's tools included concessional exchange rates, direct cash payments, permission to retain foreign exchange earnings for specified imports, and permission to borrow in foreign currencies. Banks were told to make loans for specified industries at concessional rates.

The next shift in policy came in 1973, with the heavy and chemical industries (HCI) drive—a deliberate effort by the government to rapidly change Korea's industrial structure. Six industries were chosen for support: steel, petrochemicals, nonferrous metals, shipbuilding, electronics and machinery. They benefited from tax incentives, cheap public services and preferential finance.

The World Bank concludes that unlike efforts in other countries to promote heavy industry, 'Korea was at least partly successful'. One reason is that the government made clear these industries were expected to become internationally competitive. They imported only current technology and recruited well-trained scientists and engineers.

But there were problems too. 'Interventions were so pervasive that bottlenecks emerged, large-scale debts were incurred, and labor-intensive industries were starved of credit.' So when oil prices surged with the second oil shock in 1979, inflation was already high and the exchange rate had risen. The much-vaunted heavy and chemical industries were running at low capacity and exports were faltering.

Eventually the strains on the old system became too great, and in 1980 the government changed course again. 'Support for strategic industries was curtailed and abruptly reversed. The currency was devalued, and credit allocation policies switched, with a termination of large-scale preferences to the HCI sector', the World Bank study notes. Intervention since then has aimed at restructuring distressed industries, supporting technology development and promoting competition.

Korea emerged from this process with a heavy concentration of large-scale enterprises, more marked than in probably any other capitalist country—but which now has come to be regarded as a serious problem. Having grown fat under government protection, the big conglomerates, or *chaebol*, eventually began to chafe at the bit for more independence. Growing wealth and increasing public disaffection with the oppressive and sometimes murderous military government increased the pressure for democratic reforms. As wages rose to rich world levels, workers started to demand democratic rights to influence government, which they thought should coincide with their increased discretionary spending power. The authoritarian habits that were used so successfully to force investment into export industries became increasingly intolerable.

Over the past decade these pressures have brought fundamental changes to both the political and economic environment in Korea—starting with the first democratic presidential election in 1987. (Because the two civilian candidates split their vote, the 1987 poll was won by a general, Roh Tae-woo.) As Korea's wealth grew, so did its attractiveness as a destination for foreign investment, drawing external pressure for removal of some of the protective barriers that had originally been used as an incentive for investment. Participation in the General Agreement on Tariffs and Trade and pressure from the United States also forced the pace in reducing trade barriers. But Korea's growing wealth also created an environment in which corruption flourished, inspiring the reform efforts of the next government—and helping to explain their failure.

From 1990 Korea moved further towards market liberalisation, with efforts to reduce government controls over financial markets and gradually to allow more foreign investment in Korea and more Korean investment offshore. Reform came in fits and starts. The election of Kim Young-sam as president in December 1992 was a watershed. The first civilian president in three decades, Kim made it a central goal to accelerate the shift to a market economy. Kim first spelled out his commitment to globalisation in a speech in Sydney in 1994, and elaborated upon it further in a March 1995 speech enunciating the notion of *segyehwa*—the Korean word for globalisation.

Kim argued that the past emphasis on economic development had concentrated economic power in the hands of a few business tycoons, worsened income distribution and intensified strife among different regions and classes. But by the end of his term Kim had delivered little of what he had promised, and when the 1997 Asian financial crisis struck, Korea was ill-prepared and its weaknesses were exposed.

Taiwan

Johnson and Amsden are the leading theorists of industrial policy in Japan and Korea respectively. In Taiwan the title belongs to Robert Wade, whose 1990 book, *Governing the Market*, makes a strong case that the state has played an influential role in guiding industrial development in Taiwan. What is much less clear is the extent to which that intervention has improved Taiwan's performance. Wade acknowledges the uncertainty, although his own conclusion is that there has been a clear benefit.

Taiwan seems to meet the conditions for growth spelled out by neoclassical theory unusually well, Wade notes. 'Yet other evidence shows that the government has been intervening for decades, often quite aggressively, to alter the trade and industrial profile of the nation.'[13] One of the most important earlier interventions was the massive amounts of US aid channelled into Taiwan after the outbreak of the Korean War in 1950, for reasons of defence, but with important implications for industry. 'With that much aid, who couldn't industrialize?' Wade quips.

Based on his study of Taiwan, Japan and Korea, Wade outlines what he calls the 'governed market' theory of East Asian economic success, an approach that treats capital accumulation as the principle general force for economic growth.

It interprets East Asian success as the result of a higher level and different composition of investment than in less successful countries. The difference in investment is due, in important if difficult to quantify part, to government actions to constrain and accelerate the competitive process. These actions were carried out by a relatively authoritarian and corporatist state.[14]

Wade acknowledges that much investment in Taiwan has been undertaken in response to 'relatively uninhibited' responses to price signals in the market. But he qualifies this pro-market view with the argument that the market has been influenced by the underlying social structure of investment, on which government has had a profound effect. It has influenced prices to boost industry profits and boost investment, and has used more direct methods to shape investment, especially in the large public enterprise sector. 'The governments of Taiwan, Korea, and Japan have not so much picked winners as made them. They have made them by creating a larger environment conducive to the viability of new industries.'[15]

The criticisms of Wade by neoclassical economists are broadly the same as those made of Johnson and Amsden: although they identify distinctive institutional features of these countries' development, they do not show conclusively that these features increased the rate of growth.

The World Bank identifies five stages to Taiwan's policy approach, a model derived in part from Wade's research. The first started in 1949 when the Kuomintang fled mainland China and took control of the island. The key feature of the first stage was an ambitious land reform program that fostered social and political stability and boosted farm production. Improved farm output earned foreign exchange to fund imports and machinery and raw materials, which laid the foundation for the next stage.

From 1953 to 1957 the government's goal was to achieve economic self-sufficiency through heavy investment in transportation and power networks and other infrastructure. American aid paid for almost half of all public infrastructure investment. Extensive import quotas and high import tariffs protected domestically produced goods from foreign competition. The government subsidised light industries, especially textiles, and consumer goods industries developed rapidly, including textiles, apparel, wood and leather products and bicycles.

But problems were growing. Imports of machinery and parts for manufacturing were high, but exports were penalised by the higher exchange rate that resulted from restrictions on imports of consumer products. High imports of capital goods and low exports led to a growing trade deficit. The gap between imports and exports was filled mainly with aid from the United States.

In 1958, faced with the prospect of an end to American aid, the government changed tack to a policy of lowering barriers to imports and boosting exports. It was a fundamental change of direction that laid the basis for Taiwan's economic take-off. The Bank of Taiwan offered low-interest loans to exporters and the government hired an American research institute to identify likely candidates for export industries. The industries chosen were plastics, synthetic fibres and electronic components. They were joined later by apparel, consumer electronics, home appliances, watches and clocks. Direct foreign investment replaced US aid as the main source of foreign capital, and four-fifths of it went into manufacturing. In the ten years to 1972 exports grew at an average 28 per cent a year, compared with an average 12 per cent annual increase in the previous decade. Exports had jumped from $123 million a year to almost $3 billion.

But the rapid increases in manufacturing were straining transportation, electricity and communications systems, and manufacturing faced new competition from lower wage producers abroad. Investors rushed to the newly opened mainland Chinese market at Taiwan's expense. The oil shock of 1973 added to Taiwan's woes. Growth slowed sharply, inflation soared and exports slumped. The government turned again to American consultants, who recommended heavy investments in infrastructure, upgrading industry, and promoting local industries to replace imports. The government spent $8 billion on ten large public works projects, including highways, railways, airports and nuclear power plants, with the goal of lowering hurdles to growth.

In the 1980s Taiwanese exports in traditional labour-intensive manufacturing came under increasing pressure from the newer tigers. Again the government changed tack, this time focusing on high-technology industries of information, biotechnology, electro-optics, machinery and precision instruments and environmental technology. Tax incentives were provided for research and development and for diversifying and improving production techniques. The World Bank gives Taiwan mixed grades for the latest shift. A growing number of small, high-tech firms are producing sophisticated and higher value-added products, but for most firms the transition to high-tech manufacturing has been difficult. Rich world countries are becoming stingy at exporting the advanced technology, and the emphasis of industry on smaller firms makes it difficult to undertake costly investments in research and development. 'As a result, most Taiwan[ese] . . . manufacturers are still assembling imported high-tech components.'[16]

Hong Kong

Ardent free-marketeer Milton Friedman has lauded Hong Kong's tiny territory, 1000 square kilometres adjoining China, as the world's best example of a successful market economy in which government has played an admirably limited role.[17] But factors aside from economic policy contributed to Hong Kong's prosperity, especially its role since 1949 as the *de facto*, and since 1997 *de jure*, trade and finance gateway to China.

Hong Kong was a British colony for 99 years, from 1898 to 1997, but its status as a tiger stems from the establishment of the Republic of China in October 1949. A flood of refugees from the new communist state lifted Hong Kong's postwar population from 600 000 to 2.4 million. When the United Nations imposed a trade embargo on China at the start of the Korean War in 1950 Hong Kong fell into a slump. But refugee entrepreneurs from mainland China created light manufacturing industries, aimed mainly at the American market. So began the process of Hong Kong's rapid development, with little or no input from its administrators. By 1990 Hong Kong's income per person was the third highest in Asia, after Japan and Singapore.[18]

Economist Y.C. Yao attributes the Hong Kong 'miracle' to three main factors: political stability under British colonial rule, active government provision of social infrastructure such as public housing and transport, and a well-established legal system.[19] James Wang, a political scientist, adds another factor: 'the industrious character of the people, a large percentage of them refugees from the PRC [People's Republic of China]'. About 90 per cent of Hong Kong industry is geared for export, mainly of textiles, footwear, watches and electronics. Most exporters are skill-intensive, light manufacturers with fewer than fifty employees, although trade and financial services for China have become increasingly important in recent years.

Singapore

Along with the Malaysian Prime Minister, Mahathir Mohamad, Lee Kwan Yew, Singapore's Prime Minister from independence in

1959 until 1990, is the quintessential proponent of Asian values, of a distinctively East Asian style of political and economic management.

'Individuals believe that the individual exists in the context of his family. He is not pristine and separate. The family is part of the extended family, and then friends and the wider society', Lee told the journal *Foreign Affairs*.

> We used the family to push economic growth, factoring the ambitions of a person and his family into our planning . . . We were fortunate we had this cultural backdrop, the belief in thrift, hard work, filial piety and loyalty in the extended family, and, most of all, the respect for scholarship and learning . . . We had the advantage of knowing what the end result should be by looking at the West and later Japan.[20]

In another interview Lee argued that in the early stages of industrialisation authoritarian governments are more effective than democracies at promoting rapid growth. 'Take Korea, Japan, Taiwan. In their early stages they needed and had discipline, order, and effort. They must create that agricultural surplus to get their industrial sector going. Without military rule or dictatorship or authoritarian government in Korea and Taiwan, I doubt whether they could have transformed themselves so quickly', Lee told Jim Rohwer of the *Economist*. The Philippines, India and Ceylon had democratic governments after World War II, 'but the lack of discipline made growth slow and sluggish', he said. 'But once you reach a certain level of industrial progress, you've got an educated work force, an urban population, you have managers and engineers. Then you must have participation, because these are educated, rational people. If you carry on with an authoritarian system, you will run into all kinds of logjams.'[21]

Many critics argue that Singapore, to its cost, has never made that democratic transition. American academic Christopher Lingle discovered the limits of free expression in Singapore in 1994 after he wrote an article for the *International Herald Tribune* that offended Lee. Lingle, a lecturer at the National University of Singapore, argued in the article that some unnamed Asian regimes maintained their political dominance through rigid authoritarianism. 'Intolerant regimes in the region reveal considerable ingenuity in their methods of suppressing dissent', he wrote. Their methods included 'relying upon a compliant judiciary to bankrupt opposition politicians'.

Lingle was called to an interview by two detectives, who told him they were conducting an investigation into charges of criminal defamation and contempt of court. 'The degree of social control in Singapore is so complete that such a decision could only have emanated from the highest level', Lingle maintains. The authorities demanded that Lingle pay damages for defamation and legal costs. This would have been an admission that Lingle had perjured himself in earlier statements, so he left Singapore quickly, leaving most of his possessions behind. In his absence he was tried and found guilty as charged in the Singapore High Court.

Lingle concedes that Lee's achievements are substantial. His capital-friendly policies and shrewd investments in people and public works lifted Singapore's income per head to developed country levels in less than thirty years. 'A masterly handling of his friends and foes in the independence movement eventually placed him securely at the top of a superbly coordinated and highly disciplined party structure. His strident anti-communist stance during the Cold War also made him an important figure among grateful Western allies.' Lee's dominance was marked by a 'skilfully repressive grip' that has stifled the emergence of an effective political opposition, Lingle argues. At least eleven opposition politicians have faced libel suits brought by Mr Lee or members of his party, and many were bankrupted as a result.

Rachel van Elkan, an IMF economist, argues that credit for Singapore's rapid economic growth should go largely to its sound macroeconomic policies, a willingness to accept foreign investment and a healthy level of spending on infrastructure and education. But van Elkan also gives credit to market-augmenting policies such as tax breaks aimed at promoting investment in sectors with growth potential. These policies were used widely from independence in 1959 until the mid-1970s, a time of high unemployment, to promote investment in industry. Since then, as unemployment fell, incentives to local and foreign firms encouraged state-of-the-art technologies. Since self-rule in 1959, Singapore's economy has evolved from a 'semiclosed, low-wage producer of mainly labor-intensive goods, to a very open, high-wage producer of high-technology, capital intensive products', van Elkan writes. 'Given Singapore's successful development record, the presumption must be that its policies enhanced the country's growth potential.'[22]

But which policies? Other commentators draw the opposite conclusion from the same evidence. Writing in 1982, Linda Lim argued that Singapore's spectacular success is the result more of the Long Arm of state intervention than it is of the Invisible Hand of the free market . . . While Singapore is a success story of capitalist development, this is not the same as a success story of free market development. [The Singapore state] is in fact heavily interventionist. It owns, controls, and/or regulates land, labor, and capital resources, and their allocation. It sets or influences may of the prices on which private investors base their business calculations and investment decisions.[23]

Lingle sees the promotion of Asian values by Singapore's leaders, a 'contrived notion of neo-Confucian values', as a device to justify their restrictions of individual rights. Typically, criticisms of the ruling People's Action Party are answered by the claim that its survival is necessary to the survival of Singapore.[24] The end of the Cold War has removed the bogey of the 'Red Peril' as the greatest threat to society, and hence the justification for an authoritarian regime. It has been replaced with a 'White Peril' emanating from the West, Lingle says. 'The one sided projections of images of Western decadence are common themes in the daily newspapers in Singapore.' Lingle argues that efforts to stifle individualism will hurt Singapore, not help it, by leading to a decline in the innovation and creativity that are essential to progress and economic growth. 'Singapore's authoritarian-capitalist regime has manipulated "Asian values" to pursue its own limited goals.'[25]

The new tigers

Malaysia

In the first twenty years of independence from 1957 Malaysia followed broadly free-market trade and industrial policies, while promoting rural development and investing in social and physical infrastructure. Import protection was lower than in other developing countries, with an average rate of protection of 7 per cent. This laissez-faire approach was abandoned after ethnic conflicts in 1969, which led to the formulation of a New Economic Policy with the goal of promoting 'growth with equity', aimed at boosting the economic opportunities for the majority of Malays at the expense of the Chinese, who dominated Malaysian business. Chinese dominance of Malaysia—and Indonesia—made it unlikely these countries could directly emulate much more homogenous Japan and Korea. The NEP also opened the way for institutionalised Malay corruption. Natural resource exports were promoted through income tax deductions linked to export performance and to the level of domestic resources that were used; there were also tax allowances for export promotions and accelerated depreciation for exporters. Exporters were given credit guarantees and low interest rates. The government set up export-processing zones, free-trade zones and duty-free import of materials used for producing exports. Foreign investment poured in. By 1980 approximately 70 per cent of manufactured exports came from export-processing zones, mainly from foreign-owned firms, although by 1989 this figure had shrunk to 40 per cent.

In 1986, spurred by falling world prices and budget blow-outs, the government began to move away from state-led industrialisation. Instead the government promoted private investment across a range of industries. Tax incentives for exporters were raised and import protection reduced. Average effective protection fell from 31 per cent in 1980 to 17 per cent in 1987.

Indonesia

The 1997 financial crisis was the most profound political and economic event in Indonesia since Soeharto seized power from Sukarno in 1966 amid widespread economic and social turmoil. Under Sukarno the government had nationalised Dutch enterprises and taken over all aspects of the economy. Sukarno's policy was shaped by 'a strong sense of nationalism, flavored with anticolonial and anti-Chinese sentiment', says the World Bank report. Sukarno's policies became increasingly inwardly oriented and interventionist, with a pervasive and complex regime of import and investment licences. By 1965, amid growing economic turmoil, inflation had surged to 1000 per cent, exports and foreign exchange reserves had dwindled and economic growth stagnated.

Soeharto's 1966 New Order wrought substantial economic improvements, promoting economic growth and managing inflation. Policy-makers, imbued with a strong strand of socialist thinking, sought a middle way between capitalism and socialism. Soeharto took a more pro-western stance than Sukarno, returning some nationalised businesses to private owners and offering 30-year guarantees that they would not be nationalised again. The exchange rate was devalued sharply, import licences were abolished and exports, virtually static before 1967, rose sharply. Indonesia had large oil reserves and benefited greatly from the leap in world oil prices in 1973 and 1979. With revenue pouring in, the government spent more on capital works, education, health services and family planning, and made impressive progress in reducing poverty. The government used cash from oil and commodity exports to invest in capital and resource intensive sectors such as oil refining, liquefied natural gas, chemicals, pulp and paper, fertiliser, cement and steel. Economic growth averaged 8 per cent during the 1970s and 1980s. During the oil boom controls on foreign and domestic private investment were tightened. A gradually rising exchange rate eroded the competitiveness of non-oil exports and, in response, barriers to imports were also raised. By 1985, the World Bank notes, a wide range of products had come under various forms of import controls. The system favoured industries producing substitutes for imports rather than encouraging exports.

In 1986 declining oil and commodity prices squeezed export returns and the government changed tack again towards a more open trade regime. Indonesia in 1985 had made steep cuts to import tariffs, and in 1986 introduced export incentives and simpler import and export procedures; the currency was also devalued. From 1988 production levels, exports and investment all rose and economic growth accelerated.

Indonesia scholar Hal Hill argues that it is hard to find a coherent philosophy, let alone a precise set of economic and social objectives, over the history of the New Order. Three decades after Soeharto came to power, there still remains in many quarters 'a deep-seated mistrust of market forces, economic liberalism, and private (especially Chinese) ownership', he says.[26]

The market-oriented reforms of the 1980s enabled the Indonesian economy to recover from the hyperinflation and economic decline that had been caused by the policies of the 1960s and by the 1980s slump in commodity prices, Hill says.

> Yet the country faces a fundamental dilemma in adhering to the principles of a liberal economy because notions of 'liberalism' and 'capitalism' are still very unpopular with a significant section of the population . . . Like many other newly independent states emerging from a turbulent colonial history, anti-capitalist sentiment was very powerful in the first two decades or so after independence.[27]

The issue remains potent because of strains between Indonesians and ethnic Chinese, who make up only 4 per cent of the population but dominate business.

Hill argues that the idea of an Asian developmental model, in which far-sighted activist regimes have picked winners and boosted industrial success, has much support in Indonesia, 'obviously because of Northeast Asia's undeniable success, but also because it reinforces widespread community and official distrust of markets and liberalism'.[28] Hill rejects this model.

> The notion that selective industrial promotion policies explain Indonesia's industrial success receives very little empirical support. Protection has subsidized inefficient industries, and well beyond the stage of infancy. It has also taxed some of the most successful exporters in the past, notably the garment industry. State enterprises have not played a major developmental role. Subsidized credit has helped many firms, but the schemes have been plagued by corruption and it is not obvious that they have been a decisive factor in industrial growth.

Soeharto's choice of B.J. Habibie as his vice-president amid the turmoil of early 1998 indicated the strength of support for the developmental approach in spite of intense pressure from the International Monetary Fund for Soeharto to adopt staunchly pro-market reforms. Habibie, who replaced Soeharto in May, was a strong advocate of interventionist industrial policies.

Thailand

In the early postwar years Thailand mainly exported primary and farm products. Trade was controlled, with the largest export, rice, managed by a state marketing monopoly. In 1955 abolition of the rice export monopoly and reductions in heavy export taxes on other commodities encouraged resource and farm exports. Import protection remained high in some industries, although overall levels of protection were modest. As international economic fashions changed in the 1970s, Thailand increased import tariffs on consumer goods, keeping duties on capital goods and inputs for other products low. Especially favoured were textiles, pharmaceuticals and automobile assembly.

The 1970s oil shocks forced a change of course, and in 1981 trade policy made the shift towards the typical Asian model goal of export promotion. Export taxes were cut, the exchange rate devalued and tariffs on imports reduced, although in the mid-1980s the average effective rate of protection, at 52 per cent, was higher than other East Asian countries such as Korea (28 per cent) and Malaysia (23 per cent).[29] Incentives were shifted towards labour-intensive, export-oriented, geographically dispersed activities. These included tax exemptions and rebates, cheaper electricity, easy access to finance, marketing assistance and promotion of trading companies. The result of all these policies was a surge in exports, especially in clothing, footwear, artificial flowers, jewellery and computer chips, as investment from Japan and Korea poured in.

The secret of success?

The World Bank identifies four common threads to the export push followed by all the successful countries: giving exporters access to imports at world prices, access to credit, government help in penetrating markets and overall policy flexibility. The success stories also followed macroeconomic policies sounder than in other developing countries: smaller budget deficits or surpluses and well-managed monetary (interest rate) policy.

How much of East Asia's success stemmed from selective intervention? 'The importance of this question could hardly be exaggerated', IMF economist Michael Sarel wrote in a 1995 paper. Sarel identifies several approaches to the issue. The neoclassical approach, in recent decades the most popular view among western economists, holds that markets are generally efficient, and that the role of government in economic development is important but limited. Advocates of this view, including the World Bank, see the region's success as the natural outcome of economically conservative policies.

The revisionist view argues that markets inevitably have many imperfections. In poorer countries these include credit constraints, monopolies, unfair trade practices by foreign firms and a lack of access to many markets. To counter these imperfections government should play a central role in helping to acquire technology, allocate funds for key projects, and guide the development of the economy.

Sarel himself takes an agnostic third position, which he calls neither good nor bad, but ugly. 'We cannot say anything meaningful about selective interventions, because we cannot properly identify the role that such policies play in the determination of economic growth.'[30]

Sarel points to four hurdles to reaching clear conclusions. First, researchers analysing the miracle have selected successful economies and left out the failures. In selecting the most successful economies for study, analysts knew before they started that government interventions did not inhibit growth. There has been almost no research in policies in countries that have performed badly. Second, it is usually impossible to demonstrate the 'counterfactual': what would have happened if interventionist policies had not been followed. Third, there are wide differences between the policies followed by each of the successful East Asian countries. 'There is . . . a large variation in the specific sectors and industries that were targeted for selective interventions across different countries. Indeed, the more one studies the policies pursued by the different countries, the more evident it becomes how different, and sometimes contradictory, these policies were.'[31] The World Bank report encompasses the highly interventionist strategies of Japan and Korea and the non-interventionist approaches of Hong Kong and Thailand. Only in Malaysia has government sought a deliberate redistribution of wealth. The four tigers' performance can be used to support everyone's favourite prescriptions, from intervention to laissez-faire, Sarel says.

Fourth, it is difficult to prove the 'direction of causality'. Did government policies lead to strong growth? Or did strong growth lead to desired outcomes such as small budget deficits, rising education levels and rapid industrialisation?

Spending on education and balanced budgets are often correlated with economic growth. But finding a correlation does not prove which came first. Sarel says he is not attempting to show that these policies are not important, but that 'we still understand very little about the relationship between public policy and the miraculous growth rates of East Asian economies'.

High rates of saving and investment are often held to be key factors in East Asia's economic success. But the economic evidence is that growth causes saving but saving does not cause growth, Sarel argues. High investment rates in Korea, Taiwan and Singapore and the high degree of openness to trade in Korea and Taiwan evolved only gradually, 'accompanying rather than preceding the process of economic growth'.

Indeed, there is evidence that it was not the policies they adopted but their conditions before they began that may account for much of East Asia's success, Sarel says. He cites a study which found that the best improvers up to the 1990s were countries that in 1960 had lower incomes, better primary education, less inequality of income and inequality of land distribution than the poor performers.

What are the useful elements of the Asia model? Jamie Mackie concludes that although conditions vary greatly, the common element in East Asian miracle countries is that political structures included a coalition of interests insulated from popular pressure and favourably disposed to export development. Mackie argues that laissez-faire economics does not fully explain the high growth of East Asian economies. None, except Hong Kong, practised pure laissez-faire policies. But some use of pro-market policies was important, even if it did not live up to the laissez-faire ideal.

Sadly for the democrat case you don't have to be a democrat to be a good economic manager, and contrary to the modernisation theory first espoused by Seymour Martin Lipset in 1959, good economic management doesn't necessarily increase the prospects for democracy.[32] But there is some hope in the East Asian experience, from the best and worst cases: Indonesia's problems stemmed from its undemocratic inflexibility; South Korea's underlying economic problems were as great or greater than Indonesia's, yet confidence recovered there much more rapidly in large part because a peaceful change of government achieved through an election allowed Korea to make economic decisions that, while threatening vested interests, were needed to overcome its economic crisis.

Chapter 4
Japan stumbles

Middle-aged Japanese women adore him: the kendo champion with the slicked back, jet-black hair and the booming voice of a kabuki actor. Until September 1997 almost everyone else in Japan thought well of him too. Japanese Prime Minister Ryutaro Hashimoto could do no wrong. Here was a Japanese leader prepared to confront Japan's economic problems head on, to take on the vested interests in politics and business opposed to change, to tackle seriously the problems in a country suffering six years of economic stagnation. In July 1997 the *Washington Post* declared him Japan's 'most powerful and effective premier in a decade'.

After the Liberal Democratic Party's election victory in October 1996 Hashimoto outlined a program of sweeping economic and administrative reform covering the financial system, the budget, economic deregulation, the bureaucracy, social welfare and education. The program, if carried out, would have undermined the iron triangle that has dominated Japanese postwar politics: a collusive collaboration between business, politicians and bureaucrats that served each other's interests—but not always those of the public.

A year after the election Hashimoto was coming to be regarded as a political superhero—a strong and dashing reformist who would conquer Japan's corrupt consensus politics and revive its sickly economy. His Big Bang reforms would shake up the sclerotic financial system blamed for the 1990s economic slump.

But in September 1997 Hashimoto stumbled badly, and he never recovered. Oblivious to public opinion and under pressure from a conservative group in the LDP, Hashimoto appointed a convicted criminal, Koko Sato, to his cabinet. Although appointing ministers was nominally Hashimoto's prerogative, Sato won his post as a result of factional dealing within the LDP, a reward for his long years of loyal service—paid in spite of his involvement in the 1970s Lockheed scandal. Sato in 1986 had been given a two-year suspended sentence after being convicted of receiving a 2 million yen bribe.

After two weeks of public attacks Sato was forced to resign, and Hashimoto apologised. But the move had sent Hashimoto's approval rating tumbling from 53 per cent to 35 per cent, an all-time low. The debacle destroyed Hashimoto's political authority. Sato's appointment was a reminder of the corrupt and sordid money politics that had led in 1993 to the downfall of the Liberal Democratic Party after 38 years in power.

Hashimoto's submission to the factions revealed that the same web of obligation that had shackled his predecessors remained entrenched. The short-lived hopes of a changing style of Japanese leadership—that Hashimoto would be a leader seriously prepared to undertake reform that threatened the vested interests of the ruling elite—had been dashed.

Hashimoto was in poor shape when two months after the Sato debacle he was faced with Japan's most serious economic crisis in two decades. Japan faced a crisis of accountability and responsibility. The credibility of the bureaucrats who for decades had dominated policy-making was being undermined by the economy's weak performance and the continuing corruption scandals. But the politicians have been unable to fill the vacuum. The ruling LDP was riven with factional disputes, and Hashimoto was unable to rise above the fray.

The vested interests against reform in Japan are formidable. The slowdown in the Japanese economy over the 1990s brought home the message that change was needed. While Japanese manufacturers continued to be world-beaters, other industries were increasingly dragging down the economy's performance. Even Prime Minister Hashimoto acknowledged that part of the problem was in Japan's famously influential bureaucracy. Excessive regulation was stifling new business, duplicating services and wasting resources. These were familiar problems in many countries, but they were especially galling in Japan after its amazing postwar success. The dimensions of the waste take on a scale of their own in Japan, where the close links between the construction industry and government have made spending on massive public works a traditional way to win votes, keep construction companies happy and keep political donations flowing.

The Japanese Construction Ministry has spent 3.3 trillion yen in construction and interest costs for three huge bridges linking Japan's largest island, Honshu, with its smallest, Shikoku. One of them, the 3.9 km Akashi Bridge completed in April 1998, is the world's longest bridge. But the tolls on the bridges are so high that the bridges are barely used. These projects are never subject to cost–benefit appraisal; they are the result of political deals. Politicians can get away with voting huge amounts of money on these projects in part because they have access to a huge slush fund, the Fiscal Investment and Loan Program, which is not subject to parliamentary scrutiny. Politicians everywhere like to dip their fingers in the biscuit barrel, but this one is the grandaddy of them all: in 1995 the program spent 53 trillion yen ($600 billion)—more than Australia's entire annual economic output.

It is ironic that Japan's unwillingness to take a bolder stance on the regional stage can be sheeted home, in part, to American policies in the years of the postwar occupation, from 1945 to 1950. 'America developed its own version of Orientalism after the Second World War', argues American author Patrick Smith, in his insightful account of Japan's social malaise, *Japan: A Reinterpretation*.

> We not only fixed Japan and the Japanese in our minds as a certain kind of country populated by a certain kind of people; we went on to create the country and the people we imagined . . . The version of Japan concocted after the war is still widely accepted. It is reflected in Washington's treatment of Tokyo, which resembles the way a colonial power treats a dependency; more prevalently, it is evident in the way ordinary Americans think of Japan and the Japanese. Our 'Japan' has advanced somewhat beyond kimonos and conical straw hats, though not entirely . . . In the 1970s we took to calling our imagined Japan 'Japan Inc.'—an entire nation cast as a corporation, and its people as employees rather than citizens. This conception of Japan is still taken as genuine throughout the West
> . . .
> The Japan before us today is the same one America created after the war: extravagantly corrupt, obsessed with market dominance, ecologically reckless, stifling of the individual, politically dysfunctional, leaderless, incapable of decisions.[1]

Smith traces Japan's inability to become an autonomous player on the world stage to two documents. The first was the 1947 constitution written under General MacArthur, which barred Japan from raising an army and limited its military activity to the defence of its natural borders. The other was the 1951

US–Japan security treaty, which placed Japan under American military protection. The imperatives of the Cold War induced America to devise a security treaty with goals strikingly different from those of the constitution. The constitution, in principle but not in practice, severely constrains Japan's military role; the security treaty insists that Japan provide extensive support for American forces. 'Americans were responsible for both documents, and it is remarkable that they exist side by side, for together they are a tour de force in political and diplomatic schizophrenia, the disease from which Japan still suffers.'[2]

Christmas cheer

The Japanese economic crisis of 1997 had its roots a decade before in the glorious 1980s, a time when Japan seemed ready to take on the world. Christmas Day 1989 was a turning point for Japan. It was the day that the Bank of Japan and the Ministry of Finance decided that the speculative boom of the late 1980s had gone too far. It was the day that the authorities who controlled Japanese financial policy began lifting interest rates to try and prevent the boom rising to even more dizzying heights. Another two years passed before the full effects of the interest rate hikes fully hit home in the real economy, with tumbling real estate and share prices and a slump in industrial output. But after the hikes in interest rates that began in Christmas 1989, Japan in the half decade from 1992 suffered its weakest growth in half a century.

At first it seemed Japan was suffering another cyclical downturn and that it would soon regain its composure. But the longer the slump continued the more it became clear that Japan's problems were deeper than the familiar ups and downs of economic cycles. The country that had spawned the Asian miracle and become the world's second largest economy was in deep trouble. Christmas Day 1989 marked the end of the Japanese miracle.

Japan did not cease to be a rich country with great skills and powerful industry. The bursting of the bubble revealed, however, that Japan was as susceptible to speculative excesses as any other country, and that the formula behind its postwar success no longer produced such miraculous results. Japan's economic malaise throughout the 1990s was a significant factor behind the East Asian financial crisis.

The slump in the Japanese share market began in 1989. Property prices followed share prices downwards a year later, leaving banks saddled with enormous debts no longer covered by the collateral supposed to stand behind them. Many Japanese banks were technically bankrupt, but were allowed to survive in the hope that economic growth would eventually pick up enough for them gradually to earn their way out of trouble. But they did not.

When the markets turned in the early 1990s they turned with a vengeance. By 1993 share and property values had fallen by more than half. The Japanese economy was trapped. Banks' balance sheets were shaky—and they had not brought to book anything like the true level of their bad loans. But it was not a credit squeeze that stymied lending in Japan in the 1990s. The problem was that nobody wanted to borrow, even with interest rates at record low levels.

The rupture of the bubble economy placed Japan's financial system under immense strain, with the hangover of enormous debts from the collapse of asset prices leaving many institutions technically insolvent. They were protected from collapse by the clubbish arrangements that bind financial institutions and bureaucrats in a network of mutual obligation and common interest. However, these events severely eroded confidence in the economy, compounding a self-perpetuating cycle of slow growth.

Strong yen, weak economy

The combined weight of the strong yen and slow growth had given some impetus to economic reform, the process of stripping away the heavy regulatory apparatus that made the domestic, non-tradeable side of the economy so inefficient and costly. But it was slow going. Regulations were relaxed in petrol-marketing, electricity and air transport. Changes in the financial system had been made incrementally over the previous decade. But there was little progress in many areas.

In spite of its lethargic economy, Japan's currency soared in the early 1990s, a sign of its continuing inability to consume or invest all the goods and services it produced. By the nostrums of conventional economics this behaviour was bizarre. The domestic economy was weak, yet savings remained strong. The soaring yen encouraged Japanese to continue investing massive amounts offshore. The reason for the unusual mixture of a strong currency in a weak economy was the authorities' 'massive mistakes in monetary (interest rate) policy', argues Peter Tasker, a Tokyo sharebroker and author. The Japanese authorities badly underestimated how severely the economy had contracted and kept interest rates relatively high, thinking they had to guard against the prospect of rising inflation. But with consumer prices falling by around 2 per cent, even a nominal interest rate on government bonds of 4 per cent meant a real interest rate of 6 per cent—a high enough rate to seriously inhibit new investment within Japan.

Another aspect of the problem was that many Japanese financial institutions were desperately short of cash, and the only way they could generate capital was by selling assets. With other Japanese financiers in similar straits, there were few buyers for Japanese assets, so they had to sell foreign property and shares. Repatriating the foreign currency proceeds increased demand for yen and pushed the rate still higher.

The soaring yen became an increasing burden on Japanese exporters, especially for smaller firms without large overseas operations to offset the profit squeeze at home. A high yen meant either that Japanese goods would be priced higher in world markets—which caused lost sales to cheaper competitors—or that Japanese producers would suffer lower profits, or a combination of both. With their ability to pass on costs down the chain of suppliers, larger Japanese corporations for a time were able to bear the squeeze. But the higher the yen rose the tougher life became, even for the stronger players.

With a few hiccups the yen continued to rise throughout the first half of the 1990s. The Mexican debt crisis in late 1994 and early 1995 weakened the US dollar further and so pushed the yen to levels that were becoming increasingly painful for many Japanese businesses. At the end of the Japanese business year in March 1995, investors sold off American assets they had been holding in the vain hope that the dollar would rebound, and in April the yen reached a record high of 80 yen to the US dollar.

By now both Japanese and American officials were becoming worried about the fragile health of the Japanese economy and its impact on world growth. Together they agreed to intervene in currency markets to reverse the rise in the yen that began a decade before with the Plaza Agreement. As in 1985, the currency was ripe for a turnaround, and their efforts helped it along the way.

Japanese investment in Asia

For most of the postwar years the United States was the prime location both for Japanese exports and for offshore investment. The pattern began to change markedly in the late 1980s as the rapid growth in the East Asian economies provided new avenues for investment. The Japanese investment boom in Asia came in two waves: one in the years after the 1985 Plaza Accord, another in the early 1990s. During the early 1990s Asia replaced the United States as Japan's largest destination for exports and for direct investment (in contrast to lending, which still went predominantly to the USA, where Japan was the largest customer for US Treasury bonds).

C.H. Kwan, an economist at the Nomura Research Institute, argues that in the early 1990s the character of Japanese investment changed. First, Japanese companies started to see the countries of Asia not just as production bases for exports, but as markets that are important in their own right. The search for new markets was reinforced by protectionist pressures in Europe and the United States, and encouraged Japanese investment in what could one day become the largest market of all: China. Second, to cope with the rising cost of obtaining parts and components from Japan, Japanese companies in Asia increased the content of their products sourced from their Asian subsidiaries.[3]

When the yen began to fall in mid-1995 the region's economic dynamic changed radically. Just as the rising yen inflated the East Asian investment bubble, the turnaround in the yen was a key factor in the deflation of the bubble, although with a delayed reaction. The end of the rising yen saved the skins of Japanese exporters, but it dealt a corresponding blow to other countries in East Asia. With their own factories within Japan regaining competitiveness as the yen weakened, Japanese investors had less reason to send large amounts of capital offshore. The fall in the yen led to a reduction in the flow of capital that had fuelled the East Asia boom. But South-East Asian countries had become so used to the flood of capital that they failed to adjust to the change. First, they kept spending as if the money was still pouring in at the same rates as in the early 1990s. Second, by linking their exchange rates to the US dollar, their cost advantage in world markets was sharply eroded as the American currency rose against the yen.

Bad banks

When the Japanese bubble burst, banks were left saddled with huge debts they could not service. Richard Koo, senior economist at the Nomura Research Institute, estimates the level of bad debts at 100 trillion yen, almost a quarter of Japan's entire annual output, although official figures put the level lower. But instead of responding to the problem by clearing out the dead wood, the banks, aided and abetted by the Ministry of Finance, kept trying to paper over the cracks, hoping that a gradual recovery would allow the banks eventually to write off the bad debts. But doubts about the banks' health undermined investors' confidence in the whole banking system, the strong along with the weak.

Financial rating agency Moody's Investors Service calculates that during the 1980s the value of Japan's banking assets (loans) multiplied threefold, from 264 trillion to 757 trillion yen. A large proportion of these loans were backed by commercial real estate. Many of the loans were made on the basis of what proved to be three fallacies: that the loans were backed by assets that could be sold if the lender defaulted, that the collateral would retain its value, and that there was no risk the borrowers would default so banks could lend at will. Yet even by 1997, although most of these loans would never be repaid, they were still not classified by the banks as bad or 'non-performing' loans.[4]

The 'Big Bang'

Japan had been suffering deflation—an affliction unfamiliar since the 1930s—for most of the 1990s. With their capital buffers stretched because of the fall in asset prices, Japan's banks were reluctant to lend, even if they would not admit publicly to the rising value of their bad debts. At the same time as banks lost their enthusiasm for lending, business lost the desire to borrow. With prices falling there was little incentive to buy shares or real estate. There had been over-investment in manufacturing within Japan during the bubble years, and the strong yen diminished further the incentive to add more capacity. During the late 1980s 'Japanese companies embarked on the biggest spending spree in the country's postwar history', said commentator Christopher Wood. During what Japanese call the *Heisei* expansion, from 1986 to early 1991, the Japanese economy expanded each year by the equivalent of one South Korea, said chief economist at Deutsche

Morgan Grenfell, Ken Courtis, and at the end of the period was 'one France larger' than at the start.

During the Great Depression in the 1930s economist Irving Fisher explained the two stages of deflation. In the first stage, the large amount of money spent on repaying debt depressed economic activity. If this 'debt deflation' leads to a fall in the general price level the result will be a general depression. Japan teetered on the brink of price deflation during the 1990s. Average prices across the economy fell in each of 1994, 1995 and 1996. Deflation increases the cost of borrowing and raises the 'real' amount of money owed. If prices are falling 10 per cent, real interest rates are 10 per cent even with a nominal rate of zero. 'Deflation caused by the debt reacts on the debt. Each dollar of debt still unpaid becomes a bigger dollar, and if the over-indebtedness with which we started was great enough, the liquidation of debts cannot keep up with the fall of prices which it causes', Fisher said.[5]

The financial system had already changed markedly since the late 1970s when it was an almost totally closed and regulated system. Certificates of deposit had been introduced and foreign exchange regulations relaxed in the early 1980s, and other institutions had been gradually, if only partially, deregulated. As a result of these changes, large firms during the 1980s learned they did not need to go to banks to raise capital, they could go directly to the market to issue shares or borrow. This gave them more flexibility and freedom to borrow—but it also reduced the authorities' ability to influence credit policy, and so contributed to the mismanagement of the late 1980s.

Alicia Ogawa, head of equities research at Salomon Brothers Asia in Tokyo, notes that in the mid-1990s thirteen of the top twenty Japanese commercial banks failed to generate net earnings above the risk-free rate of return—the return investors could earn from long-term government bonds. 'Those thirteen banks owned 44 per cent of the total assets of the commercial banks. That's a lot of excess capacity', she said. Almost two out of three of the top twenty sharebrokers reported losses in 1996 and 1997. In the past, the Finance Ministry had tackled banking crises by leaning on healthy banks to take over weak banks, the so-called convoy system. But the scale of the problem was so large in the 1990s that this solution was no longer tenable.

Hashimoto in 1996 announced a 'Big Bang' package of financial reforms aimed at tackling the weaknesses in the financial system. The plan was named after the British Big Bang reforms of 1986. The planned changes would be a repudiation of the Japanese postwar model of managed economic development in favour of a more market-oriented model. The goal was to lower the barriers between different kinds of financial institutions. This would be achieved by removing distinctions between commercial banks, long-term credit banks and trust banks, and allowing financiers to set up holding companies to gain entry into each other's territories. Sharebrokers' commissions and non-life insurance premiums would be removed from government control and the ban on foreign exchange dealings by non-banks would also go.

Hashimoto wanted to revitalise the Japanese financial system and restore its role as the most powerful player in the region. By increasing competition and reducing regulation the changes would also force the costly and clumsy financial system to lower its costs; and by forcing banks to consider the riskiness of their lending these changes would reduce (but not eliminate) the magnitude of a future speculative mania like that of the 1980s bubble years.

Storm warning

The Japanese share market had made a sustained bull run from mid-1995 to mid-1996, breaching the 22 000 level on the Nikkei sharemarket index, then retreated slightly in the second half of 1996 to hover around 21 000. The market slipped in early December 1996, after the warning by US Federal Reserve chairman Alan Greenspan of the 'irrational exuberance' of American share markets. Wall Street quickly recovered its composure, but the Japanese market continued to fall, spurred by the announcement in mid-December of the draft budget for the coming year. The draft made clear that in spite of continuing economic weakness the government would insist on sticking with its plans to reduce the budget deficit and persist with an increase in consumption tax on 1 April. Hashimoto regarded the promise as a litmus test of his reform credentials.

'The market thinks the economy stinks' proclaimed a market report by investment bank Salomon Brothers in early 1997. The share market weakness fuelled fears about the solvency of Japan's weaker financial institutions, whose balance sheets only returned to health with the 1996 share market recovery. On 10 January 1997 the Japanese share market suffered its worst fall in two years amid growing fears that Japan's economic recovery would stall and that the impact of deregulation on the financial sector would be negative. The Nikkei market index fell 770 points or 4.26 per cent to end at 17 303.65, its lowest close since August 1995.

The tsunami hits Japan

The markets stabilised after the January shock, but when the South-East Asian economic crisis hit in July, overseas investors started reviewing prospects for the whole region, especially when it began to appear the storm would not be confined to South-East Asia. South-East Asia takes 18 per cent of Japan's exports, but Asia as a whole accounts for 43 per cent of exports. The outlook was clouded further by Hashimoto's political stumbles.

In November the pressures on Japan came to a head. As the Asian contagion spread, investors began to doubt the viability of the Japanese financial system.

The first taste came on 3 November, when mid-size sharebroker Sanyo Securities collapsed. The real panic began two weeks later. On 17 November Japan suffered the first-ever collapse of a top twenty bank, Hokkaido Takushoku Bank, and on 22 November Yamaichi Securities, the fourth largest brokerage firm, went under, followed on Wednesday 26 November by Tokuyo City Bank, a mid-sized regional bank.

A meltdown in the Japanese financial system was a very real prospect in the week of 24–28 November, and would have been far more cataclysmic for the world financial system than anything that had happened elsewhere in Asia. In the previous week investors had queued up outside Yamaichi and other banks rumoured to be in trouble to withdraw deposits. Some banks switched off their automatic teller machines to make it harder for customers to draw out cash, although they could still do so by lining up at bank counters. On Monday 24 November Yamaichi was declared insolvent with 6 trillion yen in liabilities it could not repay. The broker admitted it had illegal, hidden debts of 264.8 billion yen. The previous week, rumours of the losses had prompted credit agency Moody's Investors Service to classify the brokers' debt as junk, making it impossible to raise funds for short-term transactions and sparking a liquidity crisis.

Finance Minister Hiroshi Mitsuzuka promised on the day of the Yamaichi collapse that the Bank of Japan would take the unusual step of providing unsecured loans to the failed broker 'in order to secure the stability of the financial system as a whole'. The promise aimed to prevent a systemic crisis—a wholesale withdrawal of investments by customers who have lost confidence in the safety of the system. But until the week was over it was touch and go whether these efforts would succeed. The crisis came less than a week after South Korea appealed to the International Monetary Fund for $20 billion in emergency support to try and staunch a damaging run on its currency. Adding to the pressure on Japan were fears that the collapse of the Korean currency would squeeze the profits of Japanese exporters as the two countries fought over their shared markets for ships, computer chips and cars.

Yamaichi had suffered worst among the Big Four brokers from a scandal over the payment of bribes to *sokaiya*, or corporate gangsters. All four banks lost substantial business to American broking houses as a result of corruption scandals—itself a sign that at least some change was afoot in the financial system. The American threat to their viability was reinforced by the slump in the share market, which had been fuelled by the exit of foreign investors amid the Asian financial crisis. Yamaichi was also damaged by persistent rumours, that it had engaged in illegal *tobashi* trading—shifting investment losses from one client to another to prevent a favoured customer from having to report losses. Yamaichi was believed to have more than 200 billion yen in these unlisted hidden debts.

The decision to allow Hokkaido Takushoku to fail meant 'capitalism has come to Japan', said chief economist at J.P. Morgan in Tokyo, Jesper Koll. For the first time, banks would be allowed to go broke without their troubles being forced onto a stronger cousin. Richard Koo at Nomura was gloomier. Until recently, foreign buying support had been the only thing keeping the Japanese share market and banking system from a total collapse, he said. The departure of foreign investors from the Japanese market in October and November had removed that prop, with potentially devastating consequences. Nomura had long been pushing for a substantial injection of government money to bail out the banking system, a prospect that had previously been politically untenable.

Foreign banks, increasingly anxious about getting their money back, demanded higher interest rates for loans to Japanese banks, and in some cases refused to roll over loans altogether. Bankers said a growing number of foreign banks were preparing blacklists of Japanese banks with which they would not deal.

On Friday 28 November the central bank, the Bank of Japan, pumped an extraordinary 3 trillion yen into the money markets to ensure there was enough cash to keep the system afloat as other sources of money dried up. This intervention showed both the depth of the crisis in the Japanese markets and the authorities' commitment to keep the system working.

Banking analyst at Salomon Brothers in Tokyo, Miharu Aizawa, said the central bank's huge liquidity injection on that Friday was a key ingredient in restoring confidence to the system and preventing a meltdown. 'Hokkaido Takushoku Bank, Yamaichi Securities and the Tokuyo City Bank all went bankrupt not because of capital deficiency problems—of course their capital was weak—but because of the very tight money market', she said as the dust settled. 'Now the Bank of Japan has shown they understand they have to support the money market, to help banks' liquidity', she said.

Risks

By November every Asian country was facing a substantial slowdown in economic growth. The growing fear among policymakers worldwide, including the US Treasury, was that a worsening crisis in Japan would sharply accentuate that process and undermine the world's economic powerhouse, the United States.

The worst-case scenario had several strands. One was a systemic collapse—a crisis of confidence that leads customers to withdraw deposits and other investments and convert them to cash, jamming the banking system, cutting bank lending and spiking growth. Another danger was that Japanese institutions, badly weakened by the falling share market and desperate to prop up their own capital bases, would make big sales of their overseas assets. This would have pricked the bubble of the overvalued American share and bond markets. A sharp fall in share and bond prices could in turn bring a slowdown in the American economy, at a time when profits were also under pressure from a surge of cheap exports from Asian goods made cheaper by their falling exchange rates. And this in turn could fuel a protectionist backlash in America, where there is always potential for a chorus of complaint against Asian exports. The final fear was that investors outside Asia would continue their flight to quality by pulling assets back home; this would put more downward pressure on

Asian currencies and spark another round of deflationary price cuts that would undermine rich world markets.

Muddling through

As the crisis deepened, it became increasingly clear that the Japanese government would have to reverse its ambition to reduce the government budget deficit, and instead boost spending to give the anaemic economy a fillip.

A longer term solution remained as pressing and as lacking in support as it always had: loosening the web of regulations that continue to stymie the domestic economy. Reviving the inefficient domestic sector of the economy will ultimately be the only way Japan will overcome its economic anorexia. But those kinds of changes can take decades to implement and bear fruit, and in the 1997 emergency more immediate steps were needed.

The debate over whether to provide a budget stimulus, and if so how much, continued for six months. The government was coming under intense pressure from the United States to kickstart the economy. The Americans feared that Japan could become the next tinderbox in East Asia, inflaming what was already a serious regional crisis into a major world catastrophe. Japan's economy alone is larger than all the rest of East Asia combined. But the Finance Ministry continued to resist, insisting that enough pump-priming had been done and that more spending now would make for worse problems later.

America's Deputy Treasury Secretary, Lawrence Summers, hammered home the point in a visit to Tokyo on 16 November. Summers told Japanese Finance Minister Mitsuzuka of his 'concern about the outlook for the Japanese economy, and the importance for the United States and for stability in this region of effective action to restore domestic demand growth'.

Edward Lincoln, economic adviser to a former American ambassador to Japan, Walter Mondale, put the American view bluntly: 'The stagnation of the past two years was the fault of the government', Lincoln said. 'For a long time the Japanese were in denial, saying things weren't as bad as everyone thought. Now it is clear that they are that bad, and they are making Asia's problems worse.'[6]

In the following months Japan made half-hearted moves to provide the stimulus demanded by the Americans. On 18 November the government unveiled a package of steps to invigorate the economy, including deregulation and measures to encourage land transactions, but without the hoped-for tax cuts. The news went down like a lead balloon. Two days later the former Prime Minister, Kiichi Miyazawa, persuaded Prime Minister Hashimoto to consider using public funds to help clean up Japanese banks' bad loan mess. But the next day a parliamentary committee passed a bill aimed at slashing Japan's annual budget deficit. After the October 1996 election Hashimoto had made reducing the budget deficit one of his top priorities, and under pressure from the Ministry of Finance he was extremely reluctant to reverse that stance. At a time when the economy was crying out for more stimulation, the bill obliged the government to reduce it by setting the goal of achieving a balanced budget in the 2003 fiscal year.

In the New Year of 1998 confidence was undermined further by a string of arrests of bureaucrats who had received large bribes from banks in return for favourable treatment. Corruption scandals are standard fare in Japan, but this one lay at the centre of bureaucratic power, the Ministry of Finance. In late January prosecutors arrested two high-ranking Finance Ministry officials, and the Minister for Finance, Hiroshi Mitsuzuka, resigned in a ritual gesture of atonement. Then in February an LDP parliamentarian, Shokei Arai, was arrested on charges of receiving bribes from one of the top four securities firms.

The government's resistance to providing a budget stimulus was gradually being whittled away. The announcements of moves to stimulate the economy and revive the banking system came in a slow trickle—there were at least sixteen statements between October and April. But the pump-priming measures announced in April 1998 still only injected back into the economy in 1998 the amount withdrawn by earlier decisions.

Neither the banking package nor the belated pump-priming addressed the deeper problem of the huge debts weighing down the corporate sector, estimated by Peter Tasker at 200 per cent of national output. The economy is likely to remain in the doldrums because rather than spend, companies and households are trying to pay off these huge debts. Some analysts predicted that in 1998 the Japanese economy would shrink for the first time since the 1974 oil crisis.

As in East Asia as a whole, the judgment over whether Japan's problems were cyclical or had more deep-seated structural features was critical to deciding the appropriate policy response. As in Asia more broadly, both forces were at work, making it especially difficult to judge the correct antidote. Adopting stimulatory budget and monetary policies should eventually provide some fillip to the economy. But these had already been tried, albeit half-heartedly, with little success in previous years.

For much of the 1990s the typical view has been that Japan was in a cyclical downturn and would soon recover. But the upturn has been a long time coming—with severe consequences for Japan, for the region, and for the world. American economist Paul Krugman in a May 1998 paper fleshed out the argument that Japan was suffering something like the deflation described by Irving Fisher in the 1930s. One consequence of deflation can be a liquidity trap in which, unusually, efforts to kick-start the economy by lowering interest rates do not work. There is little doubt that Japan is suffering from this condition, which Krugman defines as occurring when demand falls short of productive capacity in spite of nominal short-term interest rates close to zero. But while it is easy to make the case that Japan is suffering from a liquidity trap, it is harder to explain why. Krugman's explanations are tentative, but familiar: Japan's ageing population, an unwillingness to use immigration to spur growth, and the economy's structural rigidities. The two conventional remedies are fiscal expansion and structural reform. But although structural reform will improve the supply side of the economy it will do little or nothing to boost demand. And the traditional Keynesian remedy of fiscal policy has limits, theory says, because consumers know that more spending now will mean higher taxes rather later to repay today's borrowing.[7]

Krugman has a novel answer to the standard view that monetary (interest rate) policy cannot be used to cure a liquidity trap: the central bank has to 'credibly promise to be irresponsible'. In normal conditions, Japanese consumers trust the central bank to do its job of clamping down on interest rates to contain inflation. But in these dire straits the central bank ought to promise to pump enough money into the economy to create expectations of future inflation. Only that way will consumers start spending the money they have been hoarding.

It is a far-fetched cure that will almost certainly not be tried. Even without such a radical remedy, as Krugman concedes, the Japanese economy will sooner or later recover, although to a much slower growth rate than it has had in the past. But his prescription highlights the profound changes that are occurring in the Japanese economy as it confronts the prospect of a declining population, the end of the gains from technological catch-up and its other structural rigidities.

Japan and East Asia

In the early months of 1998 Japan's financial system had stabilised after the traumas of November and December, but the indicators pointed to a stalling economy, just at the time the rest of East Asia was in greater need than ever of a market for its exports. American economist Rudi Dornbusch put the argument bluntly: 'Surely the greatest paradox today is that one of the richest countries in the world, Japan, is flirting with bankruptcy', he said. Dornbusch compared Japan with the United States of 1929, when the mistakes of President Herbert Hoover and the Federal Reserve plunged America and the world into the Great Depression. 'Japan today is no different. There must be no doubt that Japan is teetering on the verge of a 1930s-style collapse of financial institutions, confidence and economic activity', Dornbusch warned. 'Japan is trapped. If everything goes well, the country will just putter along with near-zero growth. If something goes wrong—and it does not take much, as we saw when the fall of Yamaichi Securities sparked worries of a nationwide banking collapse—Japan will go over the cliff and pull down the Asian region in the process.'

It was a line of criticism becoming increasingly widespread, and a view shared—though expressed more politely—by the US Administration. For US Treasury Secretary Robert Rubin and Assistant Secretary Lawrence Summers, admonitions to Japan to apply economic steroids became routine. 'A weak Japan is a source of weakness for the region', said Rubin on 21 January. 'Japan, the second-largest economy in the world, has an especially crucial role to play.'

In April a senior Japanese businessman joined the attack on the government. Sony chairman and chief executive Norio Ohga warned that the Japanese economy was on the verge of a collapse that could cause worldwide recession. 'The Japanese economy is currently facing its most difficult time ever. I am concerned that if Japan falls into a deflationary spiral it would affect the Asian economies. In that case, not even the US economy would be able to maintain its healthy state', he warned. Japanese stimulus packages had poured money into public works instead of stimulating consumer demand through cutting taxes, Mr Ohga complained. Average households in Japan now spent only 68.6 of their income, compared with 72 per cent in mid-1997, the lowest figure since the statistics were first collected in 1970.

The day after Ohga's speech and a gloomy *Tankan* report on

business confidence, international credit rating agency Moody's Investors Service downgraded its credit outlook for Japanese debt from stable to negative—a deep symbolic blow to the country that a decade before had been predicted to overtake the United States as the world's economic powerhouse. Moody's cited 'uncertainty about the ability of the authorities to achieve a policy consensus that would help promote a return to economic growth and fiscal balance'.

Two months later, in June, Japan had its biggest economic scare since the near-meltdown of November. The Economic Planning Agency reported that the economy had shrunk 1.3 per cent in the March quarter, making a decline in economic growth of 0.7 per cent for the year to March. It was the first time the economy had gone backwards over a whole financial year since the 1974 oil shock. The hoped-for recovery was nowhere in sight.

In response to this news the currency tumbled, falling on 15 June to an eight-year low of 146.75 yen to the dollar. A lower yen would help Japanese manufacturers lift sales in world markets, but it worsened the precarious balance sheets of the Japanese banks by lifting the value of their overseas assets. To maintain the required ratio of capital reserves to assets banks would have to reduce lending, further dampening the moribund economy. For the rest of the region, a sharp fall in the yen risked sparking the much-feared round-robin of competitive devaluations in a repeat of the kind of beggar-thy-neighbour policies that contributed to the Great Depression. This risk was especially great in China, which had so far held its currency stable in spite of the great pressures on its exporters.

United States President Bill Clinton was due to visit Beijing the following week. After months of refusing to help mount a currency rescue, and only a few days after Treasury Secretary Robin Rubin ruled out the option on the grounds that it would not work without a fundamental change in Japanese policies, the United States and Japanese authorities joined in heavy interventions to support the Japanese currency, which duly recovered above the 140 yen level. It seemed the coincidence of the American change of mind and the President's visit to China was not accidental.

For his part, Japanese Prime Minister Ryutaro Hashimoto promised far-reaching reforms of the banking system, including the injection of public money, a move previously considered political suicide. But his credibility was weak. The fear remained that Japan was unable or unwilling to repair its financial system and resuscitate its economy. Hashimoto's humiliation was completed by the LDP's devastating result in Upper House elections on 12 July, when the party lost 17 of the 61 seats it had held among the half contested in the poll. The next day he resigned as party leader and Prime Minister.

The Japanese response was not simply a failure of leadership or understanding at a key moment. It was integral to the Japanese economic management style, a style at the heart of the Japanese model. The Japanese crisis showed the limits of bureaucratic ability to manage the financial system, and of the system's dangers. If Japan's banking system were more transparent, with banks forced to disclose and write off their debts instead of hiding them for years, the November liquidity crisis would not have occurred, and the size of the East Asian boom and bust would have been much reduced.

The East Asian crisis also exposed the failure of Japan's political leadership. 'Although willing to finance investment in the region, Japan has yet to play the role of market-of-last-resort for Asia. Japan may still be the head "goose", but the rest of the geese are still flocking to the US market', argued Ron Bevacqua, chief economist at Merril Lynch in Tokyo in February 1998. 'Japan is not unable to be a "locomotive" for Asia—the problems in the banking sector are mainly under control—but it is unwilling to do so . . . It is politically easier for Japan to continue following its old economic model than to switch to one driven by domestic demand.'[8]

Most public criticism of Japan was directed at its contractionary budget policies. But a boost to spending and cuts to taxes would not alone solve Japan's long-term economic problems. Some more Machiavellian analysts argued that softening the pain for Japan by allowing the yen to fall and through pump-priming would be retrograde, because they would reduce the pressure for more far-reaching changes.

Japan has another duty towards Asia: as the world's largest creditor, Japan has greater responsibility than anyone else to help restore the health of the region's financial systems, and that means writing off or at least rolling over many of its loans to the region. But with Japan's own financial system so fragile, lenders were reluctant to take a bath on their Asian exposure, even though, eventually, they may well have to do so. It is a vicious circle. Japan is reluctant to forgive or give concessions on its Asian debt while its own financial system is so weak; its financial system will not recover until its economy recovers, but the economy's fragile health has been further undermined by the Asian crisis.

There is a respectable argument that it is none of the world's business whether Japan stimulates its economy or not, that if Japan's weak economy imposes deflationary pressures on the rest of the world the proper response is for other countries to stimulate their own economies. There is no doubt that calls by the United States and Asian countries for Japanese stimulus are self-serving: it should boost their own exports. But if the Japanese economy is only suffering a cyclical downturn and is about to return to full capacity then Japanese stimulus would reduce the supply of world capital, push up interest rates and slow growth elsewhere, with no net gain. The prescription hinges critically on the assessment of what is really going on in Japan.

But even if Japan is suffering a prolonged deflationary slowdown and a liquidity trap, does the rest of the world have the right to try and impose its solutions on Japan, as America has been trying to do? There is no answer in principle to this question although in practice there are many, from Bill Clinton down, encouraging Japan to do so. Japan is a sovereign nation, and has been led to take foolish policy actions in the past under American pressure, notably the loose monetary policy of the late 1980s, which was aimed at reducing upward pressure on the yen—and which fuelled a disastrous speculative bubble. But as Kindleberger has argued, in a deflationary situation the world needs someone to act as a lender of last resort. Japan is the obvious candidate. There is a good argument that Europe could do more if it were not so constrained by its politically inspired and economically dubious efforts to establish a single currency, although Europe is a less important market for Asia than Japan. The United States is running at close to full capacity and cannot at present do more to further stimulate world demand. Japan can do as it pleases; but the consequences for the region if its economy remains weak could be considerable.

Health will not return to the Japanese economy in the long run unless it can overcome the rigidities on the supply side—getting rid of excessive regulation and protection, and halting the flow of money into huge but unneeded public works projects.

Dornbusch argues that three changes are essential. First, a huge tax cut of perhaps 3 per cent of national output. 'Small tax cuts do nothing. There is now a need to take a big leap forward, create a forceful expansion in demand, output and employment and start rebuilding confidence. When confidence is eroding, nickel-and-dime fiscal policy makes the budget worse without making the economy better.' Second, with bad loans at between 12 and 15 per cent of national output, Japan must undertake a deep cleaning of its financial system. 'Cleaning up the banks costs a lot of budget money; not doing it now will cost far more later.' Third, Japan must deregulate and open up pervasively. 'The country is festering amid an overwhelming bureaucracy that has had the last word on literally any reform . . . As long as the bureaucrats are in place they will do what they have been appointed to do—co-opt people from pursuing their market interests or conspire with them to conceal bankruptcy and misfeasance.'[9] But the prospects are low of any of these occurring.

Individualism, modernism and morality in Japan

The postwar political ethic in Japan was a kind of economic nationalism. The income-doubling policies of Prime Minister Ikeda provided a sense of national purpose in the early postwar years. The Japanese were transformed from their role as (in their eyes) victims of the war with an ambition to prove themselves to the world. Aligned with that was the continuing faith in authority. The bureaucracy was the inheritor of the revered Confucianist father, the continuation of the prewar obligations to the state as the embodiment of the nation.

But in Japan that faith in authority is fracturing. It can be seen in the tame but growing signs of youth rebellion, and in the voters' rejection of the ruling Liberal Democratic Party in the early 1990s. Voters wanted reform, but it did not happen, and in 1996, with the opposition parties fractured, they voted reluctantly for the old guard. The 1996 general election had the lowest voter turnout ever, with only 59 per cent of enrolled voters choosing to exercise their franchise—though that was still substantially higher than a typical vote in the United States.

Unlike in the West in the 1960s and 1970s, youth rebellion in Japan has not been ideologically focused by an event such as the Vietnam War. In Japan the rebellion is more sullen. Rebellion is more a passive protest at the failure of the modernist promise, at the constrictiveness of the industrialising ethos and its conflict with the cultural message of self-improvement and self-gratification. In Japan a clearer sign of the rebellion is in teenage girls prostituting themselves to buy fashion accessories and in the rise of new religions that try to overcome the hollowness of the stagnant traditional religions.

In Japan, the notion of the individual, a notion behind the western youth rebellion of the 1960s and 1970s, is much weaker than in the West. The importance of the group remains deep-seated. New religions flourish in Japan because the developmental ideology is inadequate to human needs. Japan faces its own version of the postmodern dilemma: the collapse of faith in the statist, Shintoist model, which no longer delivers cohesion, even though material affluence remains; and the growing alienation from the developmental model. Unlike the heyday of Marx or Marcuse in the West, there is no faith in a new model among Japan's intelligentsia. There is no youth protest movement adopting a New Left paradigm of a new order, there is just self-gratification. For Japan's groupthink remains too strong, even as the myths that held the group together are eroding.

There is a tension in Japan between the inexorable demands of the globalised market, of the end of the postwar developmental state, and the demands of Japanese conservatism. From its radical obsession with growth, Japan has become conservative. It beat the West at its own game but now has lost its way.

Japan at present is deeply ambiguous, desperate to imitate parts of the western model, to have earned its place in the sun, yet too proud to change. Perhaps the next generation will seize the moment. But the factors that created Japan's success could become a burden: the homogeneity and social cohesion are the flip side of the racism, intolerance and inability to become reconciled with its neighbours. A millennium of proud independence makes Japanese wonder why they should bother doing so. Their neighbours do not trust them. Some forces in Japan want desperately to hold on to the factors that create its social cohesion. At the same time others understand the need to shed them, to become more liberal, for that is the requirement for peaceful coexistence in the modern world. There is little risk of a revival of militarism in Japan; the trauma of the last militarist experiment was too great. But Japan still displays a stubborn refusal to reflect on that past. The present generation of leaders will not atone for Japan's wartime sins in the way that Germany's did.

Japan won't become a new America, it will move towards 'capitalism with Japanese characteristics'. The group ethic won't disappear; but it is weakening as the 'moral backbone' provided by state Shinto (itself invented only in 1868) corrodes. The difficulty is that in the absence of something like American nationalism or its individualist ethic, Japan has no obvious cultural and moral alternative. This is Japan's dilemma.

It is still possible that Japan will be forced to change. The optimistic view is that the Big Bang financial reforms that began in April 1998 could force Japanese government and its domestic business to become internationally competitive. Or Japan may continue to muddle along with slow economic growth, changing gradually, but not fast enough to help solve the problems in East Asia. This will put a further drag on the prospects for both Japan and the region. What seems least likely, at least without the trigger of a severe crisis, is that Japan will undertake radical change. Unemployment is rising, workers are becoming anxious about their prospects, but life is still comfortable for most in spite of the gloom. The downside risk is of a severe recession in Japan, sparked by further weakening in consumption and investment and a collapse in the share market or the currency, that could turn the Asian crisis into a global one.

Chapter 5
Meltdown

Thailand in the 1990s was a victim of the 'beauty queen syndrome', said the Thai Commerce Minister during the 1997 crisis, Narongchai Akrasanee.

> One thing in life, you never want to become [is] a beauty queen. When you become a beauty queen you have so many suitors, and they all come asking you for love, for this, and for that, and offering you everything. The temptations can be so great you can lose yourself in the process. But when you are dethroned and you are no longer the beauty queen, nobody comes to offer you anything.[1]

He was in a good position to know. Like many Thai politicians, Narongchai was also a businessman, a role he resumed when the Chavalit government stood down in November—although he did so without his finance company, General Finance, which was one of sixteen suspended in 1997 in the early days of the crisis.

> I remember one time I was raising a loan from overseas, I wanted $US50 million. We appointed an investment banker to do that for us, and the message came to us from the banker, please ask Narongchai to take $120 million. I said 'Oh, no, that is too much, please'. They came to us again, they went down onto their knees, begging, so finally, I said, 'Okay, okay, for your sake', and I took $79 million. It was so easy to have money . . . Every time I wanted to borrow money, I would have all these investment bankers offering much more than I could absorb. So I ended up with indigestion.

Narongchai was not alone. Thai businesses borrowed increasingly large amounts of money during the 1990s and as a result Thailand's external debt climbed from a yearly average of $48 billion in the first half of the decade to $78 billion by the end of 1996. Most of this amount, $70 billion, was in loans from banks, and more than half of it, $37.5 billion, from Japanese banks. The flood of foreign money fuelled an economic boom, manifested most sharply in the property market. Bangkok was dotted with new high-rise buildings, beyond what could be usefully used for many years. Investors knew this, but were spurred on by cheap and abundant money and rising property prices. By mid-1997, as the wave was about to crash over them, Thai banks were carrying an estimated $15 billion in bad debts to property investors. But the government and the Bank of Thailand insisted the currency would not be devalued, and few borrowers bothered to pay the extra cost of hedging their debts. Pressure grew during 1997 to devalue, but some observers believe that one reason for the government's reluctance to act was the knowledge that friends in business were unprotected.

As long as Thailand was a beauty queen its suitors didn't mind too much about what proved to be two serious flaws. The first was financial: a shaky banking system whose ill-health was disguised by poor and poorly enforced accounting rules and a large and growing level of unhedged short-term debt. When the crash came, these problems were magnified by the second flaw: the exchange rate system that pegged the Thai currency, the baht, to the US dollar.

A third factor that undermined Thailand's position was not so much a flaw as a fact of life: China had emerged as a keen competitor to Thailand and other South-East Asian nations both in export markets and as a site for foreign investment. From 1992 there was a substantial shift in the weight of direct foreign investment away from South-East Asia and towards China, notes Nomura Research Institute economist C.H. Kwan. In 1989 Japan invested three times as much in Thailand as in China. But by 1997 the picture was reversed. Thailand had high wage rates compared with China, and its edge was further eroded by the devaluation of the Chinese yuan in early 1994, making it increasingly difficult for Thailand to sustain its previous heady increases in exports of labour-intensive products.

Upon this shaky foundation, a sharp slowdown in Thai exports in 1996 provided the trigger for the collapse. The export slide undermined the prospects that Thai businesses would be able to service their rapidly growing debt, and increased the risk of a currency devaluation. Economist Peter Warr lists several factors behind the export slowdown, including the rise in the baht, rising wages, slowing demand in Thailand's export markets, and congested roads, transport and other infrastructure. The slowdown in exports prompted foreign investors to withdraw their capital from Thailand and sparked speculation against the Thai baht. 'Once this expectation developed and portfolio capital headed for the exit, the process was unstoppable', says Warr.[2]

At the start of 1997 there were a few signs that Thailand was about to spark a financial cataclysm that would engulf the region. Most economic indicators were looking sound. The economy was showing typically Asian growth. In the ten years to 1996 the economy grew at close to 10 per cent a year, although the figure fell to 6.7 per cent in 1996 and was tipped to slow further in 1997; inflation was manageable at 5.9 per cent; the country had been running budget surpluses for a decade. In hindsight, the growing current account deficit, the widest measure of the nation's trade position, was a warning. In 1995 and 1996 Thailand's deficit exceeded 7 per cent of annual output. When a country runs a current account deficit it has to make up the shortfall of imports over exports by borrowing the difference. Thailand, in the 1990s, was a profligate borrower, encouraged by a host of willing lenders hoping to ride on the coat-tails of the East Asian boom.

Dollars, yen, baht

Most countries in the rich West moved to floating currencies during the 1970s and early 1980s (though the European Economic Community in 1979 moved back to more tightly bound rates under its Exchange Rate Mechanism). But in the developing world there was much less enthusiasm for floating exchange rates. For smaller, poorer countries a pegged exchange rate—pegged, usually, to the US dollar—held the intangible but important benefit of engendering stability and confidence, or so it seemed. As long as the US was the main source of capital and the main market for a country's products, this was a beneficial arrangement. Investors in otherwise doubtful propositions could have confidence at least that the exchange rate would hold its value. And if, as was usually the case, the exchange rate was kept at a relatively low level, exporters would also benefit: a product sold at a given price on the world market would earn them more in their local currency.

But the growing influence of Japan during the 1980s as both

an investor and as a market for East Asian products undermined the logic of this equation. Countries with exchange rates fixed to the dollar were left at the mercy of what were enormous swings in the relative value of the dollar and the yen. From a high of 239 yen to the dollar at the time of the September 1985 Plaza Accord the American currency sank to a low in April 1995 of 80 yen to the dollar. Measured against the yen, the dollar lost two-thirds of its value in the space of a decade.

In the first half of the 1990s the rising yen was a windfall for East Asian countries. Their own relatively weak currencies made East Asian countries increasingly attractive sites for Japanese investment—and Japan, by this time, was the world's largest source of investment capital. Secondly, it made their prices increasingly competitive compared with their toughest competitor in mass manufacturing—once again, Japan. The weak dollar and its corollary, the strong yen, were key forces behind the prosperity of East Asia in the late 1980s and early 1990s.

It was too good to last. The high yen was putting increasing strain on Japan, already racked by the recession brought by the collapse of the late 1980s speculative bubble economy. When American and Japanese officials engineered the turnaround of the relative value of the yen to the dollar in mid-1995 the implications for East Asia seemed for them to be of little consequence. But for the countries affected they were profound.

Under Thailand's fixed exchange rate system, set up in 1978, the baht was effectively fixed to the US dollar. There were slight adjustments: from mid-1995 to mid-1997 the Thai baht fell 4 per cent against the dollar. But this seemingly innocuous shift masked the fact that Thailand's real effective exchange rate—that is, measured against a basket of major currencies and taking account of differing rates of inflation—actually rose 15 per cent.

As part of the effort to maintain the baht, Thai interest rates rose sharply. The Bank of Thailand knew that the flood of capital into Thailand threatened an outbreak of inflation if it were not contained. In an effort to sterilise this big increase in liquidity, the central bank made large sales of securities. But to attract sufficient funds the central bank had to offer relatively high interest rates, and this in turn increased the flow of capital into Thailand, in a self-perpetuating, self-defeating cycle—a cycle that was also being played out in Indonesia. But on the ground in Bangkok, the flood of capital was fuelling a boom the likes of which Thailand had never seen before. The first wave of investment in the late 1980s and early 1990s went into manufacturing and other productive investment. But as the money kept pouring in, investors increasingly began to invest in real estate at prices well beyond what could be justified by the potential earnings on the investment. It was a classic speculative bubble.

By 1997 high interest rates and the rising exchange rate had dented economic growth and spiked Thailand's real estate boom. At the end of 1996 more than 20 per cent of all office space in Bangkok was vacant; and there were similar gluts in commercial and residential property.[3]

Manufacturing industry and services were also under pressure because of excess capacity and increasing competition from countries such as China and Japan. The debts that had financed the investment boom began to look shaky. One early warning was the collapse in May 1996 of the Bangkok Bank of Commerce, with more than $3 billion in bad loans.

By the second half of 1996 slowing exports and a weakening economy had brought occasionally mild attacks on the baht from speculators punting it would be lowered, as it should have been. But the government resisted the pressure, arguing that a lower baht would increase the foreign currency exposure of Thai firms, many of which had borrowed in dollars without taking the usual precaution of 'hedging' their exposures, that is, taking out financial insurance against a rise in their liability due to a fall in their own currency. The authorities also feared that a fall in the baht would increase the cost of foreign borrowing as investors demanded a higher return to offset the currency's greater volatility. And a weaker baht would have lifted domestic prices and hence inflation.[4]

To support the currency the Bank of Thailand used its reserves of dollars to buy baht in the market. After the May 1997 speculative attack the central bank restricted foreigners' access to baht in an effort to limit their ability to speculate in the currency. But these tactics backfired. Most obviously, Thailand found that sale of dollars to protect the baht rapidly depleted its reserves of foreign exchange. The official figures showed reserves fell from $37.2 billion in December 1996 to $30.9 billion in June 1997. But the Bank of Thailand revealed in August 1997 that the latter figure overstated the true position substantially because of its promises to deliver $23.4 billion dollars in forward markets. Another downside was that higher interest rates dampened economic activity, further weakening the shaky balance sheets of the banks and finance companies.

Fickle finance

The exchange rate system made the shock especially sudden, but other factors helped create the 1990s boom, and so increased the size of the bust that followed. Following the advice of the IMF and in response to pressure from foreign financiers, especially Americans, Thailand in 1993 set up an offshore financial market, the Bangkok International Banking Facility, which offered tax breaks to induce foreigners to invest in Thailand. C.H. Kwan argues that establishing the BIBF was a major step in opening Thailand to international capital, but which made it much more difficult for the Thai government to control the movement of funds into the country. 'The bulk of these funds were of a short-term nature and ended up in speculative activities in Thailand's share and property markets. When the bubble finally burst in 1996, the financial system was left with massive bad debts', Kwan says.

Thailand's largest finance company, Finance One, was at the centre of the problems that eventually destroyed confidence in the Thai system. Rumours about the health of Finance One began circulating early in 1997. Finance One's managing director, Pin Chakkaphak, denied the company was facing troubles, although it later emerged he had been selling much of his own stake in the company. At the end of February the central bank organised a bail-out of Finance One by arranging a merger with a small Thai bank, Thai Danu. But the deal came unstuck amid revelations of dubious share and loan deals to various friends and affiliates. Almost two-thirds of Finance One's loans were in property, hire purchase and share market lending—all of which were at risk as the economy slowed and interest rates soared.

In early 1997 analysts inside and outside Thailand were becoming increasingly worried about the level of debt and the ability of speculators to make a one-way bet against the fixed exchange rate. The speculators were punting that the exchange rate would not hold. But none anticipated the consequences when the whole edifice came crashing down. There were some warnings. 'For Thailand, the official commitment to the exchange rate peg means that regaining competitiveness and reviving the external sector will require a harsher adjustment for the domestic economy. The difficulties of the financial sector, which stem largely from the property overhang and weak share market, are also likely to make adjustment more difficult', warned the Institute of International Finance, a Washington-based think tank, in April 1997.

The month after that warning, the strains increased dramatically. On 14 May the baht was hit by a massive attack from speculators who doubted the central bank's ability to hold the currency at the promised rate. On that occasion the exchange rate held firm. The Bank of Thailand dug deep into its coffers—too deep as it turned out—to meet the demands of everyone who wanted to sell baht and buy dollars. In spite of heavy sales of its US dollar reserves to meet the demands of speculators, the central bank claimed it still had ample reserves to keep defending the currency—reserves, it said, in excess of $30 billion.

On 23 June the government issued four emergency decrees aimed at helping the troubled finance companies rebuild. By now many of the finance companies were being kept afloat only with the help of large amounts of public money (later revealed to have swallowed more than $19 billion, or 9 per cent of national output). On 27 June the Bank of Thailand suspended the operations of sixteen finance companies and ordered them to submit merger or consolidation plans.

Stories in the Thai press claimed that a hedge fund controlled by George Soros had been a major player in efforts to sell off the baht, but warned that the Bank of Thailand would 'destroy him'. Soros denied he had been a major player, saying his trades had not been substantial and had supported the baht, not weakened it. There is little doubt that Soros was a participant, but his actions were certainly not a deciding factor.

The May rescue of the baht was based on a fiction. It emerged later that reserves were not nearly as solid as they seemed. The bank did hold $30 billion in overseas assets even after the May attack. But what nobody outside the bank knew was that almost all of this amount had been committed in forward futures contracts. The bank had bought US dollars on the spot market, covering the obligation with a promise to deliver payment at a future date. Its true position was much worse than it had admitted, and the bank had no chance of holding out against another concerted attack on the currency.

'We did not know anything about this', said Narongchai, even though he was a cabinet minister at the time. The truth emerged, he said, after officials asked the central bank to explain how it had kept reserves so high when it had clearly been spending so much defending the baht.

Another reason for the delay in floating the baht, Narongchai said, was that the central bank wanted to give banks some room to breathe by allowing them to close their books for the year on 30 June at the old exchange rate.

> Otherwise the debt exposure of the Thai baht would have been overwhelming. The business community had been demanding since the beginning of the year that the exchange rate should be more flexible. With the fixed rate they could not get money from anywhere. They would not have minded having a lower exchange rate, as long as they had the liquidity. So when the government decided to float they welcomed it. But they did not know how far it would go down.

The obvious solution was to remove the currency's peg to the US dollar. The baht would undoubtedly fall, but the fixed rate had become unsustainable. It was impossible to have a formal debate on the issue within the government, Narongchai said. 'In the currency business, if the government talks about it, the media will pick it up and there will be rumours in the market and it will cause the collapse. So ministers have to shut up', he said. 'The media is everywhere in Thailand. Also we had a coalition government. Different parties were competing for influence and favours.' Even so there were private conversations on the need for a float.

> There were private discussions between the Minister of Finance and the Bank of Thailand. And I was close to the finance minister and we had some conversations. We had the same view that the exchange rate needed to be more flexible. The Bank of Thailand agreed with us. They were waiting for the appropriate time to go flexible, but that appropriate time never came.

The Bank of Thailand jealously protected its independence. The decision on the timing of the float was the bank's, not the government's. 'If the Bank of Thailand made that kind of decision they would tell the government in the morning', Narongchai said—an extraordinary level of autonomy for a central bank. Although he was a cabinet minister with a key economic portfolio, Narongchai says he had no foreknowledge that the baht would be floated on 2 July.

On the day of the float the baht plunged 15 per cent, ending the day at 29 baht to the dollar. The Bank of Thailand, the central bank, tried to turn the tide by raising its lending rate by two percentage points to 12.5 per cent. It promised to use $4 billion to $5 billion of overseas reserves to defend the currency if it fell below an unspecified 'appropriate rate'. But once the floodgates were opened the bank could not stand against the deluge. Within a month the baht had lost 40 per cent in value; two months later it had fallen another 20 per cent.

Within a fortnight of the float a team of experts from the IMF reached Thailand, ostensibly to give advice on foreign exchange mechanisms and monetary policy. But speculation was rife that the government would swallow its pride and seek the IMF's help to arrange finance to bolster its foreign reserves. In the months after the baht collapse the government prevaricated endlessly over its response. It was struck dumb by the size of the fall in the currency, uncertain how to respond. As the currency kept falling foreign lenders were growing anxious that their debts would not be repaid. Would the central bank honour its promise to underwrite the finance companies, or would they be allowed to fail? No one knew for sure, but investors were taking no chances, and refused to roll over loans when they fell due or to offer any new credit.

A Bank of Thailand official, Thirachai Phuvanai-naranubala, was quoted in the local press at the start of the July warning that the central bank would not recognise foreign lenders to the sixteen suspended finance companies. But ten days later he sent out a missive saying he had been misreported. Lenders were unconvinced. Prime Minister Chavalit, after all, had promised three days before the float that the currency would not be devalued. By the end of July there were already signs of sharp rises in prices. The government ordered prices of 70 essential consumer items to be frozen, but this would only last until stocks ran out. Oil and cement prices rose, and Thai car-makers sought permission to lift prices by between 8 and 10 per cent.

On 5 August the government announced it had sought help from the IMF, and had agreed to a package of austerity measures in return for at least $15 billion to prop up foreign currency reserves and prevent the baht tumbling further. As the price of IMF support the government promised to achieve a budget surplus, requiring cuts to government spending of more than $3 billion and an increase in consumption tax from 7 per cent to 10 per cent. The government listed 42 more financial companies that would be suspended in addition to the sixteen already announced. On 11 August the IMF and seven regional countries agreed to the largest bail-out package since the Mexico crisis of 1993–94. Japan pledged $4 billion; Australia, Singapore, Hong Kong and Malaysia pledged $1 billion each, and Indonesia and South Korea each pledged $500 million. The last two were ironic in the light of events later in the year. China later promised

$1 billion in addition to Hong Kong's pledge—the first time China had ever contributed to an IMF rescue. By the time it was finalised the package tallied at $17.2 billion. Notably absent was the United States, which was embroiled in a Congressional debate over whether to lift America's contribution to the IMF.

These eight economies were not driven by altruism. They recognised the risks for the region if Thailand's uncertainty were to spread. But in Thailand the politicians continued to dither. As part of an effort to bolster confidence the government announced that foreigners would be allowed to lift shareholdings in financial companies beyond the previous 25 per cent limit, and a committee overseeing the bail-out of the 58 closed finance companies said foreigners could hold stakes of more than 50 per cent—but they would have to pare this back to 49 per cent after five years. Not surprisingly, this diminished their attractiveness and at the start of October only one of the fifteen banks had won such a deal. Rather than concentrating on the financial crisis, politicians were focusing on a debate to approve plans for a new constitution aimed at ending Thailand's corrupt money politics.

In September Thai Prime Minister Chavalit survived a three-day censure debate in the parliament, but his authority was weakened amid growing unpopularity over the remedies prescribed by the IMF. Three days later Chavalit won some respite when the parliament passed the vote to overhaul the constitution, by 578 votes to 16, with 17 abstentions. The new constitution forced politicians to declare their assets and restricted their ability to finance election campaigns.

But the pressure on Chavalit continued to grow. Large street protests demanded a change of government and strains intensified within his six-party coalition government. At least one thing had changed in Thai politics: in spite of the political and economic strains, the military refrained from taking control of the government. In a bid to hold on to power Chavalit on 21 October called a sudden meeting of his cabinet ministers and security officials and discussed the possibility of declaring a state of emergency and a curfew. The idea was overruled by the military, which had come to believe in the importance of maintaining democratic forms. Three days later Chavalit formed a new cabinet, and for a short time the political pressures abated. But the financial pressures remained acute. After the cabinet reshuffle the baht sank to 41 against the US dollar, 64 per cent down from its level before the 2 July float. Chavalit surprised his closest supporters when on 3 November he announced he would resign three days later, apparently at the urging of leading military figures. A scramble to form a new government ensued.

A few days later Chuan Leekpai, the leader of the largest opposition grouping, the Democrat Party, was appointed prime minister. At the time there was little optimism that the change would bring much improvement, but the change of government became a catalyst for new resolve in tackling the crisis. Before the year was out the new government had shut down permanently the 56 bankrupt finance companies that previously had been 'suspended', revealing a healthy reluctance to throw good government money after bad to keep them afloat—but at the cost of 6000 jobs.

In the new year the baht continued to fall; but sentiment was beginning to turn. In January, finance minister Tarrin Nimmanahaeminda travelled to Washington and persuaded the IMF to loosen some of the conditions on its rescue package in the wake of Asia's worsening economic situation. The government had cut its budget for 1998 by 18.5 per cent, helped by increases in some taxes, but the sharper than expected economic slowdown meant revenue would fall well short of predictions. In February the IMF agreed to the request, softening its budget target to a deficit equal to 2 per cent of national output instead of the 1 per cent surplus it had demanded previously.

In February a new bankruptcy law was passed—a seemingly arcane development, but one that would help clear the debris of crumbling businesses and allow rebuilding to begin. Under the old laws the process of selling remaining assets to repay creditors had taken years or even decades. The government established an independent Financial Restructuring Authority to sell the assets of the closed down finance companies.

Thailand, more than any other of the South-East Asian nations, and perhaps equally with South Korea, seems willing to make the difficult changes needed to overcome the crisis. But the task remains formidable. As well as rebuilding the financial system, establishing systems to make it more accountable and creating more modern institutions and instruments to allow businesses to properly manage their borrowings, the government faces the problem of paying off an enormous amount of debt.

In closing down the weakest institutions, the Bank of Thailand acquired debts estimated at between 200 billion and 400 billion baht. A royal decree promised that the Bank of Thailand will be compensated for its write-offs from the government budget, for which 50 billion baht was allocated in 1998. 'If the optimist is correct, then we have four years to write off all this debt. If the pessimist is correct, it will take something like eight years, which is very tough', Narongchai said. 'So when you talk about financial crisis in Thailand, although there are all these good developments, the worst is not over. Much depends upon how much we have to write down. In every country this is the same. Somebody has to pay for this. How much you have to pay will determine the damage.'

Bahtulism

Economic factors alone don't explain why the Thai currency fell so far, so fast, when the currency was finally floated on 2 July. Was the Thai currency really so overvalued as to justify a 60 per cent fall over the space of three months? The near universal view is that it was not.

There is an explanation, however, in the herd mentality of financial markets—which is not as irrational as it may seem. Narongchai Akrasanee explains the bull side of the Thai boom this way:

> As an economist I was concerned about the oversupply of money, of credit. But when you are in the market, if you did not do like what others did then you would lose out, your profitability would be low, you would be criticised by shareholders. Every company was competing for earnings per share. Therefore when the international money was available at low cost, everybody grabbed it, otherwise you would not have such good earnings per share and you would not be judged well by your shareholders. So we enjoyed the boom very much [even though] everybody knew that that the boom would not last forever.[5]

There was a similar logic in the sell-off in the baht. American economist Paul Krugman argues that a government can succeed for a time in stabilising a currency if its foreign reserves are large enough. But if reserves are dwindling, the day will come when the central bank can no longer sell its currency at the promised rate. Anticipating this, speculators sell the currency short, taking out loans in anticipation of repaying them back later when the exchange rate is lower. At the same time they shift their own funds offshore.

But this process accelerates the exhaustion of the central bank's stockpile of foreign exchange and brings the day of reckoning closer. 'The result is that, while the government's stockpile may decline only gradually for a long time, when it falls below some critical point, all hell suddenly—and predictably—breaks loose', Krugman argues. If the government's policies are inconsistent with keeping the exchange rate at the nominated level, speculators will not wait for the currency to fall. 'At some critical moment they will all move in at once—and billions of dollars in reserves may vanish in days, even hours.'[6]

That does not mean that speculators are blameless. Krugman comments that the herd mentality often runs rampant when a market falls.

> Everyone sells simply because everyone else is selling. This may happen because individual investors are irrational. It may also happen because so much of the world's money is controlled by fund managers, who will not be blamed if they do what everyone else is doing. One consequence of herding, however, is that a country's currency may be subjected to an unjustified selling frenzy.

Large investors can make a difference by buying baht, or pounds, or some other currency, and investing the money in another country. This is what George Soros did in the United Kingdom in 1992, giving him the odious reputation that inspired the attacks of Malaysian Prime Minister Mahathir in September 1997. But Krugman reckons Soros has pulled this trick off only once, in the United Kingdom, and was not a key player in the sell-off of the baht or of the Malaysian ringitt. The key lesson, Krugman says, is that 'abrupt runs on a currency, which move billions of dollars in a very short time, are not necessarily the result of either irrational investor stampedes or evil financial manipulation. On the contrary, they are the normal result when rational investors contemplate the implications of unsustainable policies.'

Krugman's lucid explanation of the rationality of panic and herding psychology in financial markets is widely endorsed. More contentious is his argument that 'unsustainable policies' were the root cause of the panic, a debate that is canvassed in chapter 8.

Malaysia

Mahathir Mohamad is a man of great ambition and pride. Sympathetic to capitalism, yet hostile to the West, the 1997 crisis drew out the complexities of his character. Mahathir has masterfully melded a racially diverse nation and managed its economic take-off. But at times during 1997 his hubris did his country great harm. Mahathir's imposition of restrictions on foreign investment and his call for a ban on currency trade seriously worsened investors' uncertainties, not just about Malaysia but for the rest of East Asia.

Yet in 1997 Mahathir's pragmatism and flexibility were also on show. When it became clear that his decisions restricting foreign investment had backfired he reversed them. Mahathir seemed content for his ambitious and capable deputy, Anwar Ibrahim, to play the good cop to his bad cop, to make reassuring 'clarifications' of Mahathir's more contentious comments, explaining that they really meant the opposite to what everyone else thought they meant.

Mahathir's determination to avoid the ignominy of an IMF rescue led him to implement the kinds of policies that the IMF would have demanded, but without the surrender of sovereignty and loss of face that IMF supervision would have entailed. By that crude but brutal test Malaysia fared better than Thailand, Indonesia and South Korea. Some of Malaysia's problems were similar to Thailand's, though not as severe. Malaysia's banking system was better managed, its mix of debt and direct investment was more balanced. By relying less on debt and more on direct investment Malaysia had a greater level of insurance against capital flight by nervous investors. Those who have invested directly, for example in factories or real estate, cannot pull their money out as easily as lenders. Malaysia's current account deficit in 1996 reached 5 per cent of national output—high but not necessarily excessive.

But Malaysia also suffered from the endemic East Asian disease: a speculative boom funded by high levels of debt. Although its debt was less than Thailand's it was not immune from the consequences of its heavy borrowing when confidence was shattered. The total of outstanding bank loans in Malaysia jumped to 155 per cent of GDP in 1997, from about 140 per cent in 1996, and crony capitalism was as widespread in Malaysia as in other East Asian countries.

As in other parts of the region, the main goal for policy-makers in the early 1996 had been to manage the slowdown from the boom of the early part of the decade. In March the central bank restricted loans for real estate and shares. There were growing fears that the sharp slowdown in the Thai economy would infect Malaysia. Export growth slipped in the first half of 1997 to 2 per cent, having risen 12.4 per cent over the first half of 1996. As a result Malaysia in June suffered its worst monthly current account deficit in seventeen years. Foreign investment slumped in the first half of 1997 to 5.41 billion ringgit, down from 17.06 billion in all of 1996. This had the benefit of taking some heat out of the boom, but it also made Malaysia more vulnerable to the swift change in sentiment that swept the region in July. A mild slowdown would have been healthy; the slump that occurred was damaging and disruptive.

The Malaysian ringgit came under pressure within days of Thailand floating its currency in July 1997, but heavy buying by the central bank held the ringgit firm at around 2.5 to the US dollar. But by the end of the month the currency had fallen by 5 per cent. On 24 July Mahathir launched the first of many attacks on 'rogue speculators', and two days later named George Soros as the man he held responsible. By early September the ringgit had fallen 20 per cent. On 20 September Mahathir made another attack against Soros in Hong Kong and called for an end to 'immoral' currency trading. When Mahathir repeated his call for tighter regulation on currency trading on 1 October the ringgit fell 4 per cent in less than two hours, to a low of 3.4080—down a quarter on its value three months before.

In an effort to halt the slide in the currency a budget on 17 October squeezed spending and lifted taxes, but still included a 16 per cent increase in spending on development projects. Mahathir is fond of grand projects meant to symoblise his nation's rapid technological and economic progress. The 88-storey, 452-metre-high Petronas twin towers in Kuala Lumpur is the tallest building in the world. In 1997 this monument to Malaysia's economic prowess became a symbol of nationalistic excess.

The budget also aimed to strengthen the financial system, requiring banks to declare loans 'non-performing' if no interest was received for three months, instead of six previously, and to lift their loan loss provisions. The budget promised lower restrictions on foreign property purchases to reduce the property glut, a cut in company tax from 30 per cent to 28 per cent, tax incentives for exporters, and higher import tariffs on up-market cars, motorcycles, heavy equipment, consumer durables and outward-bound tourism.

The markets delivered their judgment: the day after the budget the ringgit fell 3 per cent and the Kuala Lumpur Stock Exchange fell 4 per cent. Critics complained that of six big capital projects identified for 'deferral' only two, the Bakun Dam and the new city, Putrajaya II, had actually been started, making the supposed cuts largely illusory. 'Significant cuts in large, import-intensive projects that would rapidly and significantly narrow the current account deficit would have led to greater confidence that the currency would stabilize soon', said Morgan Stanley economist Tim Condon. The budget suggested the government considered that the financial frenzy was a 'passing phenomenon that required only some policy tinkering', said economist Premachandra Athukorala.[7] Other analysts were more scathing. The Political and Economic Risk Consultancy group warned in November that Malaysia's behaviour over the past few months 'may well ensure that it is no longer regarded as part of the crowd when foreign investors eventually return'. The report continued:

> Government intimidation of local economists and market analysts in recent months has been so effective that the credibility of economic analysis originating from Malaysia is now in serious doubt. The result is that outside observers are in danger of swinging too far in the opposite direction, overlooking genuinely positive developments and focusing on the negative ones instead.[8]

The most damaging of Mahathir's comments, the consultancy said, was his call to ban or severely curtail foreign exchange trading. Mahathir's threats to arrest local sharebrokers and other analysts who produced critical analyses about Malaysia's economic situation and his comments about the role of Jewish financiers (which he later denied) also damaged the country's international standing. In November Mahathir's flip-flops continued to muddy the waters. In that month the Prime Minister promised to proceed with a 10 billion ringgit ($3 billion) scheme to build a pipeline, highway and rail link from north-western Malaysia to south-eastern Thailand, dubbed the 'landbridge'. Also in November, United Engineering Malaysia, a profitable infrastructure company, was obliged to borrow 2.398 billion ringgit to buy a 32.6 per cent stake in its debt-ridden parent, Renong, the business arm of Malaysia's ruling party. The deal was a reminder that cronyism had not disappeared from Malaysia. Renong is the key player in the construction of two planned cities, Putrajaya and Cyberjaya, part of Mahathir's ambitious development plans. The same month Anwar announced that the government would set up a 500 million ringgit ($143 million) fund to bail out troubled share brokerage houses—the kind of policy which in Japan had prolonged rather than resolved its financial troubles. Another case of cronyism emerged in March 1998, when the state oil company Petronas announced it would buy the shipping assets of a debt-laden company, Konsortium Perkapalan, half-owned by Mahathir's eldest son, Mirzan.

In December Anwar Ibrahim redeemed himself in the eyes of international investors. His 5 December emergency economic package was a turning point in Malaysia's economic history, which repudiated Mahathir's development policies of the previous decade. The policy package was an admission of the severity of the crisis and the need for a comprehensive response. The package was dubbed an IMF program without the IMF. Anwar cancelled a large bridge project that Mahathir had been promoting only the day before. He promised to slash government spending by 18 per cent, cut back on expensive imports and restrict lending. He promised there would be 'no question of any bail-out' for troubled financial institutions. 'We have reached a stage where we must undertake further strategic but painful measures to strengthen the nation's resilience so that we can withstand any systemic risks', Anwar said. Anwar predicted growth would fall to between 4 and 5 per cent, down from earlier predictions of 7 per cent. Megaprojects like the road and rail link from Malaysia to Thailand were postponed indefinitely, as they were 'not very productive', and were responsible for 'dragging down' the country's banks.

But in spite of the reversal marked by Anwar's statement the ringgit continued falling for another month. The banking system was coming under increasing strain. In early March 1998 the central bank announced that Sime Bank, one of Malaysia's top ten banks, would need a large cash injection and that others might also need help. A week later there were reports that investment company KUB was negotiating with the government to receive a large stake in a lucrative mining company, on favourable terms, so as to compensate for losses it might incur as a result of rescuing the troubled Sime Bank.

Mahathir was determined to resist calling the IMF for help. An IMF rescue would have meant that foreign powers would impose conditions that made people worse off, force the government to increase taxes for an already impoverished nation, force up interest rates, and close down most banks and finance companies, Mahathir said. 'We'll no longer be free. The people will be left jobless and to suffer.'

Mahathir was bitter at the international reaction to his frequent ascerbic comments about the role of western capital in the crisis. Mahathir told *Asiaweek*:

> The problem we have now is something we cannot even talk freely about. The Prime Minister has lost his voice. I find that I am actually not allowed to explain. I must say the correct things. Because if you

say something that is not quite right, it will cause what is known as a loss of confidence. And when there is a loss of confidence, we suffer. We have to pay a price.

In another sign of growing tensions in the region, Malaysia had to deal with rising numbers of illegal immigrants, mostly from Indonesia. Between 9 February and 1 March 1998 Malaysian police detained 3971 illegal immigrants from 332 boat landings, almost three-quarters of the total 5432 illegal immigrants detected the previous year. Malaysian police said they believed another 5000 Indonesians were waiting for boats on islands off the coast of Sumatra, across the Strait of Malacca from the Malaysian peninsula. 'We expect the problem to get more serious as the economic situation in Indonesia gets worse', a police spokesman told the *Far Eastern Economic Review*. Malaysia has more than a million legal foreign workers in a population of 21 million, and possibly another 800 000 illegal workers. Most are from Indonesia. But with at least 8.5 million unemployed, and the number growing, the problem will intensify.

Hong Kong and China

On Monday 20 October 1997 the world discovered that the financial crisis had spread beyond South-East Asia. In four days the Hong Kong share market took its worst-ever pounding, losing nearly a quarter of its value. At the close of trade on Thursday the Hang Seng share market index had fallen 23.3 per cent to 10 426, down from 13 601 at the end of the previous week. Hong Kong is the trade and financial gateway to China, the world's most populous country and an increasingly powerful political and economic force. A financial meltdown in Hong Kong would have direct and substantial impact on the Chinese economy—a major destination for western investment and the source of a rapidly increasing share of world trade.

The slide on the Hong Kong share market spilled quickly into Wall Street and the world's other main share markets. Only when Wall Street stabilised a few weeks later did other markets around the world regain some composure. Already there had been substantial pressures on the Hong Kong currency. The Hong Kong dollar is fixed directly to the US dollar under a currency board system. This requires that the Hong Kong monetary authorities have enough reserves of foreign exchange to meet the demands of those who want to sell Hong Kong dollars. If investors believe there is a risk the currency will not be held at the fixed rate they have an incentive to sell as many Hong Kong dollars as they can, and if enough speculators share the same view there is a risk the authority's nerve will crack. On one day during July the Hong Kong Monetary Authority spent $1 billion defending the currency. In August an unnamed Beijing source told a Hong Kong newspaper that China was prepared to use $50 billion to defend the Hong Kong dollar—a report aimed at trying to bolster confidence that the rate would hold.

But that confidence was weakened by the devaluation of the Taiwan dollar on 14 October even though, like Hong Kong, Taiwan had substantial foreign exchange reserves. In an effort to defend the Hong Kong dollar, interest rates were lifted sharply. Hong Kong and Chinese authorities made clear the rate would continue to be defended at all costs. Hong Kong has high levels of debt, and the high interest rates needed to maintain the dollar can be painful for highly leveraged borrowers.

Like the rest of East Asia, Hong Kong had been experiencing a property boom. The boom was punctured by the efforts to defend the currency. But maintaining the exchange rate can be a painful exercise. Aside from speculative pressures, there are other strong reasons that the rate will eventually be abandoned, and this is likely in coming years. The fixed exchange rate has become a burden for the Hong Kong economy. But the timing of any change poses an excruciating choice. If there were any whiff of a change the speculators would come running.

The Hong Kong share market faced another bout of selling in early January 1998 when the market tumbled 17 per cent in nine days. The slump in the property market left many banks and financiers badly exposed, but they were not in straits as dire as their neighbours. Unlike Japan, Korea, Thailand and Indonesia, the issue was whether the Hong Kong banks would make profits that year, not whether they would survive. The gloom deepened on 12 January when Peregrine Investments, Hong Kong's largest investment bank, went into liquidation. It was a sign of the financial fuses linking the region's economies. The Peregrine collapse was caused by the failure of an unhedged $265 million loan to an Indonesian taxi and bus firm called Steady Safe. Later in the month Hong Kong's biggest property developer, Sung Hung Kai, suspended work on many of its construction sites.

At the time of Hong Kong's budget on 18 February 1998 the Hang Seng share market index was down 36 per cent from its 1997 peak, much less than the falls suffered elsewhere in the region. Property prices had fallen by a similar amount, with painful but not catastrophic consequences for property owners and their financiers.

Two days after the budget the US credit rating agency Moody's Investors Service downgraded its financial ratings for Hong Kong and China, citing the impact of the region's financial crisis. The agency downgraded the outlook for foreign currency loans to China and Hong Kong from stable to negative and cut Hong Kong's short-term credit ratings from Prime–2 to Prime–1. Hong Kong's financial secretary, Donald Tsang, said the downgrade was unfair and based on superficial analysis, a view echoed by a spokesman for the Chinese central bank, the People's Bank of China.

China avoided the foreign exchange crisis of its East Asian neighbours simply because its currency is not fully convertible, and speculators cannot freely move capital into and out of the country. But the pressure of the slump in East Asia's economic growth will be keenly felt. China has made impressive economic changes in the past two decades, but still faces an enormous task winding down the inefficient and highly indebted state sector, which has saddled the banking system with bad debts amounting to 30 per cent of all loans, at conservative, official estimates, and probably much more.

Song Ligang, an economist at the Australian National University, says that even though China avoided being caught in the 1997 financial crisis it faces severe economic problems. Demand is weak after the tight policies of the early 1990s aimed at containing a surge in inflation, and there is a real danger of disinflation (falling inflation) that would slow down the reform process and increase the risk of economic collapse, he argues. Unemployment has been rising as a result of measures taken to restructure state-owned enterprises. By 1997 more than 11 million workers had been laid off as a result of the reforms, and the total will rise by a million each year. The official goal of keeping unemployment under control relies on continued high economic growth and on an improving trade performance. But exports are under threat by the Asian crisis. China's competitiveness has been undermined by the falls in the currencies of its competitors in the region.[9]

China's economy is still in a serious mess, in spite of the optimism of recent years, and the Asian crisis will make the mess worse. The only question is how much worse, and what the impact of this will be on China and in the wider world. Economic growth in China peaked in 1992 at 14 per cent, and had gradually fallen by 1996 to 8 per cent, according to official figures widely regarded as highly optimistic. 'China is much nearer a stress point than just looking at the numbers would suggest', said one analyst who declined to be identified because of his company's China investments. He explained:

> The problem with Chinese numbers is that the big headline numbers are not supported by the micro data. They just don't match. It looks to us that Chinese growth has been much lower than was generally thought over the last twenty years, in which case any further slowdown on the export side could bring the country much closer to a point of stress than we'd thought.

One of the key questions over China is whether the stress on its export sector will force a devaluation that could in turn spark further devaluations in other countries in East Asia. In spite of the pressure, the consensus view in mid-1998 is that China will resist the pressure, at least until early 1999. By then exports in other countries in the region will have begun to recover and the effects will be much less severe.

The Philippines

Thailand, Indonesia, Malaysia and South Korea suffered badly in the East Asian crisis, while other countries, such as the Philippines, Taiwan and Singapore, were left bruised but not badly hurt. Narongchai reckons that the Philippines escaped the worst of the damage because it achieved 'beauty queen' status only recently, 'so it was saved from the exploitation of investment bankers'.[10]

After years of economic mismanagement and weak growth, the Philippines in the 1990s also received large flows of foreign capital. The flow of money was not as great as that going to its neighbours, so it had less opportunity to engage in their speculative excesses, leaving its banks in sounder health. But it did not avoid the boom altogether and its large debt burden still left it vulnerable. The Philippine peso crashed from 26.4 to the US dollar to 35 in the first three months of the meltdown and share prices tumbled 19 per cent. To try and bolster the currency and retard the inflation brought by the weaker currency through higher import prices the central bank tightened interest rate policy steeply, lifting average prime rates from 18 per cent to 30 per cent.

Like Indonesia, the Philippines suffered a fall in farm production in 1997 as a result of the warm weather caused by that year's El Nino episode. Economic growth was already slowing when the crisis hit, and higher interest rates will hit construction and finance particularly hard—the industries behind the recent strong growth.

As a latecomer to economic take-off, costs are lower in the Philippines than in most of its neighbours, so the Philippines will remain an attractive investment destination. But it will not escape the sharp fall in the flow of investment funds to the region as a whole, nor from the fall in demand for its exports.

Singapore and Taiwan

The 'not-yet-a-beauty-queen' syndrome doesn't explain Singapore's and Taiwan's escape from the worst of the East Asian crisis. Along with Hong Kong and Korea those two countries were among the four original tiger economies. Both Taiwan and Singapore had low levels of debt compared with their neighbours, and both had current account surpluses and substantial foreign exchange reserves.

Singapore's reaction to the crisis differed from that of its neighbours from the start. Where most countries worked vigorously to try and sustain their currencies, the Singapore Monetary Authority was happy to let it slide. By early August the Singapore dollar had fallen five per cent from its level before the Thailand currency crash, when Yeo Lian Sim, a director of the Monetary Authority, declared the exchange rate was 'appropriate'. That comment pushed the currency down another 3 per cent to 1.513 Singapore dollars to the US dollar. But even with an 8 per cent fall the Singapore currency had not suffered nearly as badly as those of Thailand, Korea, Indonesia and Malaysia, which by late 1997 had fallen by between 30 and 50 per cent.

One financial consultancy firm noted that unlike its neighbours Singapore had reacted to the crisis in a way that foreign investors regarded as highly responsible. 'No threats were made against foreign speculators, the share market remained relatively liquid, and political leaders declared boldly that they would allow the market to determine the value of the local currency. These are the things that fund managers will remember long after the dust settles', said a Political and Economic Risk Consultancy report in November 1997.

But a domestic debate about the future course of economic

policy—whether to liberalise Singapore's famously tight political and financial controls—diminished Singapore's attractiveness as a safe haven, PERC warned. As far as could be ascertained in Singapore's tightly controlled political culture, Deputy Prime Minister Lee Hsien Loong and other members of his family were key members of the liberalising camp, while the Deputy Managing Director of the Monetary Authority of Singapore, Koh Beng Seng, was a champion of the conservatives. Calls for a freer exchange of financial information seemed at odds with the government's insistence on retaining its strict Official Secrets Act. There were some signs of a more liberal stance on the need for foreign skilled labour, and of the need to widen the narrowly focused education system.[11]

By early 1998 Singapore authorities were becoming increasingly worried about the worsening political and economic situation in Indonesia, and were contemplating emergency measures to cope with a possible influx of refugees. Wealthy Indonesians are large investors in Singapore property. By some estimates 5 per cent or more of Singapore banks' loans are to Indonesia. The slump in the Indonesian rupiah sent the *Straits Times* share market index tumbling at the start of the year.

Singapore will not avoid the fallout from the region. Typical private forecasts put growth in 1998 at 1 per cent, down from an average 8.8 per cent between 1993 and 1997. In March 1998 Moody's cut the ratings outlook for all six Singapore banks because of the slowing local economy and their exposure to troubled neighbouring countries. Moody's said Singapore banks remained 'among the strongest in Asia', but warned of 'increased threats to asset quality' from the gloomy regional climate. Ratings for all six banks were shifted from stable to negative.

Taiwan, like Singapore, was less vulnerable to a capital flight than other nations in the region because of its low levels of debt, a current account surplus and substantial foreign reserves. Its chief worries were the increasing competition from Japan and Korea in a slowing regional and world market, and the perpetual concerns about China's intentions.

Taiwan was less entwined with South-East Asia than Singapore, and was less affected by the crisis. It was protected by the simple fact of having a much better managed financial system, lower debt and higher foreign exchange reserves. Non-performing loans at the end of 1997 stood at 3.8 per cent, tiny compared with Taiwan's neighbours, and it had a current account surplus of 2.6 per cent of GDP, compared with the substantial deficits of the five worst affected Asian nations. Taiwan has been gradually liberalising capital flows since the mid-1980s, although there are still limits on inward and outward investment.

Taiwan's exchange rate has floated since 1988, although at times the central bank has intervened heavily to try and support a particular rate. In the early months of the Asian crisis the central bank tried to hold the rate of the New Taiwan dollar with large sales of US dollars, but gave up the effort on 17 October 1997.

By early 1998 Taiwan had suffered a 12.5 per cent currency devaluation against the US dollar, and a 7 per cent slide in the share market, both small by the standards of most of its neighbours bar Hong Kong and China. Yet Taiwan suffered still from the general downturn. And the local economy, although partly shielded from the rest of the region by controls on capital movements, still faces the hazards caused by high domestic borrowing and a glut of commercial and residential real estate. Domestic borrowing stands at 1.6 times Taiwan's annual output, the *International Bank Credit Analyst* reported, with almost 40 per cent of outstanding loans for property investments, the same venue for speculative over-investment as in the rest of the region. Taiwan's stronger currency and falling world and regional demand slashed exports by 26 per cent in 1997, and the risk is that further falls could hit the profits of local companies.

Emerging markets

When the crisis spread worldwide with the fall in the Hong Kong share market in October, other 'emerging markets' were also hit—economies distant from Asia geographically but similar in their recent opening to western markets. In Europe these were former members of the communist bloc such as Russia, Estonia, Ukraine and the Czech Republic. The other area badly affected was Latin America.

On 27 October, the day of the large fall on Wall Street, share markets in Brazil, Argentina and Mexico all had their biggest ever single-day losses, and the sell-off continued in following days. Brazil especially came under heavy selling pressure, prompting the central bank on 30 October to almost double interest rates to defend the Brazilian currency, the real. In a few days the central bank spent $8 billion defending the currency. Weakness in Brazil prompted fears of recession throughout Latin America like that which had followed the Mexico crisis in 1994. On 7 November

Brazil's share market fell 6.4 per cent, Mexico lost 2.42 per cent, the MerVal index in Argentina fell 5.1 per cent and in Venezuela the Bursatil index fell 3.3 per cent.

By the end of the month Latin American markets had stabilised, but remained vulnerable to the growing uncertainty. From mid-November to early December Latin American markets had rallied 17 per cent against a 16 per cent fall in Asia, but turned downwards again on 11 December, when the Brazil market fell 3.7 per cent, Argentina 1.5 per cent and Mexico 1.8 per cent. Brazil's central bank was forced to take extraordinary measures to defend its 'crawling peg' exchange rate system, which limited falls to 0.6 per cent a month. As well as lifting interest rates the government spent about $10 billion selling foreign reserves to buy reals on the foreign exchange market, and cut its budget by about $18 billion. The currency held firm—but at a big cost to domestic economic growth. Growth was predicted to fall to 1 per cent in 1998 from 3.5 per cent the previous year, and unemployment to rise. Miguel Draz, a senior research economist at the Nikko Research Centre in New York, commented.

> All of this doesn't necessarily mean Brazil can survive future speculative gusts. That will depend not so much on how committed Brasilia is to the program but, in the short term, on how soon and how severe the next speculative attack will be. A crisis in China, and the unpegging of the Hong Kong dollar in particular, would put extreme—perhaps unbearable—pressure on the real.[12]

The Asian contagion spread to Russia, where the Asian troubles built on domestic uncertainties to send share markets tumbling. On 10 November and again on 2 December the central bank lifted its key lending rate to try and staunch the flow. Later in the month the central bank chairman Sergei Dubinin said foreign investors had withdrawn $5 billion from the Russian bond market in recent weeks. Russia was helped by strong signs of support from the IMF, World Bank and allies such as Germany, whose offers of support helped prevent a further rout on the markets.

Chapter 6
Korea crashes

'Down with Kim Young-sam' chanted the workers huddled around fires outside Myongdong Cathedral, where seven of their leaders were encamped to try and avoid arrest in the chilly winter of January 1997. 'Let us live like human beings', they cried in unison.

Kim Young-sam came to power in 1993 as Korea's first elected civilian president on a wave of popular support, promising sweeping political and economic reform. But by 1997 these hopes had been dashed. Kim's political authority was eroding fast and his reform agenda had crumbled. The role of class enemy was a strange reversal. For almost three decades until he became president in early 1993, Kim had been a hero in the long and bitter struggle against the military autocrats who had ruled Korea since the 1950s. But in January 1997 the champion of democracy was arresting union leaders, ramming legislation through parliament in early morning sessions, and restoring the investigative powers of his security service that he had abolished four years before. The changes Kim wanted to make to labour laws were essential for Korea's economic future, but he was not prepared to build the democratic consensus that would have allowed them to be achieved peacefully.

Unions were angry at changes to a labour law that would have allowed workers to be laid off, even though under stringent conditions. They were also furious that a proposal to allow multiple unions in each industry and nationally had been delayed for between three and five years. The law had been rushed through a pre-dawn session of parliament on Boxing Day 1996 with the opposition absent. The labour dispute was the first of two episodes in late 1996 and early 1997 that highlighted Kim's failure to achieve the changes he had promised. The second was the collapse of the Hanbo Iron & Steel Company the next month, one of the first times that a *chaebol* had been allowed to fail, although there were to be many more collapses before the year ended.

These events highlighted the strains in Korea as it tried at one turn to move away from the developmental state model, and at the next abandoned the labour market and financial reform that would have allowed it to do so. Kim Young-sam and his advisers knew these changes were important, but failed to carry through the reforms they had promised. This failure laid the basis for the crisis late in the year.

The labour dispute had its roots in Kim's promise in April 1996 to set up a new labour relations system. In negotiations to join the rich nations' club, the Organisation for Economic Co-operation and Development, Korea had come under pressure to change its labour laws to bring them into line with international standards. Previously, only one union was allowed in any industry or workplace or at the national level. The OECD insisted multiple trade unions should be allowed, and said that unions should be permitted to have lawyers represent them in negotiations.

Thanks to the boom that brought Korea's economic transformation into a relatively rich, industrialised nation, workers were in a strong bargaining position even though their rights to organise were restricted. A shortage of labour allowed workers to demand large pay rises. Every year, after the ritual strikes in annual wage negotiations, unions received agreement to be paid for the time they had been on strike. Union leaders were paid directly by the companies.

Employers wanted this to end. They wanted the right to lay off workers—especially important in labour-intensive industries like textiles and car-making which were losing their competitiveness because of Korea's rapidly rising costs. The employers' arguments were bolstered by what Koreans at the start of 1997 were already calling an economic crisis. Economic growth in 1997 had been tipped to fall to 6 per cent from 9 per cent in 1995. The unemployment rate had risen to 2.4 per cent. Most worrying was the growing trade imbalance, which had sent the current account deficit to 4 per cent of GDP.

The labour law that was passed on Boxing Day 1996 differed in one key respect from that produced by the government committee set up to reach a compromise between labour and industry.

The proposal to allow multiple unions was altered, delaying the change until 2000 for national union bodies, and 2002 for industry-level unions. The government had come under heavy pressure from Korea's large industrial conglomerates, the so-called *chaebol*, to delay the change. The leaders of the Korean Confederation of Trade Unions, vocal and influential but technically illegal, were enraged, and launched nationwide stoppages and protests.

President Kim's character fuelled the dispute, argued the Professor of Political Science at Korea University, Kim Byung-kook, in a 1997 interview. 'Kim Young-sam is a strong-willed man. Because of his strength of character he was able to stand up against the military presidents Chun Doo-hwan and Roh Tae-woo. That was a strength before 1993 when Kim was an opposition politician, but it creates a lot of problems now he's president.' Kim Young-sam had lost his way. Kim's own party members were trying to distance themselves from their leader.

Kim Young-sam's second failure was of financial reform. Discredited by the labour dispute, Kim proposed a series of financial reform bills in January 1997, but was unable to have them passed through the National Assembly. The law would have created a more independent central bank, improved supervision of financial institutions and stricter accounting rules. They were not radical changes, but could have done much later in the year to maintain investors' confidence that their money was safe and that borrowers were sound.

When he came to power Kim had said he would make financial transactions clearer so black money could not influence politics or the economy. But the only change of substance he made was to introduce a 'real name' law, which required people to use their real names for bank accounts so as to reduce money-laundering and tax evasion. Incredibly, during the 1997 crisis, the 'real name' law became one of the scapegoats. Business lobby groups had no compunction arguing that the real name changes had fuelled the crisis because they had 'forced' business people to send large amounts of money offshore to avoid declaring income and paying tax on it.

The Korean model

South Korea offers the classic illustration of both the strengths and the weaknesses of the 'Asian model' of economic development.

Until 1997 it was the strengths that shone. South Korea created an economic miracle second only to Japan's, growing for three decades at around 9 per cent a year, and in 1992 overtaking Australia as the world's twelfth largest economy.

Korea had been the closest and most successful imitator of the Japanese developmental model, in ways that contributed both to its extraordinary economic success from the 1960s to the 1990s and to the scale of its collapse in 1997. As in Japan, in Korea the state was a key agent in guiding investment towards export industries. Korea's developmental model succeeded where other statist models failed because the emphasis on exports forced its industries to be competitive in world markets—with the help of heavy implicit and explicit subsidies. Yet as in Japan, policy-makers in Korea had lost their ability to keep closely guiding economic growth. This was not simply a matter of changing fashions in economic policy or of their succumbing to pressure from the United States. Both Japan and Korea had passed a threshold in their development where the statist model no longer worked. And both countries found the transition to a more market-based model extremely difficult. Although not as techno-logically advanced as Japan, Korea was more vulnerable because of its smaller size and because of the pressures brought by the new high-tech global financial system.

Alice Amsden, the leading analyst of Korea from the devel-opmental state perspective, argues that state intervention was crucial in allowing Korea to 'catch up' with the industrialised world, by 'distorting' the market so as to force a massive level of investment. The sternest discipline was the constant pressure on all firms to export. It was enforced through the government's ownership and control of the commercial banks, through protec-tion and subsidies in new export industries, through price controls, and through controls on sending capital offshore. Discipline was applied by penalising poor performers and rewarding only good ones. Industries weakened by over-expansion were subject to government-directed rationalisation.

Korea emerged from this process with a heavy concentration of large-scale enterprises, more marked than in probably any other capitalist country. By the 1990s the dominance of the *chaebol* was viewed as a serious problem. Park Chung-hee, Korea's strongman president from 1961 to 1979, once said his goal was to allow 'millionaires who promoted the reform' to take a central role so as to 'encourage national capitalism'.

Between 1993 and 1995 the Korean powerhouse received an

extra fillip thanks to the economic weakness in Japan. Korea has a mix of exports similar to Japan's, so a soaring Japanese yen in the mid-1990s made Korea's key exports like ships, computer chips and cars especially competitive on world markets, as the Japanese equivalents became more and more expensive. Korean exports surged, and business poured the proceeds into new investments.

But there was a downside, and it was exposed in September 1995 when the Japanese yen began to fall. Korean products lost some of their price advantage over their Japanese competitors. Export growth slowed; some of the huge new investments began to seem too ambitious. The habit of heavy intervention had created an almost seamless web of interconnections between top players in government, politics, finance and business—a process that entrenched corruption and cronyism. Banks were effectively guaranteed by the government and faced little discipline over their lending. As a result Korean companies typically built up debt amounting on average to more than three times their capital (the underlying value of their companies)—about three times the ratio of western companies. When the export boom petered out in 1995, the squeeze on profits put increasing strains on companies' ability to repay their massive debts.

Hanbo Steel: the model fails

Kim Young-sam's moral authority, already weak, was destroyed in early 1997 when his son was implicated in a scandal that erupted after the collapse of the Hanbo Steel company, South Korea's second largest steel-maker and fourteenth biggest business group or *chaebol*, under the weight of a 5 trillion won debt ($6 billion).

The Hanbo collapse revealed serious failings in the Korean economy that led directly to the financial crisis at the end of 1997: enormous levels of debt and a corrupt financial system, which relied routinely on the close links between government and business. Huge loans could be made for reasons that had little to do with the likely return on the investment. The system grew directly from the ambitions of the developmental state model to beat the market, and eventually led to its downfall.

When Chung Tae-soo took control of Hanbo in 1984 his goal was to imitate the performance of Posco, Korea's highly successful state-owned steel company and the world's second largest steel producer. An ambitious plan to build a steel-making complex on the west coast at Tangjin was judged to be in line with the government's investment priorities, and was endorsed in 1986. The huge mill, with an annual capacity of 7 million tonnes, was supposed to have been completed in 1995. But as costs escalated—and, it emerged, as Mr Chung siphoned off large sums for other purposes—the project's creditors grew anxious.

Hanbo sought and received 400 billion won in emergency funds in 1996. In the first week of 1997, in spite of weak world steel prices, over-capacity in Korea and doubts about the mill's technology, the banks agreed to pay another 120 billion won. With debts valued at twenty times its capital, Hanbo's credit was already way beyond any sensible level. When, a few weeks later, Hanbo said it needed another 700 billion won to complete the project, the bankers drew the line and turned down the request. It was the straw that led to Hanbo Steel being declared bankrupt, taking with it four other group companies and risking the solvency of its main creditors, including one of Korea's largest banks, Korea First.

In Seoul, the media and the opposition went into a frenzy. The central bank, the Bank of Korea, pumped 6 trillion won into the financial system to keep it afloat. The scandal was hugely embarrassing to President Kim, and it highlighted the shaky state of Korea's banking system. The system was deeply imbued with the habits of decades of government-directed lending, and unfamiliar with the need to make independent judgments of credit risk or cash flow. Heavy regulation of the financial system had guaranteed profits, but had done little to promote financial market efficiency. The decision to allow Hanbo to fail showed that the government would not step in to bail out banks in trouble. A fundamental premise of anyone lending money to Korea had been demolished.

Critics asked how it was, with Hanbo's risks so great and its finances so parlous, that the banks had made further loans to it as recently as January. Surely there must have been political influences for the banks to have kept lending way beyond the bounds of prudence. Opposition politicians alleged that Hanbo's favourable treatment stemmed from its support for Kim Youngsam's 1992 presidential campaign.

On 20 February prosecutors indicted four MPs and six others on bribery and other charges over the Hanbo collapse, including the chief of the Korea First Bank, Hanbo's largest creditor. Hanbo's chairman, Chung Tae-soo, was charged with fraud, embezzlement and issuing bad cheques, and of diverting 218 billion won away from loans made to the group to buy new businesses, to bribe politicians and bank heads—and pay alimony to his estranged wife.

The biggest fish to be caught in the investigations was Kim Hyun-chul, the second son of President Kim Young-sam. Prosecutors in February cleared the President himself of any wrongdoing, but suspicions remained, fuelled by the President's fulsome apology for his son's involvement in the 'rumours', and his demand that his son stand down from all public positions.

In the months after the Hanbo collapse eight more of Korea's top 30 *chaebol* crashed. Most far-reaching in its impact was the downfall of the Kia Motor Corporation, whose drawn-out death throes drew the attention of foreign investors already growing nervous over the troubles in South-East Asia. Their nervousness intensified with the 20 October slump in the Hong Kong share market, which shifted the focus of international attention to North-East Asia. Suddenly the weaknesses in Korea's financial structure, the extremely high debts of Korea's companies and banks, and worsening export prospects seemed much more ominous than they had before. The panic had reached Korea.

Foreign investors began pulling their money from the share market as fast as they could; Korean banks had trouble raising money in overseas markets. The exodus sent the currency down daily to record lows—a fall halted only by rules restricting the movement of the currency on a single day. In the end, in spite of the blow to its pride, Korea had no choice but to appeal to the International Monetary Fund for help.

On Wednesday 19 November the government bowed to the huge selling pressure on the currency and widened the maximum change allowed each day to 10 per cent from 2.25 per cent. On Thursday the won fell quickly by the maximum allowed to a new record low of 1390 won to the US dollar.

Late on 21 November Finance Minister Lim Chang-yeul made a last-ditch plea to Japan for a multi-billion dollar loan to try and avert the need for an IMF package that officials feared would include harsh and unpopular conditions. However, both Japan and the United States, the only countries wealthy enough to lend sufficient money to avoid an IMF rescue, had made clear they would only offer aid to Korea under a package organised by the IMF. The government finally succumbed to the inevitable, and the announcement of the call for help was made late that night. But by February 1998 the collapsing currency meant that Korea's international ranking had fallen from eleventh to seventeenth largest economy.

Within a week of its call to the IMF, the Korean government had lifted its request from $20 billion to $50 billion. The change of heart came after the arrival in Seoul on Monday of a team of IMF officials to negotiate the terms of South Korea's rescue package. Five days after the request, in belated recognition of the message delivered by the market, the two main world rating agencies, Moody's and Standard and Poor's, both downgraded South Korea's sovereign credit ratings.

In a sign it was finally prepared to get tough with the weakest financial institutions, the government announced it would suspend eight of Korea's twelve merchant banks, the first time it had ever taken such an action. By November analysts were arguing that several of the large commercial banks and most of its merchant banks were technically insolvent, and were being kept afloat only with government guarantees.

Throughout November the Bank of Korea intervened heavily to try and defend the currency, but without success. IMF and American officials were furious at the lack of cooperation from Korea, which they felt had contributed to the continuing fall in the exchange rate during mid-December and to the rapid depletion of Korea's foreign reserves. 'There were about 10 days there where it's fair to say the Koreans were acting as if they were not going to do the program', an unnamed IMF official told the *Washington Post*. 'Instead of getting on and doing the program, they kept asking us for more money publicly—and not indicating that they would do the program. That helped destroy the confidence of the markets.'

The economic fallout from Korea's financial meltdown was far more serious than South-East Asia's because it is a much larger economy—equal to Indonesia, Thailand and Malaysia combined—and because of its direct impact on Japan, the region's economic powerhouse, and on China, a direct competitor in many exports. Even with an IMF rescue for Korea there were mounting fears that the sharp falls in the Korean won would sharply undercut the profits of Japanese manufacturers and investors in Korea, and so undermine Japan's own fragile banking system.

At the end of 1996 South Korea had $180 billion in foreign debts, of which about $130 billion was due for repayment within twelve months. The figure was not large by world standards, but foreign investors came increasingly to fear that much of that money would not be repaid, and that the pressure of falling exports and growing debt would force Korea's economy into a sharp slowdown. Six months later, in mid-1997, Korea's short-term debt was three times the size of its reserves, more than for any other country in the region.

Before the currency collapse made the figures far worse, Korea's *chaebol* had average debts of more than four times their equity. The American investment bank Morgan Stanley estimated that at the end of October Korean banks and merchant banks had non-performing loans totalling 48 trillion won—or 12 per cent of Korea's national output.

The IMF package

Details of the IMF package were announced on 3 December. The fund insisted on sweeping restructuring of the Korean economy, as well as drastic cutbacks to the budget, in return for loans totalling $57 billion. It also demanded closures and mergers of insolvent and weak financial institutions, a more flexible exchange rate regime, more open financial and product markets and, most importantly, a rapid unloading of the banks' estimated 28.5 trillion won ($27 billion) in bad loans.

The IMF package failed to staunch Korea's wounded foreign exchange and share markets. Confidence was further undermined by the failure of the Korea Development Bank to raise $2 billion in the second week of December and another failed attempt to raise money on behalf of the government a week later. Banks refused to roll over loans and the currency continued to tumble. US Treasury secretary Robert Rubin arm-twisted American banks to roll over their debts or be blamed for a global catastrophe.

Within days of the IMF deal the Halla Group, a shipbuilding and auto parts maker, was declared bankrupt after defaulting on $220 million in loans. The group was hit by rising interest rates and increasing reluctance of Korean banks to roll over debts. Halla had already foreshadowed laying off 6000 workers—a highly unusual move that went against the tradition of 'lifetime employment'. The nation's largest *chaebol*, Hyundai, had kept Halla afloat for the previous six months, but had refused to keep doing so. Halla had debts of $6.4 billion, much of it borrowed for a huge shipyard on the south-west coast.

The immediate task for the government and the IMF was to prevent the financial system from collapsing. The week beginning 8 December was the worst ever in Korean financial markets, with the won tumbling the maximum daily limit of 10 per cent for the first four days of the week. On Friday the won reached an all-time low of 1891.4 to the US dollar before climbing back to close at 1710.00 thanks to heavy buying by the central bank. But even Friday's recovery, back to the level of Wednesday's close, still left the currency 27 per cent lower than a week before.

Foreign investors had lost faith in Korea's business and financial management, and were reluctant to roll over loans to Korean businesses when they fell due. Many importers found it impossible to raise letters of credit to cover their purchases. This created an acute shortage of funds in the Korean money market, which drove overnight interest rates to 25 per cent—high enough to put healthy businesses under severe strain, let alone the weak ones. As a result the financial system came close to paralysis. Businesses and consumers no longer had faith that their money was safe in the bank, or that cheques and other obligations would be honoured.

Economist Heather Smith predicts that Korea will return to a more stable growth path more quickly than the other Asian economies in crisis—as long as it sticks to its reform agenda. 'Despite the crisis, this is an economy with huge underlying industrial strength and one of the most highly educated and motivated workforces in the world', says Smith. But the reforms will be extremely difficult to achieve. They include: an overhaul of the financial system, austere budget and interest rate policies, thus exposing business to external scrutiny, reform of the labour market, and removal of trade barriers. The process will bring widespread bankruptcies and could provoke economic nationalism and social unrest as unemployment grows. The *chaebol* are likely to resist calls for a dilution of family control.[1]

The IMF demands amounted to nothing less than a radical transformation of the Korean economic model, an abandonment of the old habits of heavy government oversight of the economy. Many Koreans were reluctant to let go of a recipe that made them for three decades until the early 1990s one of the fastest growing countries in the world. They had no real choice. Heavy intervention in lending and investment had served Korea remarkably well, but had led to growing corruption, increasingly poor investment decisions and, as a result, escalating debt. The immediate cause of Korea's meltdown was nothing more complicated than a crisis of confidence by lenders who feared they would not get their money back. But the deeper causes will be much more difficult to overcome. How quickly confidence can be restored will depend on the willingness and speed with which Koreans can make the financial and industrial systems more accountable and transparent, and shake off the shackles of the developmental state model.

Causes and consequences

The failure to undertake reforms to the structure of the Korean economy, the weakness of the Korean export markets and the decision to maintain the currency were critical factors behind the Korean crisis.

In the early 1990s Korean exports boomed as markets in China and South-East Asia expanded, and as their price competitiveness improved compared with the surging Japanese yen. But conditions worsened sharply in 1995 with the turnaround in the yen and a sharp fall in prices of semiconductors.

Economist David Hale notes that Korea by the mid-1990s had become such a big player in world markets for semiconductors, steel and petrochemicals that its own policies caused export prices to collapse. The rapid expansion of capacity in semiconductor memory chips led to a glut in the world market and a sharp fall in prices that badly undermined Korea's export performance.

For two years before the 1997 meltdown Korean economists and policy-makers had been growing increasingly concerned about the rising current account deficit. Although the volume of Korean exports was increasing, prices of computer chips and steel products were falling. Labour prices had been rising sharply since the mid-1980s. Wages rose from a very low share of national income to a level no higher than in the West, but the rise in costs contributed to the erosion in Korea's price competitiveness.

Lee In-hyung, research director at the LG Economic Research Institute, said in early 1997 that the best remedy for falling exports would have been to allow the currency to fall. But the Bank of Korea was intervening heavily to keep the currency stable. The authorities' fear was that a sharp depreciation would give foreign investors a fright and lead to a capital flight.

Despite all the talk about financial and labour market reform, change was slow. 'The Ministry of Finance has very little incentive to deregulate, because by deregulating it loses its control over the financial industry, so it emphasises stability of the financial system rather than rapid change', Lee said.[2]

Chaebol

When he came to power in 1992 as the first democratically elected non-military president, one of Kim Young-sam's promises was to tame the *chaebol*, to bring them down to size and make room for the small and medium sized businesses that had long been squeezed by the dominance of their larger competitors. The *chaebol*'s huge size restricts competition, and their huge debts were a key factor in the 1997 crisis. But Kim found that giant-taming was not as easy as he had thought. They are so dominant in the Korean economy that their tentacles spread widely. They could not be brought down to size overnight. The 30 largest *chaebol* accounted for 58 trillion won of Korea's output in 1995—16.6 per cent of GNP, compared with 13.9 per cent the year before. The *chaebol* had become the main engine of the Korean economy. 'If the *chaebol* do not perform well, the Korean economy does not perform well', said political scientist Moon Chung-in. 'If you look at the pattern of South Korean exports—semiconductors, consumer electronics, steel and steel products, automobiles—those major items cover almost 65 per cent of Korean exports, and all those items come from the *chaebol*', he said.

Chung Ju-yung, the chairman of Hyundai, Korea's largest *chaebol*, campaigned in the 1992 presidential election against the eventual victor, Kim Young-sam. After the election Kim subjected Chung to a campaign of vilification. He charged him with breaking campaign-funding rules, punished him with a suspended gaol sentence, and had his company's international borrowings restricted. Kim's response to Chung's criticisms demonstrated one change in Korea's political and economic structure: the *chaebol* and the government were no longer in each other's pockets. But past favours had made the *chaebol* so dominant in the Korean economy—they accounted in the mid-1990s for 22 per cent of the assets and 32 per cent of the sales of all South Korean companies—that they have an ologopolistic hold on many industries, posing a serious threat to the competitiveness of the domestic economy and to the prospect of finding new export industries.

Over the past decade the *chaebol* had come under increasing attack for their privileged status. Attacking the *chaebol* became the *sine qua non* of almost every politician's armoury. Yet in spite of occasional efforts to tame them, the *chaebol* continued to dominate the Korean economy, accounting for a larger proportion of economic activity than in any other capitalist country. The giants of the Korean economy, firms like Hyundai, Samsung, Daewoo and

Lucky Goldstar, have become household words around the world. They are both a symbol of Korea's unusual path to economic stardom, and a symptom of the issues it will have to tackle to return to that road. The *chaebol* grew large precisely because they were long favoured under the tightly managed authoritarian regime in its bid to promote an export-oriented economy. But now the favours that had transformed the *chaebol* into world giants had become millstones.

The paradox for the *chaebol* is that two key forces in modern Korea, democratisation and globalisation, are pushing in opposite directions. Democratisation brings pressure for reducing the influence of the *chaebol*, while globalisation brings pressure for reducing regulation to boost productivity. Because they are already in such a dominant position, deregulation would remove some of the shackles imposed in recent years on the *chaebol*, allowing them to grow larger still. The *chaebol* had grown large enough that they no longer relied on privileged access to credit that had helped their take-off.

Kim Young-sam began his term in 1993 with three goals for managing the *chaebol*. The first was to reduce ownership concentration, the very high level of control by single families; the second was to reduce the market dominance of the *chaebol*; the third was to try to reduce their dominance of such a wide range of industry. But by midway through his term he had effectively abandoned the second two goals. Following a more pragmatic line, the government in April 1996 eased credit quotas for all but the largest ten *chaebol*, one of many changes made to try to win favour with the Organisation for Economic Cooperation and Development, which Korea joined that year.

The government also tightened accounting laws for the *chaebol*. Restrictions on foreign capital injections remained, even though new equity owners would be expected to add pressure for improved disclosure and accountability. But legislating to cut the *chaebol* down to size is a futile objective. Far more effective would be measures to expose the *chaebol* to more competition, not just within Korea, but internationally. Korea is probably stuck with a skewed industrial structure dominated by *chaebol*, but the forces of international competition should eventually bring their own pressures on the uncompetitive parts of their operations. Effective anti-monopoly and fair trade laws, as well as more liberal foreign investment laws, will be far more effective than exhortations or legislation that try directly to limit the influence of the *chaebol*.

The campaign

On 18 December Koreans went to the polls to elect a new president after a year-long campaign that until its last three weeks was blissfully free of any mention of the economic crisis, or of almost any concrete policy. Did the two sons of majority party candidate Lee Hoi-chang avoid military service by deliberately failing their medicals? Did the main opposition candidate Kim Dae-jung receive illicit political donations in the 1992 campaign? These questions, not the disintegrating Korean financial system, were until late November the key issues in the campaign.

Financial problems had been brewing all year, but it wasn't until the near-collapse of the Korean banking system and the humiliating 21 November plea to the International Monetary Fund for emergency funds that candidates were presented with an issue they could not avoid. All three leading candidates had attacked the IMF bail-out to varying degrees, while saying little of how they would respond to the crisis.

The loudest critic of the IMF was the leading opposition candidate Kim Dae-jung, fighting his fourth presidential campaign. Korean politics still revolved around a semi-feudal, Confucian respect for authority, which created intensely strong allegiances to the candidate from voters' home regions. Korea's past four presidents had all come from Kyongsang in the southeast, including the nation-building dictator Park Chung-hee. In the 1997 election there was no candidate from Kyongsang, a factor that altered the political dynamic in favour of Kim Dae-jung. Kim was guaranteed almost total support—upwards of 95 per cent of the vote—from his home region of Cholla in the south-west. This gave Kim around 30 per cent of the vote nationally. But that was not quite enough to take him over the line, so he formed alliances that boosted his support in other key regions.

The election was a triumph for Korean democracy, heralding the first peaceful transfer of power to opposition forces since modern Korea was founded in 1948. Kim won 40.3 per cent of the 26 million votes cast. Kim is thought to have had a much wider margin earlier in the campaign, but his support waned in the last weeks after he called for a renegotiation of the IMF rescue package. Kim's victory came at a time of deep national crisis, just two weeks after the IMF rescue and with a banking system on the brink of collapse.

In spite of Kim Dae-jung's populist rhetoric during the campaign, the climate of crisis gave him the ability, once elected, to foreshadow some unpopular but unavoidable decisions. There was no choice but to proceed with legislation allowing companies to lay off workers, said party spokesman Park Sang-cheon. The issue set Kim at loggerheads with the unions, which had been strong supporters throughout his career. The two main union groups said they would not join a proposed consultative body unless the redundancy legislation was dropped, and threatened nationwide strikes if it went ahead. Kim Dae-jung and IMF director Michel Camdessus both pleaded with labour leaders for their cooperation, as international investors watched the dispute as a signal of Korea's willingness to reform. Unions argued that the *chaebol* and the government ministries should be reformed first.

In response to these pressures Kim Dae-jung pushed the *chaebol* to downsize. The heads of the five largest *chaebol* agreed in January to 'drastic restructuring', and said they would use their personal assets to restore the capital bases of their groups. But Kim complained that the plans announced a few days later by LG and Hyundai were cosmetic. Kim's economic emergency committee had urged the *chaebol* to announce changes before Kim's inauguration on 25 February. But the *chaebol* complained about the pressure. 'Whenever something goes wrong with the economy, *chaebol* are always blamed', said Kim Woo-choong, head of the Daewoo Group. In the face of strong resistance from business Kim backed down.

Kim was already backing away from some of his pledges for reform. He decided to delay until 1999 changes in laws to allow hostile mergers and acquisitions. 'The atmosphere for the legalization of foreign hostile M&As [mergers and acquisitions] is not yet ripe here', a Ministry of Finance and Economy official said. 'Further, there are still widespread concerns about the nation's key industrial infrastructures falling into the hands of foreign firms', he said.

After weeks of bickering, Kim achieved a breakthrough in mid-January when unions agreed to take part in discussions on the bill allowing lay-offs—a deal that would have been difficult, or impossible, under previous governments. The damage done to Kim Young-sam a year earlier by the month-long strikes showed the intensity of feeling on the issue. Kim argued that the workers' sacrifices would be 'different this time, because I will make sure that they are no longer alone in shouldering the burden under the new government and that they share the fruits after the crisis is overcome'.

Companies were to be allowed to dismiss workers only if this was unavoidable, were required to give 60 days' notice to the government, and were obliged to rehire them as soon as possible. The government promised improved unemployment insurance and welfare benefits and job retraining.

By late January financial markets had begun to stabilise, especially compared with those in South-East Asia. But in spite of the calls for austerity, the United States made sure Korea understood the terms of America's support: US Defence Secretary William Cohen warned during a visit to Seoul that any cut to the nation's defence budget would 'send the wrong signal and enhance and escalate tension on the Korean Peninsula'.

There was no question about Kim Dae-jung's authority during the two-month hiatus before he formally assumed power. Kim Young-sam was so discredited, and the crisis so severe, that there was no clash of authority during the usual lame-duck period. Kim Dae-jung was *de facto* leader right from the election. When George Soros visited Korea in early January he had a long meeting with Kim Dae-jung, but didn't bother to call on Kim Young-sam, still technically in charge.

The signs from Kim Dae-jung were much better than many had hoped during the election campaign, and he had widespread public support. But there were also signs of backsliding. Kim's political prowess was already losing its lustre. As part of the deal to form an alliance with the conservative United Liberal Democrats during the election, Kim had been expected to offer the prime ministership to the party's leader, Kim Jong-pil. But the promise didn't square with another pledge: to hold parliamentary approval hearings for all senior appointments—whose results were not a foregone conclusion, especially as Kim Dae-jung's NCNP did not have a majority in the parliament, and the opposition parties opposed Kim Jong-pil's appointment.

There was some relief for the strained financial system on 29 January, when creditor banks agreed to extend loans of $24 billion due in the coming year. As a result credit rating agencies took a more positive view of Korea's fiscal health and the IMF paid up another $8 billion in its promised loan package. But outstanding debt was now estimated at $153 billion, more than 30 per cent of GDP, and there was still $56 billion due for repayment in the next twelve months. Very high interest rates and the near impossibility of rolling over debt would bring a rapid increase in bankruptcies.

The stand-off between labour and capital worsened. In May

the Korean Confederation of Trade Unions called national strikes in protest at the growing number of lay-offs. The strikes provoked another sharp sell-off in the Korean won, as investors judged that their earlier optimism over Korea's recovery was misplaced. Kim's political strategy all year had been to try and win the support of unions by playing tough against the *chaebol*. But he could not deliver the changes, and his only hope of success was that the unions would accept something less than the revolution in the *chaebol* that they demanded. The strain reflected some deeply entrenched features of the Korean economy highly resistant to change. The *chaebol* are such a dominant part of the Korean economy that they cannot be brought down to size by legislation. Korea will have to live with the *chaebol* it has created, and accept that change will be delivered most effectively by the market.

Yet the *chaebol* were powerful enough to frighten the government from administering this kind of medicine. Three of the bankrupt *chaebol*, Hanbo, Kia and Jinro, were still operating in early 1998 in spite of their declared insolvency thanks to generous support from the banks, a phenomenon that would simply prolong the pain of restructuring, as it had in Japan during the 1990s. Keeping the *chaebol* on life-support would leave the economy with vastly more capacity than it could use and drag down healthy companies to prop up the sick. In May the government was still playing this game, lending several hundred million dollars to rescue an ailing *chaebol* in the construction industry, the Dong Ah Group.

Political failure

The 1997 crisis was a failure of Korea's fledgling democracy as well of economic management, the fruit of 'ten years of policy gridlock under an immature Korean democracy', argued Korean political scientists Mo Jongryon and Moon Chung-in. Mo and Moon place much of the blame at the feet of the Korean government and President Kim Young-sam. The government recognised but failed to solve the economic problems that caused the crisis. Financial, *chaebol*, and labor reforms had been high on the national economic agenda, but had not been implemented.

This was not simply a failing of Kim Young-sam's personal style, but reflected the immaturity of democracy in Korea, where the political process showed 'paralysis and gridlock', especially when interest groups were threatened, Mo and Moon argue. The political system failed, they say, because key figures and institutions had not shed their authoritarian habits and negotiation had not taken root in Korean political culture; because of incompetent leadership by Kim Young-sam; and because of the continuing tight links between government and business. 'Democracy requires responsible behavior and respect for the rule of law. That may sometimes involve compromise and the sacrifice of short-term for long-term gains. This simple truth has been lost largely in the first ten years of democracy, and Korea is now paying the price.'[3]

Chapter 7
Indonesia implodes

At 9.03 a.m. on Thursday 21 May 1998, President Soeharto walked into a gilded room of the presidential palace in Jakarta and began a short speech. 'I have decided to declare that I have ceased to be the president of the Republic of Indonesia', said the man who had ruled Indonesia for the previous 32 years.

Soeharto's decision to hand over to his loyal but widely disliked deputy, B.J. Habibie, ended a rule that had brought brutal repression of recalcitrant minorities and political opponents, along with exceptional improvements in material well-being for the vast majority of Indonesians.

Indonesia's first two presidents, Sukarno and Soeharto, both came to power amid violent upheavals: Sukarno in 1945 during the anti-colonial war against the Dutch, Soeharto by ousting Sukarno in 1966. Soeharto played a tactically brilliant game of dividing, eliminating or removing from contention his opponents and enemies. Under Soeharto's tutelage Indonesia was transformed from an economic backwater to one of the 'miracle' economies of East Asia, successfully overcoming economic crises that occurred roughly every decade, in the mid-1960s, 1970s and 1980s. But the crisis of 1997 proved Soeharto's undoing, provoking a political trauma as grave, though less bloody, than those that brought him and Sukarno to power. The economic crisis ended three decades of solid economic growth and destroyed Soeharto's claim to legitimacy. Soeharto's demise was the most spectacular political outcome of the Asian crisis, and a potent sign of the connections between political and economic change.

By the usual tests, Indonesia at the start of 1997 was in reasonable economic health. Inflation, at around 5 per cent, was low and falling; budget policy had been very conservative, with a budget close to balance throughout the 1990s. Indonesia's current account deficit was moderately large, at 4 per cent of GDP, but not overwhelmingly so. More problematic with hindsight was the high level of private unhedged debt in foreign currencies. A large proportion of the debt was short term, making borrowers especially vulnerable when frightened lenders refused to roll over loans as they fell due. But these factors do not come close to explaining the depth or severity of Indonesia's crisis.

The immediate trigger for the sell-off of the rupiah was an international reassessment of Indonesia's prospects when the Asian economic crisis began spreading from Thailand in mid-1997. Investors suddenly noticed danger signs they had previously ignored, especially the high level of debt and the growing inefficiency of a corruptly managed economy. Two more factors added fuel to this potent mixture: the inept political handling of the crisis, in particular by President Soeharto, and the inappropriate response of the IMF.

The sullied sultan

For several years before the financial crisis erupted the succession had been the central issue of political debate in and about Indonesia. The debate was intensified in mid-1996 by Soeharto's suppression of pro-democracy protests and riots which had focused on opposition figure Megawati Sukarnoputri, Sukarno's daughter. Soeharto was 76 and in failing health. In mid-December when Soeharto announced he would take ten days' rest, rumours—almost certainly true—that he had suffered a heart attack sparked another sell-off of the rupiah and a decline on the share market. Soeharto had been so effective at neutralising political opposition that in spite of the growing questions about his competence there was no obvious successor or process of succession.

Many Indonesians regarded Soeharto as a sultan or traditional Javanese ruler rather than an elected president, said Indonesia scholar Harold Crouch. Javanese sultans seek endorsement as the embodiment of communal spirit, and do not place great importance on popular election. Soeharto has at times shown sympathy for the traditionally mystical Javanese view of leadership that jars with western democratic ideals. For the Javanese, power is a 'concrete discernible substance that concentrates in the ruler, radiating light from a bulb', writes Hamish McDonald in his study *Soeharto's Indonesia*. 'Power has the same quality from ruler to ruler. It is limited: a powerful ruler takes power from other concentrations. Power is essentially amoral, neither legitimate nor illegitimate.'[1]

Scholar Michael van Langenberg offers another explanation of Soeharto's role. The presidency is the linchpin of the state and Soeharto, as both president and armed forces' commander-in-chief, is the core of the presidency, he says.

> Some traditional Javanese notions about ideal leadership do indeed inform part of Soeharto's own mentality. His public statements since the 1960s show convincing evidence of this. But the history of the New Order more importantly shows Soeharto as a thoroughly modernising authoritarian ruler . . . Soeharto might indeed see himself as a contemporary version of the just prince (ratu adil) of Javanese mythology, bringing Indonesia (and Java) into a golden age of prosperity. But in the Soeharto version it is a distinctly dynamic, at times even populist, notion of royalty—combining farmer, soldier and prince in the role of leading a modernising, technologically advanced nation-state.[2]

In 1998 Soeharto's leadership style crashed hard against the demands and expectations of a powerful international institution, the IMF, which had suddenly acquired enormous power over Indonesia's destiny, even though it was based half a world away and had a patchy understanding of Indonesia's political history and culture. Soeharto oscillated between ready agreement to the IMF's demands and repudiation of critical details. Critics in Indonesia and the West accused the IMF of imposing excessively harsh demands on Indonesia with the covert goal of unseating Soeharto.

Throughout the first months of 1998, as Soeharto reluctantly implemented the IMF programs, there were almost daily protests and riots throughout Indonesia. Under mounting pressure Soeharto promised gradual political reforms, and agreed that future presidents would be limited to two presidential terms. But amid rising fuel and electricity prices and mounting unemployment, and doubts about the ruling regime's willingness to reform, the protests continued.

The protests were not confined to students, but drew widespread support from academics, teachers and the middle classes. When four student protestors were shot dead by the military police, supposedly under orders to use only rubber bullets, the crisis reached boiling point. In the week beginning 11 May poor urban workers, enraged by sharp price rises induced by the economic crisis, went on the rampage, looting and burning shops and supermarkets. Hundreds died in the fires lit by looters and dozens more were killed by security forces. Foreign governments told their citizens to leave the country. When Soeharto returned from a visit to Egypt most of his closest supporters had lost their patience. On Monday 18 May Harmoko, the Speaker of the House of Representatives, called on the president to stand down. With the telling acquiesence of the military, students occupied the parliament building and pledged to stay there until Soeharto resigned. Military commander General Wiranto stood by Soeharto, who on Tuesday announced he would stay in power for as long as it took to devise new election laws and hold a new parliamentary election. But this process could have taken twelve or eighteen months, an untenable prospect in a nation suffering from economic paralysis made worse by Soeharto's reluctance to tackle reforms that would hurt his own closest supporters. The military and parliamentary factions kept negotiating, and late on Wednesday night persuaded Soeharto to stand down immediately.

The political turmoil and rioting in May dealt another heavy blow to Indonesia's economic recovery. A large number of Chinese business people left the country, taking their capital with them and further undermining recovery prospects. An IMF team negotiating the next instalment of the rescue package left the country during the worst of the riots, delaying the $1 billion payment due to have been considered on 4 June. In one sign of the worsening international anxiety, the currency fell sharply during May. The rupiah started the month at 8000 to the US dollar and ended it at 11 500. By that measure Habibie's appointment as president had done nothing to restore confidence.

According to the constitution Soeharto was succeeded by the vice-president, B.J. Habibie, a man widely mistrusted inside and outside Indonesia. The leader had changed, but the old system remained virtually intact. The crucial question for Indonesia became whether President Habibie would be capable of doing what his predecessor had failed to do: pursuing economic and political reforms that would overcome the crisis, but that would also entail dismantling the privileges of key figures in the regime.

Politics and the military

Politics in Indonesia had been strained for several years before the East Asian meltdown. Harold Crouch argues there could well have been a political crisis in Indonesia even without the economic problems. Elite opinion within Indonesia had been growing that the time had come for Soeharto to stand aside, but Soeharto's dominance of the political scene made this difficult to achieve. Crouch says most of the armed forces' elite had believed for some time that Soeharto should stand down and make way for a successor, but they were unable to say so to him directly until the rioting and looting forced their hand in May.

The top military leaders were very close personally and deeply obligated to Soeharto. In February Crouch commented:

> These people have served their entire careers under the presidency of Soeharto and they stand in great awe of him. In general they greatly respect him and admire him for his great services to the nation. They see him as the man who saved Indonesia from communism. They see him as the man who has held Indonesia together. They see him as the man who has promoted extraordinary economic development in the last 30 years.[3]

Political struggles within the Indonesian elite are usually insulated from mass politics, but the equation changed with the economic crisis. In late 1996 and early 1997 there were anti-Chinese riots in several small towns in Java, and there was considerable violence during the 1997 election campaign. In the second half of February 1998 riots broke out almost daily. The military worked hard to ensure they did not spread to the big cities, but by mid-May Jakarta, the capital, was engulfed by riots and looting.

The trigger

The Indonesian government had responded quickly when the financial crisis spread from Thailand in early July, widening the band in which its currency was allowed to trade from 8 to 12 per cent. But the central bank was unable to stem the heavy selling, and on 14 August abolished its managed exchange rate system. The rupiah fell almost immediately by 3.7 per cent, from 2655 to 2755. To try and halt the fall the government tightened both budget and monetary policy—measures that some analysts argue simply compounded the problems. In September Indonesia announced it would postpone 39 trillion rupiah ($13 billion) in construction projects to keep its budget from blowing out. The cuts had a severe impact on construction and property industries, and prompted the start of widespread lay-offs.

The collapse of the Thai currency in July 1997 sparked a

speculative sell-off of currencies and stocks in share markets throughout South-East Asia. In Indonesia several factors fuelled the conflagration. The first was the presence of a large amount of private unhedged debt. When the value of the rupiah halved, and then halved again, even the most healthy companies could not cope with a quadrupling of their repayments. 'The culprit here was the quasi-fixed exchange rate and the perceptions among borrowers borrowing abroad that it would actually continue', said Hal Hill, a leading scholar of the Indonesia economy. Investors' sanguine attitude to debt was understandable. Until the crisis erupted there was no reason to doubt the central bank's pledge to be able to hold the currency. But this confidence proved a fatal mistake.

The second factor was the high proportion of short-term debt. 'There's no problem with short term maturity if borrowers are reasonably assured of a rollover, but it's quite impossible if the creditor suddenly demands payment in full. As anybody knows with a house mortgage, you can't pay the house mortgage off overnight', Hill explained. Bank Indonesia estimated short-term private debt at $9 billion; some private analysts reckoned the figure was as high as $45 billion—the discrepancy itself a reflection of the lack of confidence in official statistics. The World Bank estimates that private debt rose from $35 billion at the end of 1994 to $65 billion in mid-1997, with short-term debt rising from $10 billion to $32 billion. A third factor was the lack of confidence in the financial sector: in the credibility of its accounts and in the soundness of prudential management and supervision by Bank Indonesia.

Australian National University economist Ross McLeod argues that the most important underlying cause of the crisis was the government's failure to recognise that it could not simultaneously control, in the long run, more than one of four key economic variables: prices, the money supply, the exchange rate and interest rates. The Indonesian government had tried to control two of these four at the same time—the exchange rate and the money supply—with dangerous results. The practice of holding the rupiah steady (more precisely in a moderate decline, of around 4 per cent a year), kept it below the level that would have been set with a free float. The result was that foreign capital was drawn in, adding to the supply of money in the economy. To avoid the inflationary consequences the central bank sterilised much of this monetary growth, selling government-backed bonds at high interest rates and borrowing from the government without paying any interest. But this imposed considerable costs on the bank and the government. These sterilisation policies crowded the private sector out of the domestic financial market, and encouraged many private firms to seek funds offshore. The surge in offshore borrowing was the key factor behind the strong growth of foreign debt, unhedged because of the promise, fulfilled for the previous decade, to keep the exchange rate steady.

There were deeper problems behind the crisis. During the 1980s Soeharto's technocrat advisers were in the ascendant, and began a process of financial market reform aimed at reducing barriers to new banks so as to attract more foreign capital. In 1998 it seemed they had succeeded too well. The problems of digesting large capital flows were compounded by the failure to properly supervise the banking system and by increasingly blatant corruption. By the 1990s Soeharto was paying less heed to the technocrats and more to his children, who had come to play a growing role in almost every aspect of the economy. The Soeharto children routinely came to demand a role in large new business projects. They figured prominently in a leaked list of large bad debts, suggesting they were given unusually lenient treatment by their lenders. Outside the financial system change was slow. A web of regulations favoured monopolies controlled by the President's family and friends, who also benefited from contracts for large infrastructure projects.

Upon this bedrock other factors made the situation still worse: there was the political uncertainty surrounding Soeharto's commitment to reform, his health and the succession; the nervousness of the Chinese business community; and Japan's inability, in spite of its dominating size, to play the role of economic locomotive to drive recovery in the region. Corruption and cronyism also added to the uncertainty. Other negative factors were the declining ability of the rural sector to provide a buffer for problems in the urban economy, unlike the crisis of the mid-1980s, and the low level of most oil and other commodity prices. And finally, in early 1998 the three key economic ministers were all politically weakened. 'In the past Indonesia has had one thing going for it and another thing against it; this time there's been a coincidence of almost uniformly negative information and impacts', Hill concluded.

Ross McLeod argues that the government's half-hearted commitment to a floating currency regime compounded the problems. 'The government's lack of commitment to the float at an intellectual level quickly became obvious when it saw the immediate large depreciation of the rupiah. In what appears in hindsight to have been a panic reaction, it chose to sacrifice its monetary targets in order to try to regain control over the exchange rate', McLeod says.[4]

In previous crises a decision to sharply raise interest rates had succeeded in averting speculative attack. But with a floating exchange rate these tactics did not work. Instead, tighter liquidity and budget cuts put a sudden squeeze on the domestic economy. Banks were forced to raise interest rates to attract funds, but found it impossible to write new loans.

In spite of the government's efforts the currency kept falling, and on 8 October the government called for help from the IMF. By the end of the month the IMF, with help from some of Indonesia's neighbours, the World Bank and the Asia Development Bank, had stitched up a $40 billion financial support package.

On 1 November, the day after the IMF package was announced, the government closed sixteen banks, and the rupiah even made a brief recovery—but not for long. Indonesia did not have the deposit insurance schemes that protect small investors in rich world countries, so the sudden closure of the banks led to a sudden and widespread loss of public confidence in the safety of their deposits. The government's promise that there would be no more bank closures was not believed, and the ensuing run on private banks exacerbated the domestic liquidity crisis. The central bank pumped in huge amounts of liquidity to keep the financial system afloat, but this fuelled inflation and increased the pressure on the exchange rate. This was the first of many blunders in which both the Indonesian government and the IMF played a part.

The reopening of a bank owned by the President's son Bambang under a new name in early November was the first of many signs that Soeharto was half-hearted about the reforms he had promised. By December hopes were fading that the IMF bail-out would solve the crisis. Fifteen of the infrastructure projects closed in September had been revived. The abrupt closure of the banks and the Soeharto family's resistance to reform were critical factors in demolishing confidence both inside and outside Indonesia and in undermining the initially favourable response to the first IMF package.

On 8 December President Soeharto began a ten-day rest, fuelling concerns about his health. The episode focused world attention on the issue of succession if Soeharto were to be incapacitated. On the same day the rupiah fell below 4000 for the first time, before central bank buying pushed it back up to close the day at 3965 rupiah to the dollar.

McLeod points to three factors apart from the President's health that undermined the first IMF package. First, in spite of the already conservative stance of policy, was the call for greater fiscal and monetary austerity, which amplified the fall in spending that was already apparent. Second was the focus on structural reforms that were bound to face political difficulties. Third, the package said little about how to restore the rupiah to a level that would allow Indonesian borrowers to meet their obligations. The economy suffered further from the lack of coherence in the government's policy responses, a problem made worse by the ill-health of one key economic adviser and by Soeharto's sidelining of others.

The currency fell sharply throughout December. On one day, 15 December, the rupiah fell 12 per cent, to a level 58 per cent below where it had begun the year, amid growing fears that Indonesia would freeze repayments on foreign loans. The government by now was admitting to $117 billion in foreign debt, but private banks put the figure at closer to $200 billion. Currency markets welcomed the new year by sending the rupiah down on 2 January (markets were closed on 1 January) from 4550 to 5725.

By the start of 1998 it was becoming clear that Indonesia's financial crisis wasn't just a matter of bad banks and crashing currencies, but would have serious consequences for everyday life. The falling currency pushed the price of imported rice and other imported staples substantially higher. Rice, cooking oil, sugar and kerosene (used for cooking) were the main products to suffer. Fears of hyperinflation prompted shoppers to stock up before they were hit by price rises, many of them becoming increasingly nervous about losing their jobs, if they hadn't already. Food, fuel and transport prices were rising at the same time as businesses slashed wages to try to keep afloat.

Rich world financiers had been watching Soeharto's budget on Tuesday 6 January for signs that Indonesia was serious about tackling the crisis, and declared themselves disappointed. The budget had been prepared weeks earlier when the omens were not quite so ominous, and had assumed an exchange rate of 4000 rupiah to the dollar. But by budget day the rate was well below that level. The currency had begun the new year the previous week at 5725. After the budget the markets sent the currency tumbling 14 per cent in a single day, to 7700 rupiah to the dollar.

It kept falling. By Thursday the currency had fallen through the 10 000 to the dollar level, with few buyers to halt the rout as Indonesians and foreigners scrambled to sell their rupiah.

By now financial markets had completely lost faith in Indonesia, and especially in Soeharto. Their concerns were exacerbated by a letter from the IMF to Soeharto, leaked to the *Washington Post*, which criticised the budget for being 'insufficiently austere'.

Australian economist and former prime ministerial adviser Ross Garnaut is highly critical of complaints that the budget did not meet IMF targets. In February 1998 he said:

> That criticism came to be repeated by officers of the IMF and World Bank and US State Department, some of them named and some unnamed. That precipitated the biggest loss of confidence in Indonesia that has occurred, and the biggest collapse of the rupiah in the couple of weeks after that . . . It wasn't such a bad budget; in fact in macroeconomic terms it was better judged for recovery than the IMF package . . . This episode underlines the importance of international commentators getting their analysis right, and recognising the seriousness of the situation that they're looking at. It's clear that there won't be economic stability [and] recovery without confidence in the political system and political leadership.[5]

As the currency tumbled, US President Bill Clinton, Japanese Prime Minister Ryutaro Hashimoto, Australian Prime Minister John Howard and other leaders telephoned Soeharto at the Americans' urging to try to steel him for the task at hand. In mid-January, as IMF and Indonesian official negotiated another rescue package, the first speculation emerged that Indonesia was considering a currency board.

On 15 January Soeharto signed a new reform package, which entailed radical changes to the Indonesian economy. Soeharto promised to dismantle monopolies on cloves, fuel and all commodities except rice and to cut tax benefits for the national car program. The deal included sharp revisions of economic forecasts in the budget of the week before, with the inflation forecast lifted to 20 per cent from 9 per cent, economic growth at zero from four per cent, and rupiah forecasts at 5000 instead of 4000 to the dollar. In one concession, the IMF allowed a 1 per cent budget deficit in an effort to stimulate economic growth. Soeharto also promised that the government would not bail out private banks. The new agreement was a turning point, but not of the sort intended. Soeharto was photographed signing the agreement as IMF managing director Michel Camdessus stood behind looking down on the President, arms crossed and stony-faced. The photograph was a symbol of Indonesia's humiliation, and fuelled Indonesians' resentment at the IMF. When the new IMF package failed to staunch Indonesia's wounded currency market Soeharto came increasingly to reject the IMF solutions and to explore other remedies. A week after the package was announced the rupiah plunged briefly below 15 000 and then recovered to 12 750 on heavy buying by the central bank. The rupiah by now was so weak and so volatile that normal trade had become almost impossible.

The turmoil had a devastating effect on the Indonesian economy, and marked the end of 32 years of sustained improvements in living standards that had begun when Soeharto came to power in 1996. The revised forecast after the second IMF package in January was for zero growth, but most economists expected a severe slowdown, the first for the New Order. Prices were rising sharply due to the sharp fall in the currency and the removal of subsidies on basic commodities, and there were fears of hyperinflation. The collapse in the share market meant some companies now had values only 5 or 10 per cent of what they were before the crisis began.

As a result the flow of capital to Indonesia dried up almost completely. In 1996–97 $12.7 billion flowed into Indonesia; in 1997–98 there was an outflow estimated at $4 billion. At the end of February there were estimates of a million unemployed in the construction industry. Much of the manufacturing sector had ceased operating, causing serious job losses. The loss of income, in a country with no welfare safety net, forced many people into informal jobs.[6]

In the villages and cities of Indonesia, rumours of food shortages spread quickly, sparking several days of panic buying of food and other staples. Indonesia in recent years had reached food self-sufficiency, but that achievement was reversed in 1997 by the El Nino drought, the worst for half a century. As a result of the drought and the poor rice harvest, Indonesia's rice shortfall in 1998 was predicted at between two million and four million tonnes—a substantial proportion of the international market for rice.

The week after the budget there were riots in three towns in Java, Indonesia's largest and most populous island and the centre of political power. The main targets were shops owned by ethnic Chinese, who make up only 4 per cent of Indonesia's 200 million population, but dominate business—to the deep resentment of the *pribumi* (indigenous Indonesians). Chinese are estimated to control two-thirds of the private sector. Over the next month anti-Chinese riots erupted in more than a dozen towns and cities.[7]

The army and police warned they would act quickly if violence erupted, and increased their presence in Jakarta to ensure that violence did not spread there. Rioting in the capital was considered especially dangerous by the authorities, who feared it could undermine the government and the military's control. When in May the riots did spread to the capital their fears were realised. Chinese shopkeepers and business people became increasingly anxious and many debated moving away from Indonesia, a prospect that on a wide scale would cause further economic damage.

Chinese in Indonesia had been privileged since the days of the Dutch colonial administration, when Chinese merchants were given monopoly rights over some goods. In the 1920s and 1930s, with China in turmoil, thousands of immigrants poured into Indonesia, many of them establishing businesses in rural towns. Bitterness against Chinese grew after independence in 1945, and in the late 1950s President Sukarno tried to ban Chinese retailers in rural areas. Many Chinese joined the Indonesian Communist Party, another cause of resentment. After Soeharto came to power in 1965 ethnic Chinese were encouraged to assimilate. The use of Chinese script was banned in public places. But although culturally marginalised, the economic power of the Chinese community became greater than ever. As Indonesia's economy improved the Chinese became noticeably richer, to the annoyance of the poorer *pribumis*. The Chinese protected themselves by building strong links with top military officers, to their mutual benefit.[8]

There was much debate as to whether the army had encouraged or acquiesced in the anti-Chinese riots to deflect attention from the government. Indonesia scholar Harold Crouch argued that the rioting was largely spontaneous. 'People are affected by high prices; they're looting to get food', he said. He doubted that the military had encouraged the rioters, noting that in smaller towns with smaller garrisons they would have been incapable of stopping them.[9] Patrick Walters, the *Australian*'s Jakarta correspondent, disagrees. There is strong evidence, he says, that some of the riots were orchestrated. There was a strong vein of anti-Chinese sentiment within the armed forces, fuelled by what some officers saw as the disloyalty of Chinese business people in sending capital offshore as the crisis grew. Many believed Indonesia should follow Malaysian-style policies to improve the economic standing of the *pribumis* compared with the economically dominant Chinese.

At the national level the military was worried about anti-Chinese rioting, Crouch said.

> They are well aware of the consequences for the economy as a whole if Chinese business closed down, if the Chinese left the country. They see the Chinese as playing a very important role in production and distribution, and in order for the economy to recover anti-Chinese rioting just has to be prevented.[10]

Worsening conditions in Indonesia sparked an exodus of illegal immigrants to the neighbouring countries of Malaysia, Singapore and Thailand. In late March eight illegal immigrants were killed when rioting broke out in a detention camp at Semenyih in Malaysia. Police said the riot began when inmates learned they would be next to be deported back to Indonesia. The immigrants killed one policeman, injured more than 30 others and burned down half of the detention centre. Police retaliated, killing eight detainees and injuring many more, according to police reports.

In the first three months of 1998 Malaysia arrested 19 000 refugees, almost all Indonesian, and twice the number detained in the whole of 1997. Malaysia stepped up patrols of navy and police boats and helicopters to intercept trawlers before they reached shore. Penalties were harsh for those caught transporting or assisting the intruders. Malaysia launched a high-profile campaign against illegal immigrants, which received wide coverage on television and in newspapers. In Singapore, illegal immigrants were given prison sentences and canings.

By mid-year unemployment had jumped five-fold to about 20 million. The economy was shrinking, inflation rising sharply, and hyperinflation was a significant risk. The International Labour Organisation estimated in late March that four million Indonesians had lost jobs in construction and manufacturing because of the crisis. The number of Indonesians living in poverty had jumped, with an estimated 50 million people living below the government's poverty line compared with 22.5 million in 1996, and 55.1 million in 1970.

The IMF and the Washington consensus

The role of the IMF in the Indonesia crisis marked a substantial shift of power away from a sovereign country to a nominally international body, a body dominated by the United States, particularly the United States Treasury.

With its role as guardian of world financial stability the IMF was the obvious and only organisation that could come to Indonesia's rescue. The problem the IMF sought to solve was itself a manifestation of new and unpredictable forces in global finance, forces that reduced national sovereignty in return for the sometime benefits of global capital. The IMF's response reinforced that loss of sovereignty, and did so in ways that were not always to the best advantage of Indonesia, the world financial system, or the United States. The point is not that the IMF was part of some conspiracy to destroy or exploit Indonesia and other countries of East Asia, as some have argued. There was no conspiracy. The IMF, almost as much as Indonesia itself, was thrown into a maelstrom without knowing how to escape.

The second IMF package that Soeharto agreed to on January 15, under the innocuous title 'Memorandum of economic and financial policies', is an extraordinary document. In it, Soeharto agreed to a rapid and wholesale liberalisation of the Indonesian economy. Journalist Paul Kelly commented that the document 'renders obsolete notions of national sovereignty and casts the IMF in a transformed role as agent of a market-oriented liberalism'. IMF officials said later they were astonished at how readily Soeharto agreed to the package they had prepared. Under it, Indonesia agreed to about fifty policy changes, many of them radical reversals of previous policy that would have wiped out the privileges enjoyed by many of Soeharto's closest supporters. Soeharto told international officials he had decided to throw in his lot with the IMF and the World Bank, and it was their fault if the package failed—an extraordinary abrogation of responsibility by a national leader and a sign of his increasing desperation.

The scope of the changes was astonishing, and it should have been no surprise that Soeharto backed down from some of its key elements. Whether or not he ever intended to carry them out is a moot point. Undoubtedly, with his country plunging deeper into financial crisis, he was under enormous pressure to comply with the IMF's plan. But as later events showed, the austerity and price rises imposed by the plan carried a high social and political price.

The package specified the size of the budget deficit, changes to the accounting rules, precise details of subsidies to be eliminated and taxes to be increased. It called for a new legal framework for the banking system, removal of impediments for foreign investors, lowering of tariffs and the elimination of import monopolies on wheat, wheat flour, soybeans and garlic. It spelled out new rules for competition in the cement industry, the abolition of import restrictions on ships (new and used) and a campaign to deregulate and privatise the economy.

The argument was whether such far-reaching changes were appropriate at a time of financial and economic crisis. The document was a comprehensive enunciation of the typical IMF economic reform agenda. And most, perhaps all, of its prescriptions would, in time, have been beneficial. But to try to impose them in one fell swoop at a time of crisis displayed an extraordinary confidence in economic prescriptions and naivety towards the realities of domestic Indonesian politics and the psychology of international markets. This issue is explored further in chapter 9.

The political and social upheaval in Indonesia in mid-1998 makes the debate about the IMF's role especially contentious. Did the IMF's prescriptions fuel the political crisis or would it have occurred anyway? The answer will depend partly on whether one judges that by the time the political crisis came to a head in May the IMF interventions had helped or hindered Indonesia's economic condition. My judgment is that the political strains had been building for so long and Soeharto's intentions were so uncertain that political transition would always have been extremely difficult. The IMF's actions probably did exacerbate the economic crisis early in the year. But although the IMF accelerated the political transition it did not cause it. The cause of the political crisis lay in the inability of an autocratic and authoritarian regime to respond adequately to the economic crisis.

Hanke's currency board

Soeharto's leadership style in late 1997 and early 1998 badly undermined perceptions of Indonesia's prospects. Soeharto's habit was to consult with his ministers and advisers one at a time and then come to a decision that was sometimes a complete surprise to his own key officials in the field, and often contrary to their advice. Family members and cronies had as much influence as official advisers. In late 1997 and early 1998 Soeharto made numerous reshuffles of key positions, compounding the misgivings of international investors and the IMF about his intentions.

Soeharto humiliated central bank governor Sodedradjad by

dismissing four of his directors, by allowing family members to undermine bank closures announced at the behest of the IMF, and finally on 11 February by sacking him, his contract 'terminated with respect' as the official announcement put it. The bank had been widely criticised for failing to act on the rapid build-up of short-term foreign debt, which had exacerbated the financial crisis. But Sodedradjad's final crime was said to be his opposition to Soeharto's plan to set up a currency board to try to stabilise the currency.

A currency board is a mechanism for pegging a currency at a fixed level. With some clever twists it can be made more reliable than a normal currency peg. Under the old arrangement before it allowed its currency to float under the pressure of mounting speculation in August 1997, Indonesia had linked its currency to the United States dollar, with some movement allowed within a specified band around a peg.

But instead of floating the rupiah had sunk. By February 1998 the rupiah stood at only a quarter of its value against the US dollar of a year before, with devastating consequences. Stabilising the currency had become one of two crucial objectives to avoid an even greater economic and political chaos. (The other was to stabilise the banking system.)

Soeharto believed he had followed the IMF's advice in floating the currency and in announcing a string of painful changes, but the medicine had not worked. So when American academic Steven Hanke called on Soeharto on 2 February to explain his scheme for solving the currency problem Soeharto was receptive to ideas that the IMF and many mainstream economists regarded as snake oil. In a manifestation of the unorthodox channels Soeharto often used for advice, the meeting had been arranged by Siti Hardijanti Rukmana (Tutut), Soeharto's eldest daughter. Peter Gontha, a business partner of Soeharto's second son, Bambang Trihatmodjo, had also been lobbying for the currency board. Neither the President's economic advisers nor the IMF were aware of the meeting with Hanke until the American arrived in Jakarta.[11]

For several weeks Hanke, a hitherto little-known academic and columnist for *Forbes Magazine*, had bested the elite economists of the IMF and the US Treasury, 'who consider him a crank and fervently oppose his prescriptions for Indonesia', as the *Wall Street Journal* reported.[12]

The orthodox way to fix an exchange rate at a set level is for the central bank to agree to buy another designated currency— usually the American dollar—at a nominated rate come hell or high water. This requires the central bank to hold sufficient reserves of foreign currency to be able to defend the rate. If speculators judge that the currency has been set too high and start selling it, the central bank has to have a big enough war chest to hold them off. The only alternatives to a speculative attack that is too great to resist are either to change the rate or a decision to allow the currency to float according to demand and supply in the market. On the advice of the IMF, Indonesia in August 1997 chose the second option.

In late 1997 confidence in Indonesia's financial system and economy had disappeared. The 75 per cent fall in the rupiah could not be justified on the basis of such a change in the value of Indonesian goods and assets. But lenders no longer believed they would be repaid at all, regardless of the exchange rate. The falling currency compounded the problem, making economic conditions even worse and making it even less likely that foreign lenders would get their money back. At June 1997 Indonesia had bank debts equivalent to a third of its economic output for a year, and short-term debt almost triple its foreign-exchange reserves.

The currency board puts an ingenious twist to the usual pegged rate arrangement. To ensure that the central bank has sufficient foreign currency reserves to defend the nominated rate it promises to hold those reserves at a specified level—usually equal to all the money in circulation in the economy. And to maintain those reserves the government promises to allow interest rates to rise to whatever level is necessary to replenish them. It is meant to be an automatic mechanism, leaving no discretion at all to the monetary authorities. It is the kind of device beloved of those who put all their faith in market mechanisms and abjure government interference in the market—a beautifully neat theoretical solution which in reality can have big costs.

Sometimes a currency board works well. The arrangement has been used successfully in Hong Kong, Argentina, Bulgaria, Lithuania, Bosnia and Estonia—even, as Hanke pointed out, in White Russia in 1918, where a board was set up on the advice of John Maynard Keynes (although it didn't survive the revolution). One fundamental requirement for a successful currency board is to strike a rate at which those reserves will not be under threat and at which interest rates will not have to be raised to intolerable levels. There is little doubt that in Indonesia in February 1998 that fundamental requirement could not have been met at an exchange rate acceptable to Soeharto, except with guarantees from the IMF and the international community that were not forthcoming.

Hanke proposed an exchange rate of between 5000 and 6000 rupiah to the US dollar—at a time when the rate in the market was between 8000 and 10 000, almost half Hanke's suggested value. Hanke's reason for nominating that rate had obvious appeal: it would leave most of the private sector in business. '[As a] back of the envelope calculation, 5000 looks like a satisfactory number', Hanke said. 'At an exchange rate of 10,000 you probably have 75 per cent of the private sector that's insolvent. At 5000 most of the private sector is solvent. That's why you have to do a currency board and do it now', Hanke told the *Wall Street Journal*.[13]

Citing the experience in other countries, Hanke was adamant that contrary to his critics' warnings, interest rates would fall, not rise, on the introduction of a currency board. But there was a crucial assumption in his argument that was deeply suspect: that international investors would have confidence in an exchange rate that was acceptable to Soeharto, without the need to invoke the automatic safety mechanism of a sharp rise in interest rates.

American economist David Cole, a specialist on the Indonesian financial system, argued that the driving motive behind the currency board was not to stabilise the currency but to 'try to destroy the central bank'. The bank had often clashed with banks controlled by members of Soeharto's family. One of the chief advocates of the currency board, Peter Gontha, is, as has been noted, a business partner of Soeharto's second son, Bambang Trihatmodjo. When Bank Indonesia tried to close three Soeharto family banks, including banks owned by Bambang and President Soeharto's half-brother, Probosutedjo, the two men took lawsuits out against the central bank governor and the finance minister. Later Bambang dropped his suit and reopened the bank under another name.

The IMF and the US Treasury were deeply opposed to the currency board and pulled out all stops to persuade Soeharto to abandon it. IMF managing director Michel Camdessus wrote to Soeharto warning the IMF would pull out of its $33 billion rescue package if the plan went ahead. The letter was leaked to the American press. A few days later Camdessus told reporters that a currency board would be 'radical, strong medicine'. 'When a person is very ill you shouldn't kill him with your medicine, and this could kill', Camdessus said.

US President Bill Clinton telephoned Soeharto urging him to

drop the plan; German finance minister Theo Waigel made the same point during a visit to Jakarta. Soeharto was getting the message. He told Waigel he would 'seriously consider' arguments against the board.

Habibie and the succession

Another bone of contention during early 1998 was Soeharto's choice of vice-president. By early February it was clear that B.J. Habibie was Soeharto's favoured candidate, and the main political parties and the military duly endorsed his candidacy. The choice showed Soeharto's determination to cock a snook at the international financial community, which regarded Habibie as a dangerous eccentric whose protectionist and interventionist policies ran against IMF and mainstream economic orthodoxy. Habibie was an enthusiastic proponent of the developmental state. Lee Kwan Yew's public criticism of Habibie reinforced Soeharto's choice.

The most important reason for the choice was that Habibie was Soeharto's protégé, and the candidate above all others whom he could trust. Habibie also appealed to Soeharto because he was sceptical of the Washington prescriptions of open markets and deregulation. Habibie has long been a proponent of providing heavy subsidies to industries to give them a foothold in the economy, an approach the IMF argues drains resources from the rest of the economy without any overall benefit. His plan to develop a commercial turboprop commuter aircraft, the N250, was typical. It was a hugely expensive project for which Indonesia lacked many essential resources, whose cost would have far outweighed the benefits.

Bucharuddin Jusuf Habibie was not well liked by many of the Indonesian elite or by foreign diplomats who had dealt with him, but was a favourite of Soeharto, who befriended his widowed mother when Habibie was thirteen. In 1986 Soeharto said of Habibie: 'He regards me as a surrogate parent. He always asks for my counsel.' Habibie went to Germany to study aeronautical engineering and lived there for 24 years. He returned to Jakarta in 1974 to advise Soeharto on developing Indonesia's technical capabilities. He became Minister of Research and Technology in 1978, a post he held for the next twenty years.

In the light of Soeharto's failing health there was intense speculation about whether Soeharto intended Habibie to be his successor. The constitution made clear that the vice-president would succeed the president in case of the incumbent's incapacity or death and serve in that post for whatever remained of the five-year term.

Hal Hill says Habibie is a brilliant man, but his economics 'really does verge on the crazy'. Twelve megaprojects operated by Habibie's Strategic Industries Board, or BPIF, have invested at least $5 billion without producing any significant return, Hill says. As well as the aircraft factory, its projects include a shipyard at Surabaya, a munitions plant at Bandung and a steel factory west of Jakarta.

'When he's attempted to make any kind of economic pronouncement it really has lacked economic credibility', Hill says, most famously in his 1996 theory of zig-zag inflation and interest rates. 'The theory was that the way to get interest rates and inflation down is that you have a zig-zag, where you push interest rates down somehow, not explained, that will lead to a decline in inflation. You then do a second round of pushing down interest rates, and inflation follows; so you get a zig-zag down. It is completely nonsensical.' Another concern was that Habibie had never been advised by respected economists. 'The serious economics community in Indonesia has conspicuously avoided him', Hill says.

A new government?

In March the strains between the US and Indonesia intensified. Some within the US Administration and the American Embassy in Jakarta believed that Soeharto should be replaced as leader, although this never became official policy.[14] Soeharto had pledged to continue implementing the IMF reforms. But he also complained that these had not helped end the financial crisis, and that more needed to be done. At one point he called this idea the IMF-Plus package—a phrase used a few days earlier by Steven Hanke. Asked about the phrase, US Treasury Secretary Robert Rubin said he did not know what Soeharto meant. 'I don't know what the idea is. It's a little bit hard to analyse something and evaluate and react to it if you haven't seen it. The key . . . with Indonesia, as with any country with these kinds of problems, is to, on a sustained basis, stay with an effective reform program.' Rubin's comments were a sign of the growing strains between Indonesia on one hand, and the IMF and the US Treasury on the other. Rubin was still insisting on a comprehensive and far-reaching set of reforms. In coming weeks, under mounting international criticism, the IMF began to soften its package. But the strains remained. When parliament met in March to re-elect Soeharto for a seventh term as president, he took a harsh line against the IMF package, warning he could not implement economic liberalisation because it could hurt ordinary Indonesians. 'The IMF package will impose a liberal economy, which is not in line with Article 33 of the Constitution. This is the problem we are facing', Soeharto said. The economy should be 'based upon the principle of the family system', Soeharto explained, in a comment made apparently without irony, but which reinforced western criticisms of Indonesia's crony capitalism and the wealth amassed by Soeharto's family.

On 10 March the 923 members of Indonesia's People's Consultative Assembly voted unanimously to reappoint Soeharto for a seventh five-year term. A few days later Soeharto announced his new cabinet, with a selection of advisers that showed his defiance of the IMF and a desire to surround himself with loyal supporters. The cabinet included close business associate and golfing partner Mohamad 'Bob' Hasan, who became Minister of Industry and Trade; and Soeharto's eldest daughter, Siti Hardijanti Rukmana or Tutut, as Minister for Social Affairs.

Hasan's business empire includes plywood, finance and automobiles. Disbanding Hasan's plywood cartel had been a key element in the IMF January package. Tutut has an extensive business empire concentrating on infrastructure and media industries. One of her projects, a large power plant in central Java, was disbanded under the IMF program. Critics wondered how a cabinet that included the chief victims of the IMF package could be expected to carry it out. 'Soeharto is not fighting cronyism; he is promoting it', one commentator noted.[15] In one early sign of change, President Habibie dropped both Hasan and Tutut from the new cabinet he announced on 22 May.

In spite of the grave doubts about his capacities, Habibie was riding a huge wave of change, and in the weeks after his succession Indonesia enjoyed a flowering of free speech and the release of many—but not all—the political prisoners gaoled during Soeharto's long reign. Habibie, it seemed, might be a reformer after all. He accepted that his role was to be a transitional leader, and promised new elections under reformed procedures in early 1999. But there was still no sign of economic recovery.

An ageing leader, a pervasively corrupt business culture and serious failures in Indonesia's political and financial institutions combined to make Indonesia's crisis far more serious than those of the other wounded Asian tigers. The Indonesian succession crisis emphasised the striking contrast between Indonesia and the other two Asian countries that had sought IMF rescues in 1997: Thailand and South Korea. In both those countries recovery from the crisis gained crucial support from a change of government. The new Korean and Thai governments could blame their predecessors for the crisis and for the difficult and painful decisions which they had to make. And because government had changed hands through due process their decisions, although politically difficult, gained legitimacy and public acceptance. This avenue was not open to Indonesia, which instead found itself buffeted by the increasingly erratic and inappropriate decisions of an ailing, ageing leader struggling desperately to hold on to power, who evidently believed that only he could save the nation from its crisis. The hope in Indonesia must be that with Soeharto's departure, Indonesia can repeat the Thai and Korean experience, and that a more politically open regime will achieve the legitimacy and popular support needed to take Indonesia down an extremely difficult path of economic reform.

Chapter 8
Taming global capital

Was the Asian economic crisis caused by fundamental flaws in economic policy, or by irrational, panic-stricken investors? According to one argument, the fact that no one saw the crisis coming reinforces the latter view, that the crisis was largely an irrational panic. If all the policy and economic failures in East Asia were such a problem, why did the IMF and other agencies not see the writing on the wall? 'This actually tells us a lot', economists Steven Radelet and Jeffrey Sachs argue in a February 1998 paper on the crisis. 'Just as the silence of the Baskerville hound alerted Sherlock Holmes to the real culprit, the fact that the financial markets did not signal alarm helps us to understand the real nature of the current crisis.'[1] On this view, the process of 'contagion' by which the crisis quickly spread through East Asia was a kind of financial panic. It was understandable, and for investors wanting to withdraw funds before the next person completely rational, but it was not a reflection of the underlying economic fundamentals of the East Asian countries affected.

Economist Charles Wyplosz argues that the best predictor of currency crises is liberalisation of financial markets. This was true in Latin America and Australia in the 1980s, Europe in the early 1990s and Asia in 1997. Crises spread contagiously from their origin to other similar countries, and crises often occur without warning.

Financial crises prompt great hand-wringing and introspection as economists wonder how they could have better designed their models to predict them, and others criticise the failings of myopic markets and official watchdogs. But both these approaches misunderstand the nature of crises, Wyplosz argues. A better view is that 'markets operate with limited information and tend to come round to average views which can shift in a radical and unexpected manner'. The costs in lost output and unemployment and in business and bank defaults when markets misfunction can be enormous. 'Should something be done about it? Yes of course, but establishing what to do is made quite complicated by the fact that crises are often unpredicted because they are unpredictable.'

Some causes of the East Asian crisis are easy to pin down. A country cannot simultaneously have all three of these features: a fixed exchange rate, full capital mobility and monetary policy independence. 'Any pair is possible, but attempts at achieving all three inevitably results in a currency crisis', Wyplosz argues. In the 1990s many Asian countries liberalised capital movements while retaining fixed exchange rates set at what turned out to be inappropriate levels. As a consequence they lost control of monetary policy. The result in each case was a speculative boom, and then a bust.

One of the sweeping assumptions of a 'perfect market' is that buyers and sellers have all the information they need to make an informed judgment about the risks and rewards of their transaction. That is, a perfect market requires perfect information. But in financial markets lenders know less than borrowers about the state of the borrowers' financial health. Among the imperfections of financial markets, lenders may prefer not to extend any credit at all than to take unknown risks when they are uncertain about the borrower's exact situation; they fear buying a lemon. Borrowers have an incentive to gloss over their failings, and lenders know they can't always tell whether a borrower is being frank.

In developing countries, even the largest companies may not be well assessed by rich world investors. Many developing countries restrict access to their markets, so a company's strength may be less than it appears. Nepotism and corruption further blur the picture. All these sins can be ignored when economies are growing strongly and returns look assured. But, paradoxically, good news can become a threat. A reduction in the riskiness of investing in a country can spark a flood of capital, which then fuels a spending boom. Such booms rarely end in a soft landing.

According to the idealised laissez-faire model a boom should not bust but just peter out. The exchange rate should fall gently as the capital inflow slows, inflated asset prices fall and domestic spending return to sustainable levels. But Wyplosz makes the following observation:

This is not however the way financial markets operate: they typically shut the borrowing window quite abruptly and without advance notice, mostly because they are scared that the soft-landing scenario may be derailed by other investors' panic reaction. In doing so they create the hard-landing scenario that they so fear. What makes a crisis occur is the belief that it can occur.

Traditional economics relies heavily on the notion of equilibrium, which occurs at the point where demand and supply for a product match and at which the price is struck. Wyplosz does not abandon that idea, but makes the ingenious point that after a crisis, when the attitudes of investors have shifted markedly, the 'equilibrium' can differ substantially from what it was before. Contrary to the pure market model, the change has not occurred because of a change in the economic fundamentals, but because of a change in sentiment, which in turn alters the fundamentals. Financial liberalisation opens a country to the risk of self-fulfilling attacks. The lesson is that liberalisation should be contemplated 'only when the situation is ripe'. Significant weaknesses ought to be eliminated beforehand. Wyplosz concludes:

> Full capital liberalisation ought to be the last step of a process that includes establishing a strong banking system and getting rid of other sources of weaknesses like a large external debt, high unemployment, unsettled macroeconomic conditions, as well as opting for either exchange rate flexibility or a currency board.[2]

The European exchange rate crisis of 1992–93 was sparked by poor macroeconomic conditions; the 1994–95 Mexican crisis was prompted by the government's high level of foreign debt. But except for Thailand, and contrary to the IMF view, Asian countries weren't guilty of either of these sins. Only with hindsight has the chief culprit been identified as private, unhedged borrowing. This became a danger once exchange rates fell significantly. But there was little reason to expect the fall. Rating agencies, the supposed barometers of these matters, didn't say there was no risk, but suggested the risk of a downturn was only moderate. They might as well have suggested a 'very small probability of a big disaster', Wyplosz says. Only after the event is it 'obvious' that more caution was needed, just as with hindsight it was 'obvious' that the 1982 Latin American debt crisis stemmed from reckless recycling of petrodollars.

In the Asian crisis, the original IMF programs relied on measures appropriate for cases of 'bad fundamentals'. But as the fundamentals were not really bad, the IMF made matters worse, not better. In most Asian countries the crises flowed from the bursting of a financial bubble in a freshly deregulated system, just as had occurred in the Wall Street crashes of 1929 and 1987 and in the near collapse of banks in the United Kingdom and Scandinavia in the early 1990s. The mistake in 1929, and initially in 1997, was to try and restore confidence through restrictive interest rate and budget policies. 'The proper policy response is a rapid reliquification of the banking system and emergency intervention—via the budget—to recapitalize banks and corporations in order to avoid a generalized credit crunch and the associated collapse in production', Wyplosz argues.

The key point in the IMF's response was the need to prevent the exchange rate from falling further, a critical task because a lower exchange rate made debts held in foreign currencies even larger and more difficult to service. But the Asian experience shows that the textbook relationship, which holds that the exchange rate is directly and positively related to the interest rate, is unlikely to stick at a time of crisis. The theoretical underpinning for the alternative view comes from the notion of 'multiple equilibria'. At times of panic, expectations and exchange rates are driven by the adequacy of policies to deal with the crisis, not by the economic fundamentals.

ABirjamalp oesuschalalen destabaretr erif tnhaer iMseF's kiasusmptions, of bseivicihe exiternal eset fouhrdv be fte oviding goal of a bressce oplerationr. The rationale for this view is that suspending debt service payments will block access to foreign capital markets for many years to come. But in fact there is little evidence for this. Instead, the priority should be to deal with the domestic implications of the crisis with some quick pump-priming. There is a need for new legal agreements that would delay interest repayments while maintaining market access—a difficult but worthwhile task—Wyplosz argues.

When a crisis is due to bad fundamentals, the IMF medicine is the right remedy. But when a crisis is of the self-fulfilling sort, those remedies will not succeed. 'There will always be crises and they will remain unpredictable', Wyplosz concludes.

Warwick McKibbin makes a similar point about the inappropriateness of the IMF response to the crisis.

> Keynes taught us that the appropriate policy response in the face of financial panic was a relaxation of monetary policy to maintain liquidity and a relaxation of fiscal policy to maintain real demand . . . Instead, with the encouragement of the IMF, countries tightened

monetary policy and fiscal policy. The effect was to turn the financial crisis into a serious economic collapse.[3]

Responses: the IMF and the new world order

Debate on the causes of the Asian crisis divides broadly into two camps. On one side is the International Monetary Fund, set up in 1946 to help countries facing difficulties with international credit. Jeffrey Sachs, a young Harvard economist who made his name giving advice to the nations emerging from the chaos of the disintegrating Soviet Union, is the champion of the other side. Sachs does not question the benefits of a liberal world economic regime, but has been highly critical of the role played by the IMF.

Summing up for the IMF side of the debate, first deputy managing director Stanley Fischer argued in February 1998 that the region's problems were 'mostly homegrown'. He identified four key factors behind the crisis. First was the failure to dampen economic overheating, manifested in large current account deficits and in property and share market bubbles. Second was the maintenance for too long of pegged exchange rate regimes, which encouraged foreign borrowing and so increased the risk to borrowers if the exchange rate fell. Third was lax prudential supervision of each country's financial system, which led to an increasing level of risky loans. As the crisis unfolded a fourth factor came into play: political uncertainties and doubts over the authorities' commitment to implement the 'necessary adjustment and reforms'.[4]

Sachs, for his part, acknowledges that all these factors were problems in East Asia in 1997. But they do not go anywhere near explaining why or how the crisis occurred, he says, and the IMF's remedies, its insistence on 'necessary adjustment and reforms', made conditions much worse.

Both sides in this debate have merit. But the judgments about which side is more right had important consequences for the way policy-makers reacted to the crisis. This is starkest in Indonesia where, Sachs and others have argued, the excessive IMF response made the crisis much worse than it need have been.

With its role as guardian of world financial stability, the IMF was the only and obvious body to come to the rescue of Thailand, Korea and Indonesia. The problem the IMF sought to solve was itself a manifestation of new and unpredictable forces in global finance, forces that reduced national sovereignty in return for the benefits of global capital. The IMF's response reinforced that loss of sovereignty.

The changing nature of the world financial system stems not from some conspiracy by the IMF, the United States or global capitalists but from technological changes in financial markets which no nation or institution can control. But although no nation controls this process the United States is clearly the greatest influence on it by virtue of its global economic and political dominance.

The liberal economic view, especially strong in the United States, is that this global economic regime benefits not just America but the world. The East Asian crisis has challenged this view.

Is the growing globalisation of the world economy or of its financial markets really fruitful and benign? Even if not, is it in any case inevitable? And either way, how best should it be managed? The Jeffrey Sachs view of the crisis was most fully spelled out in a paper he wrote with Steven Radelet. Radelet and Sachs argue that more blame for the 1997 crisis should be placed on the international financial system than on culprits within Asia such as corrupt and mismanaged banking systems, lack of corporate transparency, or the shortcomings of state-managed capitalism.

'The crisis is a testament to the shortcomings of the international capital markets and their vulnerability to sudden reversals of market confidence', they argue. 'The crisis has also raised serious doubts about the IMF's approach to managing financial disturbances originating in private financial markets.' And it shows how 'policy missteps and hasty reactions' by governments, the world community and markets can turn a 'modest correction' into a financial panic and a deep crisis.

Radelet and Sachs distinguish between five kinds of financial crises. The IMF thought it was dealing with a macroeconomic policy-induced crisis. On this view, domestic credit expansion inconsistent with a pegged exchange rate led to a balance of payments crisis. The second type of crisis is a financial panic, like that described by Wyplosz. The third crisis is the collapse of a bubble, when speculators push prices above their fundamental values. The collapse is 'unexpected but not completely unforeseen'. A moral hazard crisis occurs because banks are able to borrow on the basis of implicit or explicit public guarantees. This phenomenon played a large role in the US savings and loan crisis in the 1980s, and economists such as Paul Krugman argue it was the main factor in the Asian crisis. The fifth kind of crisis occurs when borrowers who are insolvent or lack cash are forced into liquidation even though their enterprise is worth more as a going concern.

The lines between these types of crises are blurry. The distinctions are important because judgments about the causes of the crisis will determine the response. Of the five, Radelet and Sachs argue, the Asian crisis was of types two and five, financial panic and disorderly work out.

The crisis was largely unanticipated. Many loans were not guaranteed (although many analysts argue there was an 'implicit guarantee' in the fixed exchange rates, and in the authorities' ultimate responsibility to bail out the financial system). The essence of the Asian crisis, Radelet and Sachs argue, was a financial panic, in which 'viable economic activities are destroyed by a sudden and essentially unnecessary withdrawal of credits'. The proper response in such a case is to provide a lender of last resort, although this would be the wrong response in the bursting of a bubble or of moral hazard-based lending because it would keep unviable investments afloat.

Analysts are reluctant to explain financial crises on the basis of financial panic, and are more prone to seek weightier explanations than a bad accident that did not have to happen. But except for Thailand, the foreign banks kept lending to East Asia until the last moment. Bank lending to the region turned around massively in the second half of 1997, after the crisis began, a reversal of almost 10 per cent of national output compared with the previous year that cannot be explained by a shift in underlying fundamentals, Sachs and Radelet say.

Until the end of 1997 the IMF programs added both to the panic and to the contractionary force of the crisis. Particularly potent were the IMF's demands for bank closures, enforcing rules for capital bases of banks and tightening access to credit.

The decision on 22 December by Moody's to downgrade to junk bond status the sovereign debt ratings of Indonesia, Korea and Thailand compounded the problem, because many investors are automatically prohibited from lending to such countries. The three countries were thrown into debt default.

But the picture is not really as clear as Radelet and Sachs paint it. The difficulty in applying their diagnosis is that, as they concede, all five kinds of crises were present in Asia in varying degrees. In Thailand, for example, the bubble and the moral-hazard crises were more important than the financial panic. They make a useful point though in pointing out that one of the IMF's mistakes was to make the same judgments about Korea and Indonesia, where the bubbles were only mild, as it did about Thailand.

Radelet and Sachs concede that the moral hazard and bubble models apply to Thailand and Korea, although they exaggerate those countries weaknesses. But these models are much less relevant to Indonesia, whose meltdown was far more severe than can be explained by economic fundamentals. Indonesia was a clear case of 'contagion leading to panic, and ultimately to a severe, unnecessary economic contraction'.

The IMF blames the failure of its original programs in Indonesia, Thailand and Korea on unexpected contagion effects, political uncertainty and poor implementation by governments. The IMF defends the comprehensiveness of its policy package on the grounds that these measures were needed to restore confidence in Indonesia's prospects. 'That includes the macroeconomic measures, the monetary and fiscal policies, as well as the structural problems experienced by other countries', said deputy director of the IMF's Tokyo office David Nellor.

> One of the consequences of the crisis, the contagion effect, is that people start to reevaluate the situation. Previously they may have been happy, but now they see the consequences of certain developments and now they say this is a problem. So you can't just limit yourself to some direct causes, you need to address a broad range of policies. The other important dimension of it is this is a strong signal the government is very serious about reforms. Confidence is an intangible concept, but it's clearly very important. The strong implementation of comprehensive reforms is a critical ingredient.
>
> The IMF has to treat all countries uniformly. We're not asking any more of one country or another, we're asking for reforms which will deliver sustainable growth.[5]

Radelet and Sachs disagree. The design of the IMF's programs, they maintain, made things worse. In particular, they criticise the call for abrupt bank closures without a more comprehensive financial reform program; the insistence on rapid increases in the banks' capital bases at a time of economic distress; the demand for budget surpluses; and demands for tighter monetary (interest rate) policies.

As Charles Kindleberger noted in his 1978 classic 'Manias, Panics and Crashes', tight money can attract funds or repel them. In usual times, with no fear of crisis or of currency depreciation, tight money attracts funds. But in times of turmoil, with falling prices, bankruptcies or exchange rate falls, raising interest rates may suggest to foreigners that trouble is brewing, and they should pull their money out.

'The worst of the crisis could have been largely avoided with a relatively small correction and moderate policy changes', Radelet and Sachs conclude. 'The search for deeper explanations that attribute the entire massive contraction to the inevitable consequences of deep flaws in the Asian economies—such as Asian crony capitalism—seem to us to be misguided.'

The picture Radelet and Sachs paint of their opponents' views is a caricature. Nevertheless their key point, that the IMF misjudged the crisis and offered inappropriate remedies, is persuasive, although to its credit the IMF did markedly soften its stance in the early months of 1998 as the crisis deepened in Indonesia. The Asian crisis came at a bad time for IMF politically, when it was under fire from an unusual alliance of Left and Right as the US Congress debated a bill to lift the US contribution to the fund by $3.5 billion. The chief argument on the Right—aside from the isolationist view that America owes the world nothing—was that the promise of support created a moral hazard, inducing borrowers to act rashly knowing they would eventually be bailed out if things went bad and governments were to go soft on reform. The argument on the Left came from the opposite stance, that the IMF's programs were too harsh and undermined national sovereignty in favour of US financial interests. Sachs is making a different point again, arguing rather that the IMF is needed, but that its policies are mistaken.

There are wide differences on these questions, which are crucial to the debate over both the causes and consequences of the Asian crisis, and the lessons for future crises. My judgment is that Radelet and Sachs paint too rosy a picture of economic conditions in East Asia, overlooking the growing evidence of corruption and mismanagement in both the 'real' economy and in the financial sector. They are right to point to the importance of panic in the crisis. But if a panic sell-off is an inevitable consequence of a boom, can we complain that the markets overreacted? Here the argument is whether the IMF's policies made the panic worse than it otherwise would have been, and in my judgment their argument is well made. The point is not, as some argue, that the IMF is not needed, but that like any human institution it is fallible; its judgments under pressure were not ideal.

The IMF's response was heavily influenced by the debate over whether the United States, the IMF's largest shareholder, should replenish its contribution to the fund. With the IMF so dependent on the United States for capital and facing the risk that the replenishment would be rejected by an isolationist Congress, it was inevitable that senior figures in the IMF would be heavily influenced by the views of Congress. And Congress had little sympathy for Indonesia, the most contentious of the IMF East Asian rescues. Indonesia was a marginal issue in American politics, and came to attention mostly over the issues of controversial political donations to the Democratic Party and its 1975 invasion and later annexation of East Timor.

'It is not surprising that the IMF would try to impose a whole lot of policies that show that they are taking on Soeharto. But I don't believe that the structural reforms that they emphasise so much are inherent to the crisis or necessary to its resolution, except that the IMF says they're necessary to its resolution', says Australian National University academic Ross McLeod.

Noted American economist Martin Feldstein argued in *Foreign Affairs* in early 1998 that the IMF's emphasis on imposing major structural and institutional reforms, as opposed to focusing on balance-of-payments adjustments, would have adverse consequences.

> In deciding whether to insist on any particular reform, the IMF should ask three questions: Is this reform really needed to restore the country's access to international capital markets? Is this a technical matter that does not interfere unnecessarily with the proper jurisdiction of a sovereign government? If the policies to be changed are also praticed in the major industrial economies of Europe, would the IMF think it appropriate to force similar changes in those countries . . . ? The IMF is justified in requiring a change in a client country's national policy only if the answer to all three questions is yes.[6]

A further line of attack against the IMF, widely made in the US debate, does not stand up to scrutiny: that by bailing out the mistakes of profligate lenders and borrowers its policies create 'moral hazard', an incentive to make rash loans in the belief that they will be ultimately repaid by someone else. The first answer to this point is that very few lenders to failed companies in East Asia will get anything like all their principal back, let alone the interest. Many will be lucky to get half, and some will get nothing at all. The second answer is Kindleberger's point that panics are a form of market failure that can have catastrophic and destabilising consequences, and that the IMF or a large country like the

United States or Japan is needed as a 'lender of last resort', an insurance against still worse catastrophe.

Two cases in East Asia—Malaysia and Japan—point to opposite conclusions in this debate, and suggest that finally the issue is a matter for case-by-case judgment. Malaysia, although suffering many of the same symptoms as Thailand, Indonesia and Korea, had in mid-1998 succeeded in avoiding an IMF rescue package. Two factors were important in this achievement: the determination of Prime Minister Mahathir Mohamad to avoid the humiliation of an IMF rescue; and the ability of his deputy, Anwar Ibrahim, to implement policies tough enough to persuade the international community that Malaysia could tackle its problems on its own, even though many of them had long been opposed by Mahathir. The lesson is that with effective leadership, countries can do for themselves what sometimes they ask the IMF to do for them.

Japan, by contrast, is too big to be rescued by the IMF, and is in any case not suffering the usual affliction for which IMF help is sought: a large and unsustainable current account deficit. But Japan today is suffering from a failure of political leadership, and would benefit greatly from the kinds of reforms the IMF imposes elsewhere.

The most pointed part of the judgment of Radelet and Sachs is that the Indonesian financial crisis need not have occurred. They blame the IMF, arguing that the crisis could have been mitigated if the IMF had taken a different tack. But the response of the markets to the Indonesian crisis surely would also have been much less destructive if Soeharto had reacted with greater acuity.

Although there is disagreement about the roles of panic and economic fundamentals, there is broad agreement on one point: that the conditions for the crisis were set by the massive capital inflows into Asia during the 1990s. The greatest signs of growing risk, with hindsight, were in the financial sector, where credit had grown rapidly, much of it headed for speculative real estate investments. And increasing amounts of this credit were raised from short-term debt, borrowed offshore.

In the region as a whole capital inflows surged from 1.4 per cent of GDP in the second half of the 1980s to 6.7 per cent between 1990 and 1996. In Thailand, capital inflows averaged an extraordinary 10.3 per cent of national output between 1990 and 1996. Government borrowing made up less than half a per cent of GDP in each country except the Philippines.

Radelet and Sachs trace the huge increase in capital inflows to changes in both internal economic policies and in world markets. Strong capital flows led to rising exchange rates, and the declining competitiveness of exports led to the expansion of non-tradeable sectors of the economy. This also put underdeveloped financial systems under increasing pressure, creating the conditions for excessive risk taking, poor judgment and sometimes outright fraud.

Before the crisis, the IMF had expressed some concerns about the Asian economies but was still broadly optimistic about their prospects. The only signs of concern in the markets before the crisis struck were in share prices, most clearly in the case of Thailand, where share prices had fallen continuously since January 1996.

Once the panic began, there were triggers aplenty: in Thailand the failures of finance companies; in Korea the weaknesses in the conglomerates; and in all of Korea, Thailand, the Philippines and Indonesia, political uncertainty.

At first, investors seemed to regard all the countries in the region alike. The blow to Thailand's credibility after first promising to support but then abandoning Finance One, its largest finance company, undermined the credibility of governments throughout the region. Comments by Malaysian Prime Minister Mahathir compounded the anxiety, but so did the behaviour of the IMF. Radelet and Sachs maintain that the IMF recommendations for immediate closure of financial institutions 'actually helped to incite panic'.

When investors started to withdraw their funds the panic developed quickly, and was compounded by policy mistakes. Thailand and Korea futilely tried to defend their exchange rates even after exhausting most of their foreign exchange reserves. In Indonesia and Malaysia, grand public works projects were postponed and then restarted. Malaysia announced and then abandoned plans for controls on foreign exchange transactions and to use government funds to buy shares. Thailand and Korea invested large sums in failing financial institutions.

Paul Krugman and the myth of the Asian miracle

But although financial crises, panic and IMF mismanagement were proximate triggers for the crisis, there were deeper reasons why East Asia's growth should sooner or later have slowed.

Economist Paul Krugman provoked intense controversy three years before the crisis erupted with an article in *Foreign Affairs* entitled 'The Myth of Asia's Miracle'. Krugman admits now that he was not predicting that Asian economies would suddenly hit the wall. His claim was more modest, that they would not sustain the growth rates they had enjoyed in the recent past.[7]

Krugman's 1994 article began with a parable about a time when western opinion leaders found themselves impressed and frightened by the extraordinary growth of a group of eastern economies. These economies displayed such rapid economic growth, technical achievements and growing self-confidence that a young Democratic American president felt the need to make a pledge to 'get the country moving again'.

Where was this, and when? 'The time, of course, was the early 1960s. The dynamic young president was John F. Kennedy. The technological feats that so alarmed the West were the launch of Sputnik and the early Soviet lead in space. And the rapidly growing Eastern economies were those of the Soviet Union and its satellite nations.' Krugman asked rhetorically whether there were parallels between the growth of the Warsaw Pact nations and recent spectacular Asian growth. 'At some levels, of course, the parallel is far-fetched', Krugman said. But just as the potential of the Soviet economy was exaggerated, so today 'popular enthusiasm about Asia's boom deserves to have some cold water thrown on it', Krugman wrote. 'Rapid Asian growth is less of a model for the West than many writers claim, and the future prospects for that growth are more limited than almost anyone now imagines.'

After that provocative preamble Krugman launched into the meat of his argument with a discussion on the causes of economic growth. Economists separate the factors driving economic growth into several components. Growth can come from an increase in inputs—investment in physical capital and also in labour, training and education, and growth can come from producing more output from existing inputs—that is from improved productivity. What was different about the Soviet Union was that its growth was based overwhelmingly on the first component, a massive increase in inputs, and not on improvements in productivity. The same thing, Krugman argued, had occurred in Asia.

But growth stemming from increases in inputs rather than improvements in productivity is an inherently limited process. Growth of this kind must slow down when inputs become scarce. Quoting figures by Stanford University researchers Jong-il Kim and Lawrence Lau, Krugman argued that in the case of Singapore especially, and to a lesser degree in South Korea, Taiwan and Hong Kong, 'there is startlingly little evidence of improvements in efficiency'.

The data Krugman used was not his own, but he brought the issue to widespread notice with his provocative style and the choice of America's most influential foreign policy magazine as a vehicle. Asian opinion leaders took great offence at his article and set about dismembering it. His target though, as the article makes clear, was not so much Asians as the American revisionists who argued that the success of the Asian tigers came from their rejecting orthodox economics and instead following more interventionists industry policies. 'If Asian success reflects the benefits of strategic trade and industrial policies, those benefits should surely be manifested in an unusual and impressive rate of growth in the efficiency of the economy. And there is no sign of such exceptional efficiency growth', Krugman said.

Many economists disputed Krugman's style of growth accounting, rejecting the view that perspiration and inspiration could be so easily separated. These economists said the critical issue was the quality, not the level, of investment. C.H. Kwan, a senior economist at the Nomura Research Institute in Tokyo, says that even if Krugman was right that the miracle economies showed low productivity growth earlier in their development—which he disputed—this does not mean they would not lift their productivity later.

Even granting that there are technical shortcomings in Krugman's growth accounting, these do not undermine his fundamental points. His argument was a useful antidote to the overexcited optimism surrounding East Asia. Some (but not all) of the arguments for and against Krugman come down to a question of whether the glass was half empty, or half full. Some of the growth Krugman attributed to raising inputs could by other lights be seen as improvements in productivity. But these arcane disputes do not invalidate Krugman's underlying point, that there are not shortcuts or miracle answers to achieving economic growth, and that contrary to the claims of some Asia boosters, the growth rate of any economy will slow as it approaches the technological frontiers of the most advanced nations. Excessive reliance on inflows of capital is not sufficient for sustained growth, and Asian countries manifestly were suffering from that condition. Asian countries have not discovered some new model of economics, but have applied some of the existing tools especially well—and like the rest of the world, they can also make mistakes.

Another depressing deflation?

In the West, the East Asian crisis prompted fears of a worldwide economic slump. In 1997 the term deflation re-entered economic debate after an absence of more than half a century. In the post-World War II world, especially since the 1970s, inflation was a major preoccupation of economic policy.

As with inflation, a little deflation may not be a bad thing. In industries such as computers where productivity is improving rapidly, prices are falling constantly and the industry still thrives. Prices of some assets—real estate and shares—are almost as prone to sharp falls as they are to rises. If the falls are not large and widespread the consequences for the real economy may not be great.

The classic definition of deflation is of a sustained and general fall in prices of goods and services. Falls in asset prices such as shares and real estate comprise a narrower case, but one which can nevertheless have serious effects. The first risk of asset price deflation is that economic activity contracts as borrowers devote resources to paying back loans instead of spending and investing; the second risk, if the deflation is widespread, is to the health of the financial system.

Deflation can extend beyond assets to prices in general, to food and other consumer goods and services—and wages. The price of labour is a particularly contentious issue. Workers and their unions resist attempts to cut wages. In technical terms, wages are sticky downwards. But when a business's prices and profits are falling, either profits will have to fall or the cost of inputs will have to fall, or both. Wages are often a substantial cost. The wage bill can be reduced by reducing overtime payments. But if the squeeze persists something else has to give: wages will fall or jobs will be cut.

Just as inflation is caused by too much money chasing too few goods, deflation is caused by too little money chasing too many goods. Deflation occurs when an economy is producing more than it consumes, when it has excess capacity. Excess capacity in Japan and Asia and the consequent deflation were key factors behind both the Asian crisis and the long American boom of the 1990s. America's boom had gone for so long and sent share prices so high that some commentators claimed to have identified a 'new economic paradigm' or 'new age economy', the result of a secular shift in productivity, which they believed gave credence to the long bull market on Wall Street. A more plausible explanation was that deflation in Asia gave the American economy more breathing space by lowering the price of many inputs.

The excess capacity began in Japan in response to the surge in investment during the 1980s. When the Japanese bubble burst in 1991 Japanese investors turned to South-East Asia, and then to China, investing heavily in capital equipment, and later in real estate. Japan has been suffering the effects of this excess capacity and deflation throughout the 1990s. Japan exported its excess capacity to its neighbours. The boom turned sour in Asia in 1996, as it had in Japan in 1990. The currency crisis simply drove the point home. There were considerable mistakes made in each of the afflicted East Asian countries that compounded the problem, but the export of Japan's excess capacity to the rest of the region was a key contributing factor.

There had been mutterings about deflation since the crisis began, but the issue shot to prominence when the chairman of the US Federal Reserve Board, Alan Greenspan, made it the subject of a speech on 3 January 1998. In typically cautious terms, he said: 'Some observers have begun to question whether deflation is now a possibility, and to assess the potential difficulties such a development might pose for the real economy'.

'Historically, it has been very rapid asset price declines—in equity and real estate especially—that have the potential to be a virulently negative force in the economy', Greenspan said. The danger was in the speed of the fall. Slowly falling prices could be absorbed without marked economic disruption. But the sharp economic slowdown of the 1930s probably would not have occurred without the steep asset price deflation that started in 1929 with the Wall Street crash.

Greenspan made a technical but important distinction between the two forms of deflation. Asset deflation, he said, could have several causes. But general deflation is necessarily a monetary phenomenon. The implication was that the solution to deflation, or the way to avoid it, was to follow appropriate monetary policy. The risk of global deflation has greatly diminished in the 1990s compared with the 1930s because the world has shifted from a gold standard to a floating exchange rate system where most countries have discretion over their monetary policy, he argued.

The *International Bank Credit Analyst*, a finance industry journal, has argued that there are three factors that could fuel deflation worldwide if policy-makers fail to adopt sufficiently stimulatory policies. First, inflation was already very low before the Asian crisis began, in the world's 25 largest economies running at about 2 per cent; second, the crisis had tipped the world economy into conditions of general excess supply; and third, central banks, still fighting the last war, were more concerned about inflation than deflation and were unlikely to take sufficient countermeasures.[8]

General price deflation is unlikely in the United States and the rest of the West. Deflation usually occurs when economic growth is weak; America is growing strongly. Although the prices of products are low in the United States, services make up a much greater part of economic output that manufacturing or agriculture and mining, and there is no deflation in the price of services. Falling prices for the commodities produced in Asia need not spill into general price deflation in the US. In early 1998 consumer confidence in America was at its highest in thirty years. Unless confidence takes a serious dive then proper monetary management will prevent deflation becoming serious. That Greenspan is looking seriously at the question is itself reassuring: on his past excellent record there is good reason to hope he will manage the US monetary system so as to avoid it.

But although deflation in the strict sense is unlikely, many of the problems associated with deflation pose big problems for Asia. In 1998 every East Asian economy was suffering from asset deflation and the consequent bust in their booms in real estate and share prices. Except for Japan, East Asian countries have avoided deflation in the strict sense of the word by allowing their currencies to fall sharply. A weaker currency lifts import prices, and pushes prices higher, effectively removing the risk of price deflation. But although avoiding general deflation, a round robin of currency devaluations can still be damaging. Measured in world prices the prices of most goods produced in Asia have fallen sharply.

As each country struggles to revive its industry there will be a temptation for some to allow their currencies to fall further still, to improve the relative prices of their products on world markets. This round robin of competitive devaluations was a key feature of the Great Depression of the 1930s, and could well be repeated in Asia in the late 1990s. One critical question is whether China will join the fray in an effort to revive its own exports—even at the cost of undermining the prospects for its neighbours.

Globalisation and the new high-tech international financial system

One of the greatest concerns provoked by the Asian crisis is the fear of 'globalisation', the sense that in a world of increasing economic, financial and technological integration, powerful and malign impersonal forces are undermining the autonomy of individuals and nations.

Dramatic improvements in computer and telecommunications technology have radically altered the way capital can flow around the world. David Hale notes that in 1930 a telephone call from New York to London cost $800 in today's prices. Today a short call costs less than a dollar. The cost of making international transactions has fallen close to zero, and as a result the volume of financial traffic has increased exponentially. While transaction costs have virtually disappeared, the amount of money available for investment has increased dramatically thanks to the swelling of pension funds as the baby boom generation draws closer to retirement age. In the United States, the assets managed by pension funds have leapt from less than $1 trillion in the early 1980s to $4.5 trillion. A third factor behind the transformation of world financial markets, Hale argues, is the growth of derivative markets and the new kinds of financial institutions to manage them: the infamous hedge funds that Mahathir blamed for the meltdown. (Hale concurs with the IMF view that it was not hedge funds that caused the crisis, but the unhedged [uninsured] borrowings of Asian businesses.)

These three factors can work for good or for ill. Potentially, they provide a 'great opportunity to allocate global savings more efficiently and bolster the growth rate of the world economy', Hale argues. But the downside was demonstrated in the Asian crisis, when the new dynamic of the global financial system showed the risk of massive overshooting in financial markets 'on a scale with can generate economic and political shocks that are simply unacceptable'.[9]

Alan Greenspan describes this as the 'new high-tech international finance system'. The increased prevalance of financial shocks, first in the Mexico crisis of 1994 and three years later in the Asian crisis, may be a defining feature of this new system, Greenspan argues. 'I do not believe we are as yet sufficiently knowledgeable of the full complex dynamics of our increasingly developing high-tech financial system', Greenspan said. But the Mexican and Asian crises showed that this new system created 'critical tendencies toward disequilibrium and vicious cycles that will have to be addressed if our new global economy is to limit the scope for disruptions in the future'. Greenspan is firmly on the side of those arguing the primary cause of the Asian crisis lay with poor government policy. But the consequences were magnified because of the effect of the new financial technologies. Where some condemn this new technology as a malevolent force working in the interests of malignant US capital, Greenspan regards them as an irreversible fact of life.

> With the new more sophisticated financial markets punishing errant government policy behavior far more profoundly than in the past, vicious cycles are evidently emerging more often. For once they are triggered, damage control is difficult. Once the web of confidence, which supports the financial system, is breached, it is difficult to restore quickly. The loss of confidence can trigger rapid and disruptive changes in the pattern of finance, which, in turn, feeds back on exchange rates and asset prices . . . At one point the economic system appears stable, the next it behaves as though a dam has reached a breaking point, and water (read, confidence) evacuates its reservoir.[10]

George Soros is one of the most unexpected critics of globalisation, unexpected because he has made so much money by exploiting it. In articles in *The Atlantic Monthly* in 1997 and 1998 Soros argued that globalisation is responsible for the ultimate manifestation of laissez-faire capitalism: excessive individualism. Because communism and socialism have been so thoroughly discredited, he commented, 'I consider the threat from the laissez-faire side more potent today than the threat from totalitarian ideologies'.

Soros has his own variation of the 'financial panic' argument, that supply and demand cannot perfectly allocate resources as long as markets are imperfect, and markets are always imperfect. Soros emphasises the way expectations influence the behaviour of players in financial markets, a process he calls reflexivity.

Soros makes a point similar to that of Kindleberger, the definitive theorist of financial panics. Kindleberger argues that the world financial system needs a dominant power to provide stability and to act as the 'market of last resort'. The Great Depression occurred because in the 1930s the United States was the only country in a position to play this role, but it would not do so.

Soros bemoans the failure to create a new world order to replace the brutal but simple exigencies of the Cold War. 'We have entered a period of disorder. Laissez-faire ideology does not prepare us to cope with this challenge', Soros says.

His antidote is the notion of an open society, whose members recognise their own fallibility, and the fallibility of their social institutions. It is an admirable model of a liberal, civil society in which individual wants are constrained by a strong sense of social obligation. A 1997 article in which Soros first made this argument was widely cited, and almost as widely misunderstood. Mostly it was seized upon as an apostate confession by a high priest of capitalism, and caricatured as a repudiation of free markets. It was nothing of the sort, as Soros tried to make clear in another article a year later. Global integration, he noted, had brought tremendous benefits: an international division of labour, the rapid spread of innovation from one country to another, and increased freedom in trade and in ideas. But the system also had problems that had to be understood and tackled. 'By focusing on the problems I'm not trying to belittle the benefits that globalization has brought, as some readers of my previous *Atlantic* article assumed', Soros wrote. The failure of the laissez-faire system was not due to its fundamental character, but to weaknesses that could be corrected.

Walden Bello, an economist at Chulalongkorn University in Bangkok, is another thoughtful critic of globalisation. Thailand exemplifies the perils of fast-track capitalism, Bello says. Thailand could not digest the massive inflows of capital that occurred in the late 1980s and early 1990s, and which created a sense of euphoria and hubris that could not be justified or sustained.

> This capital never found its way into the domestic manufacturing sector or agriculture—low-yield sectors that would provide a decent rate of return only after a long gestation period. The high-yield sectors with a quick turnaround time to which foreign money gravitated were the share market, consumer financing and, in particular, real estate.

Bello paints a harsh picture of American goals in the region: to 'level the playing field' for US corporations through liberalisation, deregulation and privatisation of Asian economies.

> [America] has used IMF and World Bank 'structural adjustment' programs, a harsh trade campaign threatening retaliation so as to open markets and stop unauthorized use of US technologies; a drive to create an Asian-Pacific free-trade area; and a push to implement GATT agreements eliminating trade quotas, reducing tariffs, banning the use of trade policy for industrialization and opening agricultural markets.

The disturbing side of US capitalism, Bello argues, is that it has the most unequal distribution of income among advanced industrial countries, and that its policies in Asia 'do nothing to build on the strengths of the existing economies but simply establish an arena in which the economic actors that followed one particular historical road to advanced capitalism—the free-market/minimal-state road—will have an unparalleled competitive edge'.[11]

There are no one-size-fits-all solutions to the question of economic development. But there are some important guiding principles. The Asian crisis reinforces, not undermines, the importance of following market-oriented policies. There is no doubt that another aspect of the liberal model, the move towards free trade, has been a powerful force for prosperity in East Asia and elsewhere. But at the same time it also shows the need to implement those policies carefully, taking account of the readiness of domestic culture, politics and institutions to manage them. In some areas that will mean moving more slowly than did the countries of East Asia in the 1980s and 1990s; in other areas it will mean moving faster.

The opening of financial markets was too rapid in Thailand, but too slow in South Korea. In both cases the opening of capital flows was not matched by appropriate management and supervision. Financial markets do not work well when they are completely untrammelled. They need watchdogs. Effective watchdogs evolve over time and on the basis of years of experience. They cannot be created overnight.

Are the prescriptions of the IMF and the World Bank in the interests of American capital? Frequently. The United States is the world's greatest economic and military power, and by dint of its size will benefit more than any other country from expanded opportunities for trade. That does not mean those prescriptions are against the interests of the countries persuaded to adopt them, nor that this is their intention. The United States is a benign hegemon. But as a hegemon it is still prone to bouts of hubris and arrogance that sometimes undermine its own purposes, and lead to policies and practices that are neither in its own interests nor in those of its clients.

Chapter 9
The economic consequences of the crash

For the rich world—for the United States, Europe and other western countries—the implications of the Asian crisis are serious, but not catastrophic, as long as China and Japan can keep their heads above water. All the relatively benign forecasts for world growth in the first half of 1998 were predicated on Japan and China continuing to resist the Asian contagion. But if either or both of those countries became embroiled in the turmoil, the consequences will be much greater.

With its growth slowing and its exports threatened, China was under immense pressure from its own exporters to follow its neighbours in allowing its currency to fall. This was one of the nightmare scenarios that could have made the Asian crisis far worse than it already was. Another was an economic or financial collapse in Japan.

China's exporters wanted a devaluation, but the risks put China's leaders under strong pressure to resist. America's thinly veiled promise of easing China's entry into the World Trade Organisation was a powerful incentive for China to cooperate, and cooperate it did. Chinese leaders made clear from early on in the crisis that they would resist the pressure to devalue.

Chinese Vice-Premier Li Lanqing was the star turn at the World Economic Forum at the Swiss ski-resort of Davos in February, with his pledge that the currency would not be devalued in the next twelve months, and his promise of a massive economic stimulus package that would keep drawing in imports from China's neighbours and further ease the pressure on world markets by absorbing more of China's own substantial output.

China promised to spend $337 billion on construction of roads, rail, ports and water treatment facilities, and over three years would spend about $1 trillion. Critics complained that details were scarce and that on the broadest measure of infrastructure spending this amounted to only a 5 per cent increase on previous plans. But sceptics' doubts went unnoticed. There was a sharp contrast between China's response and Japan's. The official *China Daily* echoed western commentators, describing the package as 'somewhat reminiscent' of Roosevelt's New Deal, the huge 1930s job program that helped America recover from the Great Depression. While Japanese leaders seemed paralysed, China's were delivering exactly the message the West wanted to hear.

China's Vice-Minister of Foreign Trade and Economic Cooperation, Long Youngtu, spelled out the strategy. 'We hope that this decision will help the international community increase their awareness of China's attitude and image in international trade and affairs. In this sense it will contribute to the process of negotiations on China's accession to the WTO.'[1]

China has sometimes been blamed for providing one of the initial sparks for the Asia crisis with its 1994 decision to devalue the yuan—but this argument does not stand up to close scrutiny. Economists at the Institute for International Economics argue in a January 1998 paper that although China's exchange rate did experience a large depreciation in nominal terms (that is, according to the face value of the yuan against the dollar), its much higher level of inflation eroded the gains from the fall in the currency. After adjusting for inflation the currency actually rose during the 1990s.

The researchers have also calculated the benefits for China from lowering its exchange rate, and argue that a modest 5 to 10 per cent fall would be enough to re-establish the relativities that existed before other regional currencies began to tumble in mid-1997. 'Given the relatively minor impact on China of the events observed thus far, and the likelihood that a devaluation in China could spark another round of financial turbulence in the region, this result surely argues for restraint on the part of the Chinese', the researchers pleaded.[2]

In spite of the pressure on exporters, there were strong domestic reasons for maintaining the level of the yuan. A sharp devaluation would have badly undermined confidence in the Hong Kong financial system, the chief conduit for capital into and out of China.

The transmission mechanisms for the Asian financial contagion were not as immediate in China as in countries such as

Thailand and Indonesia, which had the deadly combination of a fixed exchange rate and open capital markets. But although China's capital market restrictions could muffle the impact of the outside world, they could not prevent it. The pressures, though they built up more slowly, were still substantial.

As other countries' currencies fell, their exports became cheaper and more attractive on world markets. Chinese producers were at a growing disadvantage. Korea was the gravest threat. 'There is a significant risk that China's exports would actually fall if China's exchange rate is maintained and the Korean won weakens considerably more', Andy Xie of Morgan Stanley noted in November 1997—when the Korean won still had much further to fall.

It is remarkable to hear Chinese officials talk about their economic agenda. There are faint echoes of the old command economy conceit that managers can finely control the economy, but mostly they sound as if they have come straight from Chicago University (indeed many have). 'China is determined to continue this economic reform and open to the outside world, including attracting more investment', said Long Youngtu when he travelled the world in early 1998 to promote China's stance. China would hold the currency stable and would continue to grow strongly, he pledged. 'We firmly believe that if China can keep a relatively high growth rate it will be a positive economic element for East Asia as well as the world.'[3]

China's insulation against the Asian crisis is sturdy, but not impregnable. It has a fixed exchange rate, set by the central bank. And unlike its cousins in South-East Asia, investors in China cannot freely move capital into and out of the country. So even if they were concerned about prospects in the wake of the Asian crisis, the risk of a speculative capital flight is greatly diminished. Investors cannot liquidate their assets in China the way they can in other countries, and cannot freely exchange yuan for a foreign currency.

Why don't other countries follow China's example and set rigid controls on capital movements? One argument is that with such strict controls, investors would be unwilling to send their money in the first place. China was such a favourite destination in the 1990s that this factor carried less weight than usual. China was the leader among East Asia's beauty queens in the 1990s. Reforms in 1994 had relaxed capital controls considerably, and in 1996 China had agreed to allow the free flow of capital for trade, although not for financial transactions.

As investors grew chary of prospects in South-East Asia, China became more attractive than any other destination, drawing more foreign investment in the first half of the 1990s than South Korea, Malaysia, Indonesian and Thailand combined ($158.1 billion compared with $137.2 billion from 1991 to 1995, according to World Bank debt tables). In response to this surge of investment China's exports grew at breakneck speed. The fear in the early 1990s was of a runaway economy with surging prices. Inflation in 1990 reached 24 per cent but was tamed in 1997 to a much sounder 5 per cent. China's share of world manufactured exports almost tripled from 1.2 per cent in 1983 to 3.4 per cent in 1995, a huge gain.

But exports were hit hard by the Asian crisis; growth in exports was predicted to slow to around 5 per cent in 1998 compared with 22 per cent in 1997. In spite of its insulation China was suffering from similar over-capacity in manufacturing plant and speculative excesses in real estate as the rest of the region. Shanghai, the epicentre of China's real estate boom, boasted plans for a skyscraper in the city's Pudong district that at 460 metres would beat Malaysia's 452-metre Petronas Towers as the tallest building in the world. Hundreds of skyscrapers were built in Shanghai in the 1990s—220 in 1995 alone. The city was said to boast a third of the world's giant cranes. But unofficial estimates were that more than half the floor space in the new Pudong district was vacant. Shanghai agency Colliers Jardine predicted the city would have 7.5 million square metres of office space for rent to foreigners by 2000, the same as the whole of Hong Kong in 1997.

China's exports were threatened both by the more sophisticated manufacturers in North Asia and by the lower level producers in South-East Asia. The sharp fall in the Korean won was particularly damaging. 'China has been shifting its export into higher value added products, mainly into machinery and mechanical appliances. While Korea has been retreating from industries that China is marching into, the current devaluation has changed the dynamic and would allow Korea to gain back market shares from China', Morgan Stanley economist Andy Xie noted in November 1997.

There was no chance the slack would be made up by increased exports to the United States and Europe. Increased competition from South-East Asia meant that even if the volume of exports could be increased, profits would likely be lower. Exports were crucial both to China's economic strategy and to its ability to maintain political and social stability. In 1997 exports made up 17 per cent of national output, but were significantly more important than that figure suggests, for it was exports that had produced nearly all the growth in China's economy since the market liberalising reforms began in 1978. It was exports that bought the Chinese regime social peace while they attempted to continue the economic restructuring and modernising, and which eased the strains of growing unemployment from the hopelessly inefficient state sector.

The United States

The shock of the Asian crisis reached the United States in October 1997, when the slide in the Hong Kong share market sparked the largest ever plunge on Wall Street when measured in points, although measured in percentage terms the 7.2 per cent fall on 29 October 1997 was much less than the 22.6 per cent collapse almost exactly a decade earlier, on 19 October 1987. With more Americans than ever owning shares, many through their mutual or pension funds, there were fears that the fall could inflict severe damage on the real economy. But American markets soon shrugged off the news and regained their momentum. In early 1998 Wall Street was again setting new record highs. The irrational exuberance that Greenspan had warned of a year before was back in full force, along with renewed talk of a 'new paradigm' American economy that had beaten inflation and lifted productivity to a higher plane.

In mid-1998 the US had mainly benefited from Asia's troubles, which can take some of the credit for the remarkable eight-year economic expansion and the surge in American share markets. The Asian deflation has been a critical and overlooked factor in the American economy's 1990s strength. America had effectively imported Asia's low prices and excess capacity through imports of Asian consumer products, cars and textiles, delaying the day when the US reaches its own capacity limits, the point where inflation begins to rise and the economic cycle turns downwards. The risk is that the American producers competing with Asia will eventually be hit by the same over-capacity being felt in Asia. This would propel an American slowdown close on the heels of the more severe crunch in Asia.

Alan Greenspan offered a sober and thoughtful commentary on the market's exuberance. In testimony to Congress in February

1998, Greenspan noted the remarkable strength of the American economy. There was good reason for investor enthusiasm. Corporate profits were at levels not seen since the 1960s; the rate of output per worker, or productivity, was rising faster than usual. Inflation in 1997 had been only 1.75 per cent. Spurred by these factors, most share price indices had risen more than 20 per cent during 1997. And there would be benefits for America from the increased competition as Asian producers lowered their prices. But Greenspan sounded again his caution that markets could not keep rising forever, though in more cautious terms than his 1996 warning of the market's 'irrational exuberance'. 'Twelve or eighteen months hence, some of the securities purchased on the market could be looked upon with some regret by investors', Greenspan said in typically understated terms.[4]

Investors, however, took little heed, and the market's exuberance continued. Wall Street kept setting new records. 'Speculative manias can continue against all apparent reason', commented one analyst. 'Irrational speculation by definition does not end at a rational point.'[5]

On 3 April the Dow Jones industrial average rose through 9000 for the first time. Pundits warned yet again that the market was overvalued, but the market kept rising. But although profits were high, share prices were so inflated that earnings per share were very low. Those earnings are likely to decline further as falling prices in Asia start affecting the earnings of America's largest companies: multinationals with big exposures to the region. Asia provides the market for 30 per cent of all US exports. Other pressures will come from the rise in US wages, and continuing strong investment will start to erode profits as capacity exceeds demand and competition increases.

The outlook for the United States is for some slowing of growth and profits, but nothing like the cataclysm in Asia. McKibbin's economic model suggests the Asian crisis will be a net benefit for the American domestic economy, even though US companies and shareholders are likely to be worse off because of falling profits offshore. Manufacturing will be hardest hit by competition from Asia, but accounts for only 20 per cent of total American output.

But it is the variations from the regular patterns that are not predicted by economic models. Here, the risk is greater that the Asian crisis will make things worse rather than better for America. Consider some of the risks. The first is that the American share market in mid-1998 was overdue for a fall. The trigger could be a withdrawal of funds by Japanese banks as they try to restore their own fragile balance sheets, or it could be an increase in American interest rates as Greenspan judges that the US new age economy has finally reached its speed limit.

Although conditions are already far worse in Asia in mid-1998 than a year before, there is a risk that conditions in Japan and China, more important markets to the US than South-East Asia or Korea, could worsen further. There are some new signs of weakness that could finally trigger the collective realisation that American share prices are way too high. The two challenges for the United States in the Asian crisis are to make sure that along with Japan and China it provides enough economic stimulus to offset the dampening effects of the sharp slowdown in demand, and to guard against a protectionist backlash.

Australia

No western country has more at stake in Asia than Australia. For a generation Australian political leaders have been gradually but steadily trying to draw closer to Asia economically and strategically. At the crudest and most obvious level, a larger proportion of Australia's exports have gone to Asia than from any other country in the West. Equally important culturally, immigration from Asia to Australia increased sharply during the past two decades, starting with an exodus of refugees from Vietnam and Cambodia after the end of the Vietnam war in 1975. Since 1990, 43 per cent of immigrants to Australia have come from east and South Asia.

But by the time of the Asian financial crisis, Australia was undergoing a backlash against this engagement with Asia, manifested most crudely in the anti-Asian stance of populist politician Pauline Hanson, but also in the approach of the conservative coalition government of John Howard elected in March 1996. Howard set the tone for his administration during his first visit to Indonesia in September 1996, when he stressed that Australia was not Asian, not part of Asia, and not a bridge to Asia. Supporters of Howard's caution towards Asia argued it reflected domestic political realities: the backlash against his predecessor's emphasis on boosting links with Asia. Critics said the Prime Minister was neglecting a region that would continue to grow in importance for Australia, and with which political leaders should work to improve links in spite of popular resistance.

Ironically, the adversity of the Asian crisis inspired in Howard and his government a more heartfelt engagement with the region. Australia and Japan were the only countries to contribute to all three IMF bail-out packages—for Thailand, Korea and Indonesia. Australia was very active in lobbying the IMF and the United States to soften their stances towards Indonesia.

The Asian crisis has deflated the most prosaic argument for Australian engagement: the economic benefits. Initial assessments that the economic impact of the crisis would be slight had given way by mid-1998 to a more pessimistic view.

But the crisis has also underlined the importance of Australia achieving relationships that go beyond the immediately economic. The political transformation of Indonesia, in particular, has reinforced the importance of Australia having close political and personal links with its neighbours, to help and understand, and to defend against any backlash and uncertainties.

Australian governments in the 1990s invested enormous energy and prestige into building up political and economic institutions in Asia, especially the Asia Pacific Economic Cooperation forum, originally proposed by Australia in 1989. But in 1997 APEC was unable to do anything of substance to ameliorate the crisis, nor was the smaller South-East Asian grouping, the Association of South-East Asian Nations. Neither ASEAN nor APEC had given warning of the crisis, and their responses were ineffectual. It was the IMF that provided the rescue vehicle. The former Australian Prime Minister, Paul Keating, in March 1998 was dismissive of APEC, in which he had previously invested much energy. One problem was the lack of an APEC secretariat able to bring issues and current data to members' attention. More critically, APEC had been hobbled by the decision—he called it an 'act of international vandalism'—to include Russia as a member. Russia was not part of the Asia-Pacific economy, and its strategic and political priorities were vastly different from those of other APEC members. Russian membership made it impossible to consider using APEC to create a financial fund for the region, because its own potential demands would be so great.[6]

Asia and the world

Aside from the lessons for economic policy, the key question arising from the Asian crisis is its economic impact: how quickly will Asia recover, and what effect will the crisis have on the rest of the world?

There were warnings about rising debt and current account deficits in early 1997, but no one predicted anything like the crisis that unfolded. All sorts of excuses were made, but some things cannot be foreseen. Economic modelling assumes more or less regular patterns, but these patterns are sometimes upset by factors no one had considered. With hindsight, economists have identified a host of factors that contributed to the crisis: falling exports, high levels of short-term debt and fixed exchange rates. But no one had an economic model that predicted the effects they would have.

In the wake of the Asian crisis economic forecasters worldwide lowered their predictions of economic growth, although nowhere near the depression levels predicted initially by the gloomiest pundits. The IMF's December 1997 forecast for world growth in 1998 was 3.5 per cent, down from 4.3 per cent two months earlier—cause for concern, but not excessive gloom.

The forecasters' answer to the problem of how to deal with unforeseen shocks like the Asian crisis is to run the model first on its baseline projection, then introduce a 'shock' or dummy variable as a deliberate alteration to the calculations.

A shock like the Asian financial crisis or the 1994 Mexican debt crisis raises the interest rates investors demand before they will lend to those countries. To assess the impact of the 1997 crisis economist Warwick McKibbin fed two extreme assumptions into an econometric model. The first assumption was that the risk premium on loans would disappear quickly, the other that it would be permanent. Reality, McKibbin speculates, will probably lie somewhere between these two.

There is no surprise in McKibbin's finding that the Asian crisis will reduce exports outside Asia, because Asian exporters will steal more of the world market through lower prices as a result of the falls in their currencies. More surprising is the fact that the weakness of investment and growth in Asia has some benefits for the rest of the world. This occurs because the fall in investment in Asia reduces worldwide demand for capital. This in turn lowers world interest rates and so boosts economic activity elsewhere. However, that gain is not enough to offset the losses in Asia, leaving the world as a whole worse off, McKibbin figures.

The overall impact of the crisis on any country depends on the level of its trade with Asia. One important conclusion with ominous political implications is that the crisis will widen the current account deficits in countries outside Asia as they take advantage of lower interest rates to draw in higher levels of investment. McKibbin warns that efforts to prevent this occurring will be costly both for the Asian economies and for the rich world outside Asia. Even the temporary, best-case, shock brings a 60 per cent fall in consumption in Indonesia and a 40 per cent fall in investment, McKibbin's calculations show. But there is also a beneficial response: a sharp increase in demand for exports that results from the fall in the currency.

For countries outside Asia the increase in capital flows lifts the exchange rate, reduces exports and increases imports. Whether the net effect of the crisis brings a rise or fall in economic growth in the United States and Australia, for example, will depend on whether the reduction in exports to Asia is fully offset by the increase in investment demand produced by lower interest rates. McKibbin figures that even the temporary shock has negative effects for both countries, although more so for Australia (where growth falls by 0.25 per cent) than for the US, because of Australia's greater reliance on Asian trade. Even with the temporary shock, non-Asian countries' gross national product (which includes offshore as well as domestic production) is permanently reduced.

The impact of the permanent shock on the domestic economy is surprising. For Australia, the fall in domestic output is smaller than the overall effect, and for the US it actually rises as the result of the flow of capital to new locations outside Asia. But neither country is better off, because income from investments in Asia has declined.

Shifting balance

The Asian crisis has brought a subtle shift in the balance of power in the region, away from Japan and the United States and towards China. Of the three strongest powers in the region, Japan and the United States both fumbled while China responded decisively. Japan, beset by its own financial and economic weakness and political inertia, was unable to provide the economic stimulus needed to revive the region's economies. The United States remains the most powerful force in the region, but it misjudged the political and economic dimensions of the crisis, undermining its own influence with heavy-handed insistence on radical pro-market solutions. America's political influence, and that of the proxy in its ideological contest, the IMF, have been diminished by the crisis, although America remains the dominant economic and political power and provides the largest market for Asian exports.

China has done everything that the international community asked of it, in spite of the considerable cost to its own exporters, and its own widespread economic problems. One of the gravest fears arising from the crisis was that China would devalue its currency to restore the price competitiveness of its exports with those of the rest of the region. This in turn could have sparked a round of competitive devaluations, leading to a beggar-thy-neighbour spiral like that which fuelled the Great Depression in the 1930s. China's decision to defend the currency was not an easy one, but was made quickly and with resolve. And as long as it is maintained the world will hold China in its debt.

But the rise of China poses more subtle and complex changes in the exercise of power and influence in the region. Military analyst Paul Dibb argues

> China has still to demonstrate that it is a responsible, cooperative world power that will abide by the rules of the international community including the strategic rules. In the past it has been an old-fashioned power with regard to the use of military power, whether occupying the Taiwan states and slinging missiles in the general direction of Taiwan, or occupying reefs and territories in the South China Sea and claiming it owns the whole South China Sea. That is a slightly imperial point of view.

The Chinese don't accept the western rules of the strategic game, and they are acutely conscious of what they regard as 200 years of insults. 'When they get there, as a great power, they'll behave like a great power. That doesn't mean to say they're going to use military force, although clearly against Taiwan and Tibet and other contiguous areas they may well. It's an argument about the balance of power and influence,' Dibb predicts.

During the Cold War, power relations in the region were overwhelmingly dominated by the rivalry between the United States and the Soviet Union. With the demise of the Soviet Union, the East Asian region lost its fundamental strategic importance to the United States. America remained the region's dominating hegemonic power, but the force of its commitment came into doubt. It no longer needed China as a bulwark against its great enemy. In the first phase of the post-Cold War order, South-East Asia comprised a 'stable, cooperative group of non-threatening powers who were a strategic shield to Australia's north. ASEAN increasingly became a cooperative, self-confident group of countries which could handle problems and were extending that sense of confidence into the ASEAN Regional Forum', Dibb argues.

But ASEAN after the crisis is badly bruised. Like APEC and the ASEAN Regional Forum its response was weak. Dibb contends

> There's a real risk now that ASEAN will become a more inward-looking, suspicious, xenophobic organisation. Indonesia, the natural long-term leader of the region, suddenly looks a very diminished power. Thailand, which saw itself not as the natural leader but the leading power in mainland Southeast Asia—showing the way to recalcitrant communist powers like Vietnam, Cambodia, Laos and military juntas like Burma—all of a sudden their model doesn't look so good. And that isn't good for the West or its values.

Hopes that Asian countries would move inevitably towards more democratic and liberal political and trading systems as they became wealthier have been undermined. Some fundamental tenets of the liberal model have been challenged. The arguments for free trade and capitalism look questionable from the vantage point of East Asia in the wake of the crash.

Dibb argues that one of ASEAN's past successes has been to sweep under the carpet many tensions in the region. But the crisis will fall unequally on different countries and will leave these tensions exposed. There will be more localised strains as leaders try to protect and extend the boundaries of their economic spheres of interest or seek scapegoats for their economic troubles.

The meltdown is likely to undermine the status of Asia's political elites, whose legitimacy rested largely on their economic success. The most striking manifestation of this process is in Indonesia, but it may be repeated elsewhere, perhaps in Malaysia, where Prime Minister Mahathir placed such weight on emulating Japan in his Look East policy.

Japan, the inspiration for the Asian model and the origin of the developmental state, has stalled. It retains its economic supremacy, but is passing political dominance to China. The crisis has sparked differing reactions among countries of the region. Thailand and Korea seem prepared, under heavy persuasion from the IMF, to follow its liberal precepts. The future of Indonesia remains dark and uncertain. Malaysia, Singapore and the Philippines were less badly affected and will recover more quickly, but their growth rates will be retarded for several years at least as their customers in the region remain weak and as they recover from the bursting of their own bubbles.

In every country in East Asia the crisis should have demolished the hubris that led to the fall, but has also weakened the sense of collective purpose and pride in Asia's achievements. The United States' influence has been damaged, as its overbearing response to the crisis has provoked resentment. It is doubtful that Japan will regain its poise soon, although its prospects could improve if the next generation of politicians has more enthusiasm for reform. The rise of China could be undermined if it does not deal well with the extremely difficult process of managing its continuing economic transformation. The era of the Asian miracle has ended, but it is not at all clear what will take its place.

Chapter 10
After the miracle

The argument of this book is that the Asian miracle was a myth—but like many myths, its effects were potent. The economic crisis of 1997 has destroyed the myth and so, in that symbolic sense, ended the miracle. This is not to say that Asia has not achieved and cannot resume strong economic growth. But it is to say that when that growth returns it should be accompanied by a more sober and prosaic understanding of the elements of growth, an understanding that Asia's growth was not so miraculous. The appeal of the myth was that it held out the hope that the rest of Asia, and ultimately the rest of the developing world, could achieve economic take-off by emulating the Japanese model and, later, the Asian model.

Did they not succeed? Was Mahathir Mohamad right in asserting that the crisis was a conspiracy imposed on East Asia by the West, or was George Soros right when he said that it flowed from home-grown policy failings? Was the IMF correct to demand radical restructuring of the economies of Thailand, Korea, and especially Indonesia? Or did it misjudge the importance of speculators and panic and make matters worse with its insistence on radical reform? Was the crisis a warning of the dangers of globalisation and global capital, or of the failure to apply properly the lessons of free-market economics?

Is there a distinctive model of East Asian economic growth, and if so did the 1997 crisis support or undermine it? What is the nature of the Asian model? Does it deserve to be called miraculous? Was the crisis a vindication of the neoclassical economic models and a repudiation of the Asian model? Was it irrational panic, or rational concern, that caused investors to shun East Asia after years of adulation?

It would be tempting, but wrong-headed, to try and answer these questions by applying some template that gave clear and unambiguous yes-no answers, neatly divided into pro-market and anti-market views. But useful answers cannot be so easily found; the story is too complex. If the answers were clear and widely agreed the crisis would likely not have occurred in the first place. That said, the answers to these questions have important implications for economics, finance and politics.

In my judgment many of the answers tend towards the free-market view, but others to the idea that markets do not always work according to plan, and that free-market prescriptions in 1997 and 1998 made matters worse. The free-market principle is sound: that markets are generally the best way of allocating resources. But that simple statement begs some important questions. Markets may generally be the best way of allocating resources, but what is the best policy on occasions when they are not? And what is the test of the *best* way? These are the main battlegrounds of economic and political debate, and while the answers can sometimes be found by appeal to economic principle, more often they are found by trial and error, by experience. There is no *a priori* reason why centrally planned economies could not deliver better outcomes than market economies. But the experience of the twentieth century is blindingly clear: they don't. Experience teaches that the best policy for making economic decisions is to start with a presumption in favour of a market outcome. The onus of proof should be on those who would intervene. But the devil is in the detail; there is plenty of argument and often no one simple answer when circumstances do not fit a perfect market model.

There are distinctive features to the economic history of every country and the region, and Asia is no exception. There are some features of Asia's economic development that distinguish it from the West; but equally there are many more elements that reinforce the usefulness of traditional neoclassical economic models. There is such variety of economic management styles in East Asia that any model that tries to encompass them all in a unique model of economic management does not deliver many useful prescriptions beyond those that are also true of orthodox free-market economics. The distinctive features are concerned with questions of culture and history that can deeply influence economic performance, but that do not thereby undermine the standard economic models.

The most potent lesson of the 1997 Asian crisis is its

demolition of the conceit of the Asian model and its corollary, the Asian miracle. After decades of strong growth, East Asia has been shown to be subject to the same economic forces as other economies. Some countries have performed poorly in the crisis, others better. Although none of the models is so powerful as to have predicted the crisis, the free-market model does a much better job of explaining it. Yet the crisis also shows the limitations of free-market prescriptions. The two clearest examples are in the role of panic and the role of the IMF in the crisis. Then there is the debate over how fast developing countries should open their capital markets. There are sound explanations as to why panic occurs—a sudden change in sentiment or confidence, produced perhaps by some extraneous event, but just as often by a shift in judgment about prospects. Although many of the preconditions can be identified, panic, by definition, defies reliable prediction. One of the worrying aspects of recent economic history is that panics have become more frequent as world financial markets have become deeper, wider and more intertwined, a phenomenon encompassed in the notion of globalisation.

The IMF, the international epitome of free-market orthodoxy, emerges from the Asian crisis badly tarnished. When it came to applying free-market principles the Asian crisis was difficult to fit to the IMF's model. The IMF, as much as the countries it was seeking to help, was caught up in its own political struggles. The IMF's determination to enforce widespread structural reform in Indonesia worsened the crisis there. Its approach was driven by the IMF's political battles in the United States. The IMF's prescriptions would, in time, have improved Indonesia's economic performance, but the manner of enforcing them failed to take account of political constraints.

The IMF's failures in Indonesia shed light also on the debate over how rapidly, or even whether, developing countries should open their financial markets to global capital. The lesson from Thailand especially, but also of the other East Asian crisis countries, is that too rapid opening of financial markets can be destructive. Thailand opened its doors to foreign capital without having the institutions to manage the consequences: sound management of monetary and exchange rate policy and effective supervision of banks.

Do the failures of financial management in East Asia undermine the case for globalisation of capital? Are there the same benefits from free trade in capital as there demonstrably exist in free trade in goods and services? Here the argument swings back to the free market, but with some qualifications. The main caveat is that the flow of capital has become in recent years much more volatile than trade in goods and services can ever be. The technological changes in telecommunications and computing behind the phenomenon that Alan Greenspan calls the new high-tech international financial system have made capital transactions almost costless. United States mutual or pension funds in 1998 overtook the entire American banking system in size. Their growing influence creates enormous pools of capital seeking the highest return. The risk is that the velocity and volatility of capital flows created by these changes can be destructive, as the Asian crisis and the Mexico crisis of 1994 demonstrate. Are the animal spirits that Keynes wrote about so powerful in capital markets that they should not be unleashed? It is sobering that the world's foremost proponent of free trade, Jagdish Bhagwati, has argued that the benefits of free trade in goods and services cannot equally be enjoyed from free trade in capital. He had better be wrong: if only because the globalisation of capital cannot be escaped; the genie cannot be returned to the bottle. The task is better to manage the flows of international capital, and in developing countries to open capital markets only gradually, as the necessary institutions are built. Properly managed, open capital markets should be beneficial—though perhaps not as much as free trade—by exposing financial markets to competition and providing capital for investment that will boost a nation's output and productivity, and so improve its general welfare. How much capital does a country need? The flood of capital in the 1990s to East Asia—a region already notable for its high level of savings—may have been too great to have been usefully invested.

In the spat between Mahathir and Soros the weight of the argument lies with Soros: that much of the problems of East Asia were home-grown. But Mahathir's argument does have some merit. The crisis was worsened by the effects of foreign money: not as Mahathir claimed as the result of a deliberate conspiracy, but as a by-product of the effects of increasingly volatile global capital markets, and was worsened by mismanagement of a body seen by some outsiders as an agent of global capital, the IMF.

What next?

The region's economic giant, Japan, is beset by gloom inside and outside, by a failure of leadership, by weak economic growth. The recovery touted throughout the 1990s has still not arrived. It is increasingly clear that Japan's potential growth rate has made a secular shift for the worse, probably to somewhere between 1 and 2 per cent a year. Japan's own peculiar circumstances mean that even that potential will be difficult to realise for several years, because of Japan's failure still to tackle resolutely the problems of the financial and distribution systems and the labour market. Changes will come, but slowly, and Japan will likely never regain the heady optimism of the late 1980s bubble. Japan is caught between the growing burden of an ageing population and the demands, from inside and out, that it apply more budget stimulus to try and solve the immediate problem of its economic slump. Whatever balance is found between these opposing demands, the best prognosis is that Japan will muddle through; and the worst that failure to tackle some of the deeper structural problems will spark another financial crisis.

Of the three worst-hit economies of East Asia—the three which sought help from the IMF—conditions are much worse in Indonesia than in Korea and Thailand. The Indonesian experience is a blunt reminder that the political dimensions of an economic crisis can have an extraordinarily large impact, just as did the economic consequences of the peace of 1919. In all three countries, the main goal of the financial rescue teams has been to stabilise currencies, but progress has been just as difficult in the other crucial ingredient for recovery: repairing paralysed banking systems. Indonesia in particular was suffering from the inability of exporters to secure letters of credit for their customers, or for their own imports of inputs.

Malaysia escaped an IMF rescue, but its economic health is still highly precarious, with growing doubts about Mahathir's willingness to recognise economic problems and act on them and his readiness to rely instead on populism. The Philippines was lucky to have escaped the worst of the crisis simply by having been such a late participant in the boom.

Hong Kong, with its currency board and high level of reserves, did not suffer a prolonged currency crisis, but real estate and share prices have fallen sharply, and there are doubts about the prospects for economic recovery in the domestic economy. Of more concern are the risks of a sharper slowdown in China, upon which Hong Kong depends heavily. China was not directly affected by the Asian contagion, but is suffering just the same from the fall in demand from Asia, and from its own grave problems of transition from a command to a market economy.

Even Singapore and Taiwan, which like Hong Kong had better protection against the regional contagion because their economic and financial health was much sounder, will suffer from the general slowdown in growth and investment.

By mid-1998 there were some positive signs. After the $12 billion capital outflow from Asia in 1997, the Institute of International Finance in May predicted capital flows would roughly balance in 1998, with equity investors in particular returning in force—but it will still be a far cry from the massive capital inflows earlier in the decade.

In all three countries under IMF supervision, deals among creditors for rescheduling debt were beginning to emerge in mid-year, but there was still only faint recognition that large levels of debt would have to be written off altogether. In Indonesia especially, but also in Korea, Thailand and Malaysia, financial systems were still close to paralysis a year after the crisis began. Until the financial systems begin to function properly and banks are able to lend readily to exporters, importers and domestic businesses, it will be extremely difficult for normal trade to resume. Until that happens the economists' assumption that a currency depreciation will boost exports will stand for little.

Interest rate policy highlights another of the dilemmas facing policy-makers in the worst affected countries. A true laissez-faire approach would be to let currencies find their own level, and not to try and prop them up with high interest rates. But no central bank anywhere is prepared to follow such a policy with complete abandon, for the good reason that they have learned that markets 'overshoot'. This is one case where the IMF prescription of tight monetary policy is decidedly illiberal, and arguably ill-suited for the purpose. It is a moot point whether supporting the currency with high interest rates really helps the economy as a whole. It may be that the liberal view is correct, but nobody is game to find out. In the meantime high interest rates continue to stifle recovery.

In all the countries of East Asia it is possible to paint a more or less rosy picture of long-term prospects. But the immediate prognosis is gloomy. The euphoria of the boom years has given way to pessimism, and will not easily be restored. The end of the boom was a psychological as much as a rational response to what may have seemed only slight changes in prospects. Similarly, it will take some years before the mood turns brighter again. Social and political strains throughout the region are greater than they have been for decades, with rising unemployment and heavy-handed treatment of the large numbers of illegal immigrants who a few years earlier in Malaysia, Thailand and Singapore were welcomed with open arms to overcome labour shortages.

What of the argument that the economic fundamentals in the region are sound, and will recover once investors come to their senses? Whatever the merits of that argument, investors will remain chastened for several years to come, and many of the fundamentals are not as sound as they seemed during the glory days. Political cronyism, corruption and shaky banking systems will not easily be brought to health.

In a decade's time, will East Asian growth rates have returned to the levels of the late 1980s and early 1990s? The answer will vary from country to country. My guess is that on average—even excluding the undoubted drag on the average from Japan—growth will be markedly lower in the 1990s among what had been the high performers. This is simply an extrapolation of the notion that a country's growth rate tends to slow as its income rises—a simple and well-founded proposition, but one which was forgotten by many during the Asian boom years. Whether China is in this group is one of the most difficult and important questions to answer, and I will not attempt it. China's prospects hold bigger uncertainties and bigger risks than any other country. Whether or not China does recover its growth momentum will be fundamental to its own political stability and to the prosperity of the region. The range of possibilities for China is much wider than that for the other great economic force in the region, Japan, because the challenges it faces in transforming its grossly inefficient state sector are so immense. Among some of the poorest countries of the region—Vietnam, Cambodia, Burma, Laos—growth rates may be close to or higher than the 10 per cent a year that the high performers once achieved. If there is a benefit from the 1997 crisis it may be that the countries in the region that never made it to miracle status will not be so easily seduced by some of the miracle cures.

The miracle model

There are distinctive features of the East Asian tiger culture that have had a big impact on their economic development. It is likely that these differences were one of the key factors in their success. Yet this same success is diminishing that cultural distinctiveness. Growing affluence leads to growing individualism and self-centredness. For the first time, people can afford not to have to worry about their social or family obligations as much in the past. Their survival no longer depends on those links. For all the complaints of the Asian traditionalists, western culture is highly attractive to most Asians. Western fashion, especially American fashion, is the dominant symbol of material aspirations for young Asians. Western popular culture, especially American culture, is for many Asians a promise of something intensely desirable, both for its affluence and its emphasis on individual fulfilment.

The paradox is that this individualism, the ultimate fruit of the rationalist impulse behind the industrial revolution, is a force for immense cultural stress in the West. Another paradox is that rationalism itself is under threat in the West from postmodernism—most apparent in the weakening of the belief that science can answer all questions and technology solve all problems.

East Asia has won the material advantages of industrialisation in a cultural framework different from that of the West. Veteran Japan-watcher Murray Sayle argues that Japan's Shinto nationalism was the cultural foundation of the old order, instilling discipline and the deferral of consumption. But the old order is fading, and as yet there is no new moral or cultural order to replace it. Without a new moral foundation there will be no democratic or economic rebirth in Japan, Sayle argues. The failure of the cultural realm to adapt will also lead to failure of economic and political realms to perform as well as they have in the past.

The signs of growing individualism are readily seen in Japan and Korea. Individualism is one key aspect of modernism and of westernism. But the growing individualism of Japan and Korea does not mean those countries will become western in the specific cultural sense. Many young Koreans and Japanese have little interest in their own traditional culture, but their deeper traditions and habits are deep-seated. The social dimensions of their lives remain very different from those of the West. In the workplace, for example, there is no tradition of sharp division between capital and labour that still pervades many western workplaces. A worker's interest is the firm's interest, creating a relationship that many in the West would regard as exploitative.

Japan and Korea are the classic examples of developing economies which appeared not to obey the rules of classical economics and yet achieved extraordinary economic success—they were the two most rapidly growing economies in the half century after World War II. Yet both countries, although at different stages in the development process, face the failure of the developmental state model. In Korea, enormous economic growth was achieved partly through severe discipline imposed by the state, as well as through harsh repression of dissent and of the democratic impulse. After decades of startling growth, the classical objections to the statist model are beginning to apply. The developmental state model works during the process of industrialisation, but does not work so well once the stage of advanced industrialisation has been achieved.

One area where the changes are clearest is in the role of women in Japan and Korea. Affluence and birth control have given women in those countries much greater choice about when to marry and have children. Yet women do not have the same professional opportunities that are available in most Western countries, and mostly they do not seem to want them.

Western feminism is a logical outcome of Western individualism and liberalism, and its absence in East Asia shows how little those notions have taken hold. The roots of Western feminism can be found in the liberal ideas of self-actualisation and individual growth and development. But although the seeds of these ideas have been planted in East Asia, they have not flourished. Even in Japan, one of the richest nations in the world, very few women expect to have professional careers after they marry.

The Koma Feminist café in Seoul, a few blocks away from Yonsei University, doesn't look much different from any of the dozens of others among the boutiques and fancy shops. It has the usual soft pastel furnishings, cuddly huggable bears, and Celine Dion on the sound system. The customers are as immaculately dressed as affluent Koreans usually are—with just a touch of student scruffiness. It does not seem so unusual that the customers are all women. Feminism is an oxymoron in Korea—a nation steeped in Confucian notions of filial duty and distinct and separate roles for men and women. 'Most men don't take feminism seriously. They haven't been accused of anything—yet', says one of the café's owners, Lee Sook-yeong.

> Most men would think of feminists as women with a relaxed life style and nothing else to do. A few might think of us as subversive; maybe some would just look at us as if we were a little strange. I would say about 2 per cent of the whole women's population are university graduates, and about 0.01 per cent of those graduates would consider themselves feminists.

South Korea's growing affluence has given women for the first time a chance of some independence, but not many yet aspire to break out of the traditional woman's role of mother and housewife. The first stirrings of feminism were faintly heard in Korea about twenty years ago. Interest grew in the 1980s, when some universities began teaching courses in women's studies, Lee says, though feminism is still on the margins of intellectual culture. 'All these different theories of feminism have been imported in a very short time, just ten years. There are many different sides of feminism, and these elements coexist right now in a very chaotic state.'

Democracy

One of the main battlegrounds of the debates about the Asian miracle and Asian values has been the question of democracy: whether it is a universal or merely a western value, and even if universal, whether there are distinctly Asian variants.

Democracy has had growing appeal in East Asia in the postwar years, though often the notion has been applied in forms different from those in the West. Many Asian leaders—from Jiang Zemin in China, Mahathir Mohamad in Malaysia to Kim Jong-il in North Korea—endorse democracy in principle, but argue that the western version is unsuitable for their circumstances. All their countries purport to be democratic, but in ways vastly different from anything resembling western democracy.

Political scientist Arthur Stockwin identifies five elements in the Asian model of democracy. First, economic and social democracy are often seen in Asia as more important than political democracy.

> Free and fair elections, fully representative government, government responsible and responsive to the electorate through regular tests of opinion, freedom of speech, a free energetic mass media, these are the classic elements in the western model of democracy, [which] tend to take a back seat in the Asian models to ideas of social and economic advancement.

Second, whereas western models of democracy are based on the concept of the rights of the individual who lies at the centre of western political theory, in the Asian model emphasis is given to individuals' duties to the family, to the local community, to the industrial organisation, the company and to the broader society and nation. Third, so-called Asian values, often derived from Confucianism, are seen as the principal source of social, political and economic order. Fourth, western notions of democracy are seen as inappropriate in Asia, because they are founded in an alien culture of individualism and permissiveness, and in a context where Asian nations are on the rise compared with those in the declining West. Fifth, the Asian model is seen as capable of delivering sustained, rapid economic growth with relatively low levels of social disruption.

Democracy isn't always an easy choice. It is difficult to operate a democracy in severely divided societies, or during the transition from a long period of dictatorship in a country with no experience of democracy. Asia has an extraordinary diversity of cultures, religions, languages, ethnic groups and ways of life. But there are also some common features: their economic openness and their intensive connections with other parts of the world. Asia also has a great variety of governmental and political systems. South Korea and Taiwan have recently begun the shift from authoritarian to democratic systems 'of fairly orthodox kinds, although with some local characteristics', Stockwin says. China has been undertaking economic liberalisation since the late 1970s, but has made little progress towards 'anything recognisable as a classic democratic institution such as contested elections'. Singapore is a semi-authoritarian, one-party state. Hong Kong has been a free-wheeling economy with little state involvement in the economy. Japan is undergoing a transition from a one-party dominant democracy with a powerful bureaucracy to something 'which may or may not be rather different'. Malaysia is a 'semi-authoritarian semi-democratic state' with quite effective laws to secure ethnic equality; Indonesia is an authoritarian state with the armed forces extensively involved in the political system and the economy, now becoming more democratic. Thailand has had periods of democracy or semi-democracy, but has experienced repeated *coups d'état* by the armed forces.

In spite of all these differences, are there common features justifying the notion of an Asian model? Common features include the high value given to the community over the individual, the emphasis on duties over rights, the emphasis on 'economic democracy' over 'political democracy', and the emphasis on political stability over political change. Other differences compared with the western model are the tendency in Asia towards a paternalistic notion of government, in which government's responsibilities go beyond representing the community's will as determined by elections to a broader social trust to manage the economy. Another distinction is the relatively lax attitude towards corruption. 'The interests of government tend to be regarded as superior to considerations of abstract morality; the assumption is made that a degree of money politics is natural, or culturally sanctioned.'

Although not universal, many Asian countries share the notion of bureaucrats having a mission to rule, a notion which clashes both with the principles of democracy and of neoclassical or free-market economics. And finally there are the questions of freedom of the mass media and human rights and freedoms such as the right to criticise or the right to put forward alternative ideas. Asian countries tend to temper these freedoms with a view of the importance of the state, and of the need to discourge criticism of the 'national welfare' and hence of the government.

But in spite of all these distinctive Asian features, these problems for democracy are universal, Stockwin argues. 'Despite the obvious differences that exist, the history of the development of political systems in Europe, North America, Australasia and elsewhere is full of hard-fought battles over all of these very issues.' These questions have been resolved not according to absolute standards, but by striking a balance between competing principles. If there is a specifically Asian element in this, it is the tendency to emphasise values such as hierarchy, group, family, and stability, Stockwin argues. And whether or not these values are genuine values of the region, they are subject to manipulation and re-creation by governments.

Stockwin notes that many of the critical economic issues in the debate over the Asian miracle—its high rates of capital accumulation, relative equality of income distribution, mainly competent government oversight of the economy, and working with, not against, the market—can coincide with various authoritarian political forms. These issues of economic management are on a different plane from those of how democratic a political system is.

> The most important lesson of recent decades in East and Southeast Asia is that genuine democracy of a moderate kind, with all its imperfections and uncertainties, is proving the most viable way of organising a political system over the longer term. Already the most prosperous societies in Asia—Japan, though there are qualifications; the Republic of Korea, though there are qualifications; Taiwan, though there are qualifications—have moved from some form of authoritarian regime . . . to one based on a moderate form of democracy, based on some sort of popular choice . . . This is not the Asian model of democracy that Dr Mahathir understands, nor

is it what is sometimes denigrated as western democracy. But it is well within the range of democracy as a universal concept.[1]

Many of the distinctive features of the Asian model of democracy are benign, and provide a good foundation for resolving some of Asia's democratic problems—problems of a sort inevitable in any democracy, whether eastern or western. Asian democracies should aspire, Stockwin argues, to gradually increasing personal freedoms, while keeping and fostering the mechanisms of social and family solidarity. Although social change has diminished the role of the extended family in favour of the nuclear family, 'family loyalty retains an impressive strength which should be regarded as a social merit'. Hard economic times are bringing changes in labour relations and undermining permanent job contracts. 'Nevertheless, the concept of firms taking responsibility for their employees and employees feeling responsibility for their firms continues to prevail widely, and has great advantages in terms of incentives and stability.' But as Stockwin notes, these virtues are coming under increasing pressure as economic stress grows, and can be a negative force if allowed to inhibit innovation and creativity.[2]

The precepts of democracy have had some clear victories in the East Asian crisis. In Indonesia, the lack of responsiveness of a blatantly undemocratic regime made conditions much worse than elsewhere in the region. But even Indonesia's prospects began to improve when a gradual move began towards more democratic forms with Soeharto's departure in May.

But the crisis has also put democratic aspirations under stress. In South Korea between the 1960s and 1980s, the main political imperative aside from economic development was the campaign for democracy. A brutal authoritarian government created the conditions for economic take-off, but at the cost of significant political repression. The democracy movement was a powerful and ultimately successful force that unified disaffected workers and intellectuals. The goal of creating a democracy was achieved in stages beginning with the first democratic presidential elections in 1987. But once democracy was achieved, politics in Korea fell back into its old patterns. Political candidates campaigned on the basis of their regional allegiance, not their policies; and its rulers assumed a Confucian-style authority and arrogance.

The absence in Asia of the West's liberal philosophical tradition means that most Asians are sceptical of precepts that westerners take for granted: the philosophical underpinnings of a rationalist, legalistic, individualistic political and economic system. And the western ethic has been further undermined in East Asia by the economic crisis of 1997, and there is every chance that other ethical and political formulations will arise to contest the western liberal model. This has been an explicit purpose of the prescriptions of Mahathir in Malaysia and Lee Kwan Yew in Singapore.

Animal spirits

The end of the East Asian model does not mean the end of the distinctiveness of East Asia, but the end of the idea that this distinctiveness is miraculous—miraculous not in a literal sense, but symbolically, as a myth of a special, unique road to growth. The crash of 1997 does not mean the end of East Asia as a region with good potential for growth. Clearly East Asia has been doing something right for the past half century. The task now is to pick out what was good and what was bad in the East Asian development path. There is right and wrong in the view of East Asian exceptionalism: right in that a unique combination of factors in East Asia enabled an extraordinary economic performance; wrong in the belief that these provided a model that could overrule the normal rules of economics. The exceptionalist view is right in asserting that there is more than one way to achieve economic development; it is wrong in asserting that the Asian way is always a better way.

The best explanation for East Asia's success is not that it was a miracle, but that partly by design, partly by accident, and partly as a matter of history, it did many things right, and sometimes may have even managed to beat the market. But the conditions which seemed to allow Asian countries to 'beat the market' have changed fundamentally, and will no longer deliver the same positive results.

Within East Asia itself there are vast differences, especially between the North-East and South-East Asian models. In South-East Asia the developmental state model was more mythic than real. And in the countries where it was more closely applied, in Japan and Korea, the model has now clearly failed.

Against the neoclassical orthodoxy, one key lesson of the Asian crash is that liberalising markets is not a panacea, and that if done badly it can have damaging consequences. In general the pro-market decisions are preferable to interventions. But that view does not justify rejecting all government regulation. Failures of regulation and government were just as important in the East Asian crisis as the excesses of government.

Investors are prone to panic in all kinds of economies, whether markets are greatly or only minimally constrained. That of itself does not undermine the utility of the market model, although it does suggest the need for caution. Another way of viewing the propensity for panic is to say that maintaining confidence is crucially important in any economy. Confidence, like panic, is an intangible quality, not easily fed into an econometric model. In healthy doses confidence is a crucial ingredient in economic success, but in excess it is a precondition for panic.

The Asia crisis shows that markets, as Keynes noted, contain animal spirits. Some markets get closer to the ideal type of a free market than others, but every market operates in social, historical and cultural circumstances that have profound influences on the way it functions. Markets sometimes need to be tamed; and markets sometimes tame those who would master them.

Appendix: The crash by numbers

The miracle was still in full swing in the first half of the 1990s. In the region's eight superstars—Japan, Korea, Taiwan, Hong Kong, Singapore, Thailand, Malaysia and Indonesia—average growth rates were higher in the first half of the decade, at 6.8 per cent, than the average for the quarter century to 1990, 5.5 per cent.

The average figures disguise a slowing in growth rates through the decade, but nothing to forewarn of the crash that came in 1997. Japan's growth peaked early, reaching 5.1 per cent in 1990, before coming to a standstill by 1993. The year 1990 was also the peak year for Thailand with growth of 11.7 per cent, easing to 8.7 per cent in 1995 and falling more sharply to 5.5 per cent in 1996. Indonesia's and Malaysia's growth hovered between 7 per cent and 9 per cent right up to 1996; Taiwan's GDP was between 6 per cent and 8 per cent; Korea slowed from near 10 per cent in 1990 to 5 per cent in 1992, but recovered to 8.4 per cent in 1994.

Singapore also dipped in 1992, to 6.3 per cent, but recovered to record a 10.4 per cent rate in 1993. Hong Kong had a serious slowdown in 1991, with growth of only 0.5 per cent, but the next six years recorded growth levels of between 4 and 8 per cent. There was little sign in East Asia of another common element of overheated economies: a high level of government spending. The exception was Thailand, whose government budget deficit was high in the early 1990s at around 4 per cent of national output, and was still high, for a booming economy, at 2.6 per cent in 1996 and 2.3 per cent in 1997. But this does not explain the 1997 crisis.

What of the other standard indicators of economies growing

Appendix: The crash by numbers 209

Figure 1   Asia-Pacific economic growth

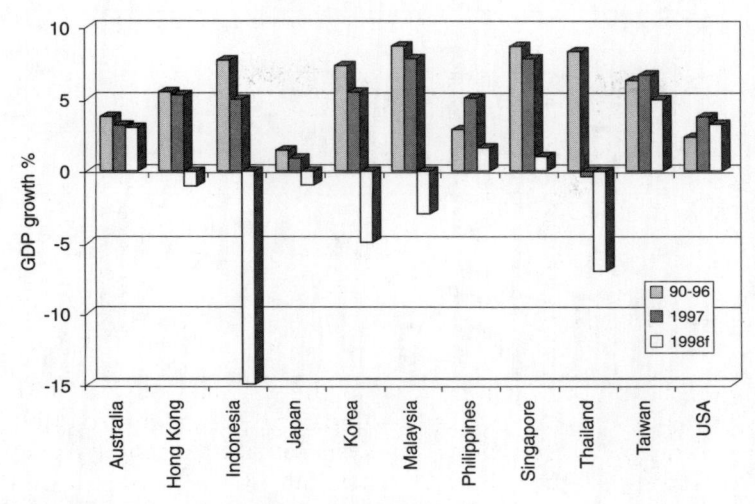

Source: World Bank, IMF, Asia Pacific Economics Group

Figure 2   Current account balances

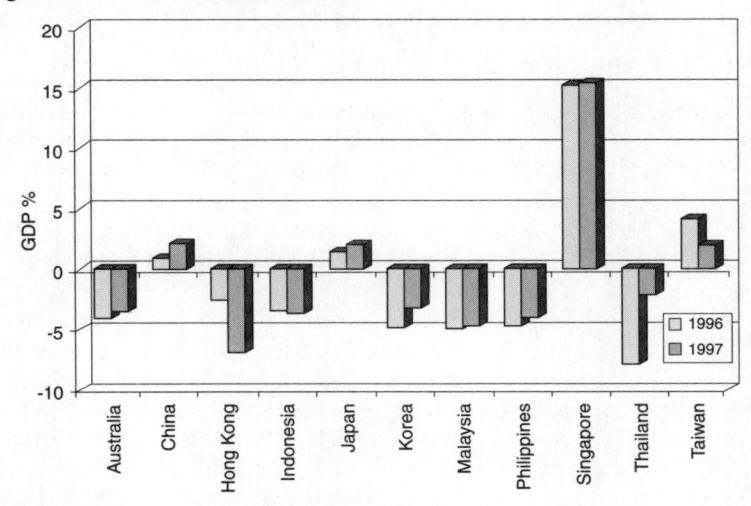

Source: World Bank, Asia Pacific Economics Group

at levels that cannot be sustained: the current account deficit and inflation? There were warning signs in Thailand's current account, which reached 8.1 per cent of national output in 1995, and in

210   *Tigers tamed*

Figure 3   Inflation

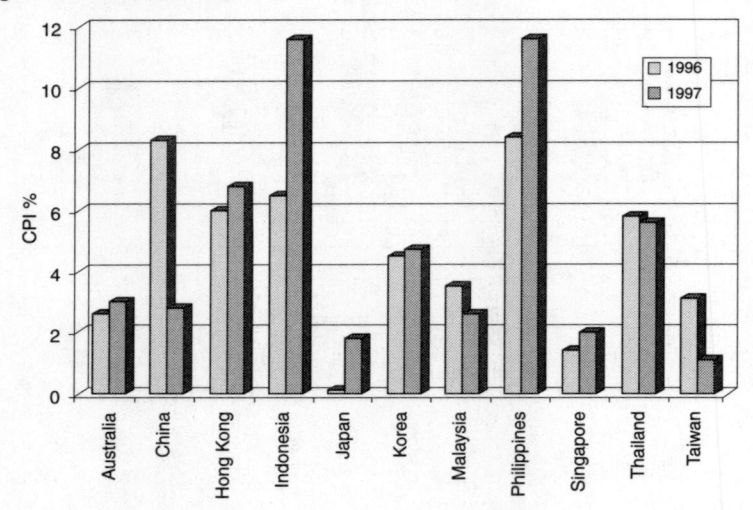

Source: Asia Pacific Economic Group

Figure 4   Currencies against the dollar 96–98, per cent fall

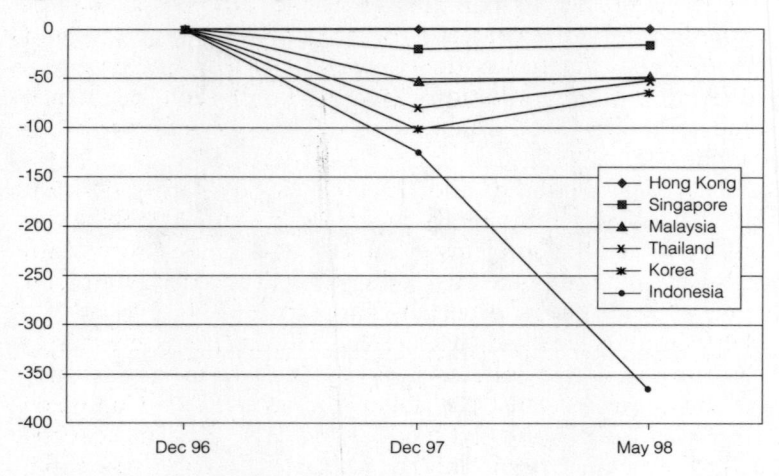

Source: Pacific Exchange Rate Service

Malaysia, where it reached 10.2 per cent of GDP in the same year, but there was nothing out of the ordinary in other countries in the region. Indeed both countries' deficits improved in 1996,

Figure 5   Short-term debt as a percentage of foreign reserves

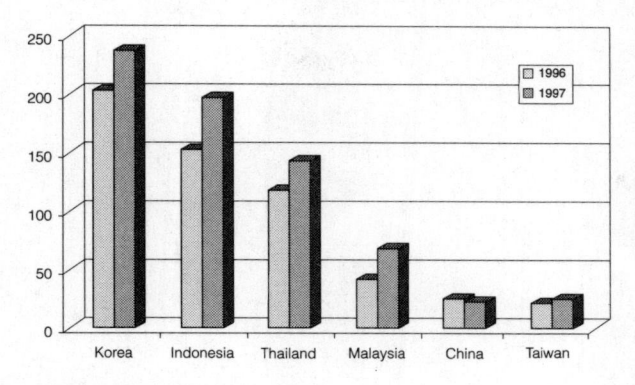

[Bar chart showing 1996 and 1997 values for Korea (~205, ~240), Indonesia (~150, ~200), Thailand (~120, ~145), Malaysia (~40, ~65), China (~25, ~25), Taiwan (~25, ~30)]

Source: Asia Pacific Economics Group

Thailand's falling to 7.9 per cent, Malaysia's showing a marked improvement to 4.9 per cent.

Inflation in the region was higher than in the developed world, but not at especially worrying levels. Hong Kong, the Philippines and Indonesia were at the high end of the range, with inflation rates between 8 and 10 per cent, while Singapore and Taiwan kept inflation below 6 per cent. Korea, Malaysia and Thailand were in between. Japan was the exception, with its stalled economy delivering official inflation figures close to zero, and which by some reckonings was experiencing deflation—falling prices—throughout the 1990s.

Aside from Thailand and Malaysia's unhealthy current account deficits, which in any case were improving by 1996, there was no sign of serious problems in the traditional indicators. With hindsight, it is clear that two other signals carried warnings: exchange rates and debt, especially short-term debt.

Malaysia and Thailand, with their exchange rates effectively fixed to the US dollar, suffered a significant loss of competitiveness as the yen fell against the dollar from mid-1995. Compared with 1990, the Thai baht had held its ground exactly against the dollar by the end of 1996, and the Malaysian ringgit was 8 per cent stronger. Indonesia's and Korea's exchange rates were more flexible—by the end of 1996 their currencies were 22 per cent and 15 per cent down on the dollar compared with 1990—but not flexible enough to prevent the devastating adjustment forced on them in 1997.

212   *Tigers tamed*

Figure 6   Source of bank loans (mid-1997)

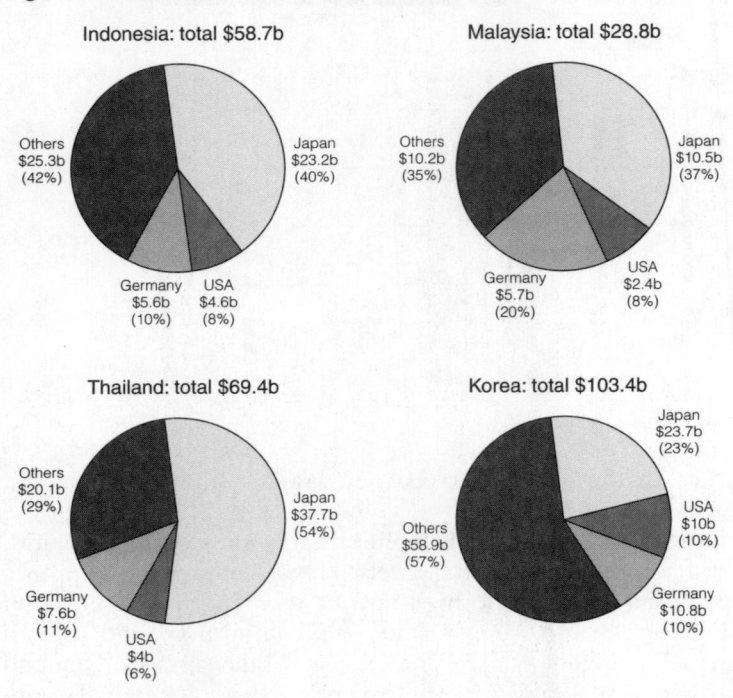

Indonesia: total $58.7b

- Others $25.3b (42%)
- Japan $23.2b (40%)
- Germany $5.6b (10%)
- USA $4.6b (8%)

Malaysia: total $28.8b

- Others $10.2b (35%)
- Japan $10.5b (37%)
- Germany $5.7b (20%)
- USA $2.4b (8%)

Thailand: total $69.4b

- Others $20.1b (29%)
- Japan $37.7b (54%)
- Germany $7.6b (11%)
- USA $4b (6%)

Korea: total $103.4b

- Japan $23.7b (23%)
- USA $10b (10%)
- Others $58.9b (57%)
- Germany $10.8b (10%)

Source: BIS

Figure 7   Foreign debt as a percentage of GNP, 1996

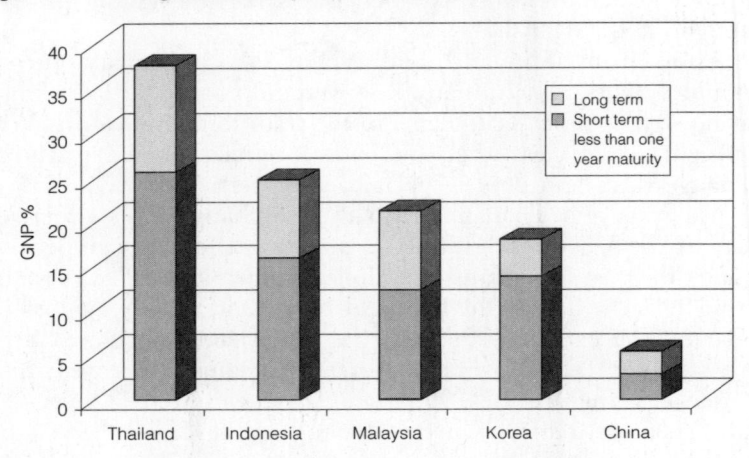

GNP %, for Thailand, Indonesia, Malaysia, Korea, China (Long term; Short term — less than one year maturity)

Source: Asia Pacific Economics Group, World Bank

Figure 8   Economies of size—GDP $b, 1996

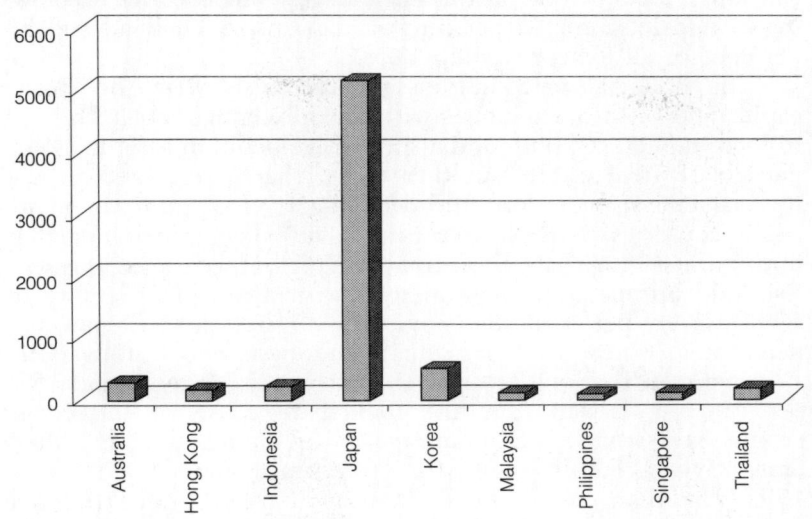

[Bar chart showing GDP in $ billions for: Australia, Hong Kong, Indonesia, Japan, Korea, Malaysia, Philippines, Singapore, Thailand. Japan's bar dominates at over 5000, while all others are well under 1000.]

Source: World Bank

Even the figures for gross external debt did not give any clues, with Thailand, Indonesia and Korea all holding debt at approximately the same levels throughout the decade: around 50 per cent of national output in Indonesia, falling sharply to 38.9 per cent in 1996, around 30 per cent in Malaysia, and around 20 per cent in Thailand.

The most plausible *ex post facto* explanation for the crash, the region's high level of short-term debt, did not reveal itself by increasing during the late 1990s when measured across the region as a whole. Only when debt is examined at the level of individual countries do the warning signs seem obvious. Short-term debt for the five Asian countries most affected—Thailand, Indonesia, Korea, Malaysia and the Philippines—almost doubled from 82 billion in 1993 to $152 billion in 1996.

Japan was by far the single largest source of lending to the region, and to the most troubled economies, although the proportions declined slightly in the mid-1990s. Lending by European banks grew rapidly between 1995 and 1997, making up 43.8 per cent of all loans in mid-1997 compared with Japan's 31.8 per cent. It was European banks, not Japanese, which were most responsible for the last big burst of lending to Asia as a whole.

But Japan remained by far the single largest single lender, accounting in mid-1997 for 54 per cent of all loans to Thailand and 23 per cent of all loans to South Korea.

The financial preconditions for the crisis were the strong capital inflow into economies with fixed exchange rates. This led to loose monetary policy and a speculative boom in asset markets, particularly real estate. Another factor that contributed to the reversal in sentiment was the declining level of profit in many Asian countries before the crash. David Hale points out that during the 1990s the US corporate sector outperformed those of Asia and Europe by a large margin, with a return on equity in 1995 of 19.2 per cent, compared with 2.7 per cent in Japan, 6.3 per cent in Korea, 11.4 per cent in Indonesia and in Singapore, 12.6 per cent in Hong Kong, 14.0 per cent in Malaysia and 15.7 per cent in Taiwan. But the immediate cause of the crisis, economist Warwick McKibbin argues, was the rise in the United States' Federal Funds Rate by 0.25 percentage points on 25 March 1997. This change in the direction of world interest rates triggered a change in direction of world capital flows by causing a fall in world share markets, including those in East Asia (except in Thailand, where the share market had been falling since 1996). The rest is history.

Endnotes

Introduction

1 World Bank, *The East Asian miracle*, Oxford University Press, Oxford, 1993.

1 The end of the Asian miracle

1 Mahathir Mohamad and Shintaro Ishihara, *The voice of Asia*, Kodansha, Tokyo, 1995.
2 'George Soros, Scourge of Asia?', *Fortune*, 29 Sept 1997.
3 *Hong Kong Standard*, 25 Aug 1997, quoting Malaysia's national newsagency Bernama.
4 *Far Eastern Economic Review*, 2 Oct 1997.
5 Jean-Pierre Lehmann, *Greater China and the East Asian Economic Crisis*, http://www.saf.ethz.ch, Swiss Asia Foundation, Lausanne, 1998.
6 Robert Wade and Frank Veneroso, 'The Asian financial crisis: the unrecognized risk of the IMF's Asia package', paper, 1998.
7 Ken Courtis, author interview, January 1998.

2 Japan rises

1 Chalmers Johnson, *MITI and the Japanese miracle*, Tuttle, Tokyo, 1986.
2 ibid.
3 ibid.
4 World Bank, *The East Asian miracle*.
5 Kent Calder, *Strategic capitalism: private business and public purpose in Japanese industrial finance*, Princeton University Press, Princeton, 1993.

6 Eamonn Fingleton, *Blindside—Why Japan is still on track to overtake the US by the Year 2000*, Houghton Mifflin, New York, 1995.
7 Richard Katz, 'Japan's Self-Defeating Trade Policy: Mainframe Economics in a PC World', *Washington Quarterly*, Spring 1997.
8 ibid.
9 McKinsey & Co, quoted in Katz, ibid.
10 This account draws on R. Taggart Murphy, *The weight of the yen*, Norton, New York, 1997.
11 Alexander Kinmont, Dead Fukuzawa Society listserve, 4 April 1997.
12 Richard Cookson, 'A whopping explosion', *Economist*, 28 June 1997.
13 C.Y. Horioka, 'Why is Japan's household saving rate so high? A literature survey', *Journal of the Japanese and International economies*, no. 4, pp. 86–107.
14 Rikki Kersten, *Democracy in postwar Japan: Maruyama Masao and the search for autonomy*, Routledge, London, 1996.

3 Flying geese and tigers

1 Khoo Boo Teik, *Paradoxes of Mahathirism*, Oxford University Press, Oxford, 1995.
2 ibid.
3 ibid.
4 ibid.
5 B. Higgins, *Economic development*, 2nd edn, W.W. Norton, NY, 1968, quoted in Hill, 1996.
6 Saburo Okita, 'Pacific Development and its implications for the world economy', in Saburo Okita, *Japan in the world economy of the 1980s*, Tokyo, University of Tokyo Press, 1989, quoted in Terry.
7 C.H. Kwan, *The rise of Asia and Japan's hollowing out problem*, Nomura Research Institute, Tokyo, 1996.
8 Edith Terry, *The East Asian miracle—one paradigm too many?*, Institute of Southeast Asian Studies, Singapore, 1997.
9 Walter Hatch and Kozo Yamamura, *Asia in Japan's embrace*, Cambridge University Press, Cambridge, 1996.
10 ibid.
11 ibid.
12 J.A.C. Mackie, 'Economic growth in the ASEAN region: the political underpinnings', in Helen Hughes, ed., *Achieving Industrialization in East Asia*, Cambridge University Press, Cambridge, 1988.
13 Robert Wade, *Governing the market*, Princeton University Press, Princeton, 1990.
14 ibid.
15 ibid.
16 World Bank, *The East Asian miracle*.
17 Milton Friedman and Rose Friedman, *Free to choose*, Pelican, Harmondsworth, 1980.
18 James C.F. Wang, *Comparative Asian politics: power, policy, and change*, Prentice Hall, Englewood Cliffs, 1994.

19 Quoted in Wang.
20 Lee Kwan Yew, 'Culture is destiny', *Foreign Affairs*, March/April 1994.
21 Jim Rohwer, *Asia rising*, Nicolas Brealey, London, 1996.
22 Rachel van Elkan, 'Singapore's development strategy', in *Singapore, A case study in rapid development*, Kenneth Bercuson, ed., International Monetary Fund, Washington, 1995.
23 Linda Y.C. Lim, 'Chinese economic activity in Southeast Asia: an introductory review', in Linda Y.C. Lim and L.A. Peter Gosling, eds, *The Chinese in Southeast Asia, Volume I: Ethnicity and Economic Activity*, Singapore, Maruzen Asia, 1983.
24 Christopher Lingle, *Singapore's authoritarian capitalism*, Edicions Sirocco, Barcelona, 1996.
25 ibid.
26 Hal Hill, *The Indonesian economy since 1966*, Cambridge University Press, Cambridge, 1996.
27 ibid.
28 ibid.
29 World Bank, *The East Asian miracle*.
30 Michael Sarel, 'Growth in East Asia: what we can and cannot infer from it', *Conference on productivity and growth*, Reserve Bank of Australia, 1995.
31 ibid.
32 Daniel A. Bell, 'After the tsunami', *New Republic*, 9 March 1998.

4 Japan stumbles

1 Patrick Smith, *Japan: a reinterpretation*, Pantheon Books, New York, 1997.
2 ibid.
3 Kwan, *The rise of Asia*.
4 Moody's Investors Service, 'Comments on rating implications of recent Japanese market developments', paper, Tokyo, 17 Jan. 1997.
5 Courtis and Fisher quoted in Christopher Wood, *The bubble economy: the Japanese economic collapse*, Tuttle, Tokyo, 1993.
6 *New York Times*, 22 Feb. 1998
7 Paul Krugman, *Japan's trap*, Paul Krugman homepage, May 1998.
8 Ron Bevacqua, Dead Fukuzawa Society listserve, Feb. 1998.
9 Rudiger Dornbusch, *Far Eastern Economic Review*, 26 Feb. 1998.

5 Meltdown

1 Author interview, February 1998.
2 Peter G. Warr, 'Thailand: what went wrong?', in Ross McLeod and Ross Garnaut, eds, *The East Asian crisis: from being a miracle to needing one*, Routledge, London, 1998.
3 Ramon Moreno, 'Lessons from Thailand', *Economic Letter*, Federal Reserve Board of San Francisco, vol. 97, no. 33, Nov. 1997.

4 ibid.
5 Author interview, Feb. 1998.
6 Paul Krugman, 'Bahtulism: Who poisoned Asia's currency markets?', *Slate*, http://www.slate.com, 14 Aug. 1997.
7 Premachandra Athukorala, 'Malaysia', *The East Asian crisis: from being a miracle to needing one*.
8 Political and Econonomic Risk Consultancy, *Country Risk Report: Malaysia*, 4 Nov. 1997.
9 Song Ligang, 'China', *The East Asian crisis: from being a miracle to needing one*.
10 Narongchai Akrasanee, National Press Club, Canberra, 24 Feb. 1998.
11 Political and Economic Risk Consultancy, *Country Risk Report: Singapore*, 4 Nov. 1997.
12 Nikko Research Center, *Capital Trends*, vol. 3, no. 3, Feb. 1998.

6 Korea crashes

1 Heather Smith, 'South Korea', *The East Asian crisis: from being a miracle to needing one*.
2 Author interview, 26 March 1997.
3 Jongryn Mo and Chung-in Moon, 'Democracy and the ROK Economic crisis', *Democracy and the Korean economy*, Chung-in Moon and Jongryn Mo, eds, Hoover Institution Press, forthcoming.

7 Indonesia implodes

1 Hamish McDonald, *Suharto's Indonesia*, Fontana, 1980, citing American scholar Benedict Anderson.
2 Michael van Langenberg, from a longer version of an article in the *Australian*, 13 Aug. 1996.
3 Harold Crouch, speaking at a seminar on Indonesia, Australian National University, Canberra, 26 Feb. 1998.
4 Ross H. McLeod, 'Indonesia', *The East Asian crisis: from being a miracle to needing one*.
5 Ross Garnaut, speaking at a Westpac International Exporter's Summer School on 'Strategic issues affecting business in regional markets', Australian National University, Canberra, 22 Feb. 1998.
6 Hal Hill, speaking at a seminar on Indonesia, Australian National University, Canberra, 26 Feb. 1998.
7 Patrick Walters, *Australian*, 21 Feb. 1998.
8 ibid.
9 Crouch, Indonesia seminar.
10 ibid.
11 *Wall Street Journal*, 10 Feb. 1998.
12 *Wall Street Journal*, 23 Feb. 1998.
13 *Wall Street Journal*, 11 Feb. 1998.
14 The IMF and the United States emphatically deny that this was

official policy, but there is no doubt that this view was held by a number of key officials. Confidential interviews.
15 Paul Kelly, *Australian*, 16 March 1998.

8 Taming global capital

1 Steven Radelet and Jeffrey Sachs, 'The Onset of the East Asian financial crisis', draft paper, February 1998.
2 Charles Wyplosz, 'Globalized financial markets and financial crises', paper, Graduate Institute of International Studies, Geneva, March 1998.
3 Warwick McKibbin, 'The crisis in Asia: an empirical assessment', paper, Research School of Pacific Studies, Australian National University, 1998.
4 Stanley Fischer, 'The Asian crisis: a view from the IMF', speech to Bankers' Association for Foreign Trade, Washington DC, 22 Jan. 1998.
5 Author interview, May 1998.
6 Martin Feldstein, 'Refocusing the IMF', *Foreign Affairs*, March/April 1998.
7 Paul Krugman, 'The Myth of Asia's Miracle', *Foreign Affairs*, November/December 1994.
8 Quoted in Martin Wolf, 'The deflation nightmare', *Financial Times*, 24 Feb. 1998.
9 David Hale, 'A new financial crisis? It's only natural', *Weekend Australian*, 21 Feb. 1998.
10 Alan Greenspan, testimony to House Banking Committee, 30 Jan 1998.
11 Walden Bello, 'The end of the Asian miracle', *Nation*, 12–19 Jan. 1998.

9 The economic consequences of the crash

1 *Financial Times*, 10 March 1998.
2 Ligang Liu et al., *Asian competitive devaluations*, Institute for International Economics, Working Paper 98–2, Jan. 1998.
3 Long Youngtu, speaking at a Westpac International Exporter's Summer School on 'Strategic issues affecting business in regional markets', Australian National University, Canberra, 22 Feb. 1998.
4 Alan Greenspan, testimony to House Banking Committee, 24 Feb. 1998.
5 David Levy, *Financial Times*, 2 Jan. 1998.
6 Paul Keating, 'The perilous moment: Indonesia, Australia and the Asian crisis', public lecture at the University of New South Wales 25 March 1998.

10 After the miracle

1 This section is based on a talk by J.A.A. Stockwin, 'Reflections on the Asian model of democracy', at the Deutsches Institut für Japanstudien in Tokyo, 17 April 1997, later published by the Institute of Social Science, University of Tokyo in January 1998 under the title 'Is there such a thing as the Asian model of Democracy?'
2 J.A.A. Stockwin, 'Beyond the Asian model of democracy?', *Japanstudien*, no. 10, Deutsches Institut für Japanstudien, 1998 (forthcoming).

Bibliography and sources

Much of the material here is based on interviews during my two and a half years reporting on Japan and Korea for the *Australian* and on my return to Canberra in February 1998. Endnotes have been kept to a minimum. Quotations not otherwise attributed come from interviews or from news reports, which have not been referenced unless they offered unique information or special insight. News sources include the *Australian*, the *Australian Financial Review*, the *Daily Mainichi*, the *Daily Yomiuri*, the *Economist*, the *Far Eastern Economic Review*, the *Financial Times*, *Foreign Affairs*, the *Japan Times*, the *New Straits Times*, the *Straits Times*, the *International Herald Tribune* and the *Wall Street Journal*. Researching this book and keeping pace with the debate would have been far more difficult without the Internet. Especially useful were the Asia Crisis Homepage of Nouriel Roubini at the Stern School of Business, New York University and the Dead Fukuzawa Society listserve. Also invaluable were three seminars on aspects of the crisis at the Australian National University, Canberra, in February, March and May 1998.

Amsden, Alice H. *Asia's Next Giant*, Oxford University Press, Oxford, 1989
Beasley, W.G. *The Rise of Modern Japan*, Tuttle, Tokyo, 1990
Bello, Walden 'The end of the Asian miracle', *Nation*, 12–19 Jan. 1998
Calder, Kent, *Strategic Capitalism: Private Business and Public purpose in Japanese Industrial Finance*, Princeton University Press, Princeton, 1993
Chen, Edward K.Y. 'The total factor productivity debate: determinants of economic growth in East Asia', *Asia Pacific Literature*, vol. 11, no. 1, May 1997
Clifford, Mark L. *Troubled Tiger: Businessmen, Bureaucrats, and Generals in South Korea*, M.E. Sharpe, Armonk, 1994
Dale, Peter N. *The Myth of Japanese Uniqueness*, St Martin's Press, New York, 1990

Eckert, Carter J. et al. *Korea Old and New: A History*, Harvard University Press, Cambridge, 1990
Fallows, James *Looking at the Sun: The Rise of the New East Asian Economic and Political System*, Vintage Books, New York, 1995
FitzGerald, Stephen *Is Australia an Asian Country?*, Allen & Unwin, St Leonards, 1997
Hartcher, Peter, *The Ministry*, HarperCollins, Sydney, 1997
Hatch, Walter and Yamamura, Kozo *Asia in Japan's Embrace*, Cambridge University Press, Cambridge, 1996
Hill, Hal *The Indonesian Economy Since 1966*, Cambridge University Press, Cambridge, 1996
Johnson, Chalmers, *MITI and the Japanese Miracle*, Tuttle, Tokyo, 1986
Kersten, Rikki *Democracy in Postwar Japan: Maruyama Masao and the Search for Autonomy*, Routledge, London, 1996
Khoo Boo Teik, *Paradoxes of Mahathirism*, Oxford University Press, Oxford, 1995
Kindleberger, Charles P. *Manias, Panics, and Crashes*, 3rd edn, John Wiley & Sons, New York, 1996
Krugman, Paul *Pop Internationalism*, MIT Press, Cambridge, 1997
Lingle, Christopher *Singapore's Authoritarian Capitalism*, Edicions Sirocco, Barcelona, 1996
McCormack, Gavan *The Emptiness of Japanese Affluence*, M.E. Sharpe, Armonk, 1996
McDonald, Hamish *Suharto's Indonesia*, Fontana, 1980
McGregor, Richard *Japan Swings: Politics, Culture and Sex in the New Japan*, Allen & Unwin, St Leonards, 1996
McLeod, Ross and Garnaut, Ross *The East Asian Crisis: From Being a Miracle to Needing One*, Routledge, London, 1998
Mahathir, Mohamad and Ishihara, Shintaro, *The Voice of Asia*, Kodansha, Tokyo, 1995
Murphy, R. Taggart *The Weight of the Yen*, Norton, New York, 1997
Ravenhill, John, ed. *The Political Economy of East Asia*, Edward Elgar Publishing, Aldershot, 1995
Reischauer, Edwin O. *The Japanese Today*, Tuttle, Tokyo, 1988
Rohwer, Jim, *Asia Rising*, Nicolas Brealey, London, 1996
Radelet, Steven and Sachs, Jeffrey 'The onset of the East Asian financial crisis', draft paper, February 1998
Schwarz, Adam, *A Nation in Waiting: Indonesia in the 1990s*, Allen & Unwin, St Leonards, 1994
Smith, Patrick *Japan: A Reinterpretation*, Pantheon Books, New York, 1997
Stockwin, J.A.A. 'Is there such a thing as the Asian model of democracy?', Paper F-67, Institute of Social Science, University of Tokyo, January 1998
—— 'Beyond the Asian model of democracy?', *Japanstudien*, no. 10, Deutsches Institut für Japanstudien, 1998 (forthcoming)
Terry, Edith, *The East Asian Miracle—One Paradigm Too Many?*, Institute of Southeast Asian Studies, Singapore, 1997
van Elkan, Rachel, 'Singapore's development strategy', in Kenneth

Bercuson, ed., *Singapore: A Case Study in Rapid Development*, IMF, Washington, 1995

Wade, Robert *Governing the Market*, Princeton University Press, Princeton, 1990

Wang, James C.F. *Comparative Asian Politics: Power, Policy, and Change*, Prentice Hall, Englewood Cliffs, 1994

Wood, Christopher *The Bubble Economy: The Japanese Economic Collapse*, Tuttle, Tokyo, 1993.

World Bank *The East Asian Miracle*, Oxford University Press, Oxford, 1993

Wyplosz, Charles 'Globalized financial markets and financial crises', paper, Graduate Institute of International Studies, Geneva, March 1998

Index

Aizawa, Miharu, 83
Amsden, Alice, 50, 56
Anwar Ibrahim, 107, 109–10, 169
Argentina, 117–18
Asia Pacific Economic Cooperation (APEC) forum, 187
Asian economic crisis
  see East Asian economic crisis, 193
Asian economic miracle, 1–2, 193–6, 206–7
  see also Asian model
Asian model, 3–5, 12–14, 17, 30, 49–54, 199–207
Asian values, 43, 202–6
  influence of crisis on, 18
  Lee Kuan Yew on, 62–4
Association of South-East Asian Nations (ASEAN), 187, 191
Athukorala Premachandra, 109
Australia, 186

Bambang Trihatmodjo, 144, 152, 154
Bangkok International Banking Facility, 99
Beasley, W.G., 24
Bello, Walden, 178–9

Bevacqua, Ron, 89
Bhagwati, Jagdish, 196
Brazil, 117–18
Bretton Woods system, 25

Calder, Kent, 31–2
Camdessus, Michel, 146
chaebol (Korean conglomerates), 122–5, 127, 130–1, 133, 135
Chavalit Yongchaiyudh, 102, 103
China, 95, 111, 113–14, 175
  and East Asian crisis, 17, 19–20
  and regional security 189–91
  exchange rate, 95, 113–14, 181–2
  political system, 203
  response to East Asian crisis 180–4
Chrysanthemum Club, 9
Chuan Leekpai, 104
Chung Ju-yung, 130
Chung Tae-soo, 124
Clinton, Bill, 88
Cole, David, 154
Condon, Tim, 109
Confucianism, 44
contagion, 159
  see also financial panic
Cookson, Richard, 41

Index

Crouch, Harold, 138, 140–1, 148–9
currencies *see* exchange rates
currency board, Indonesia, 152–5
Czech Republic, 117

deflation, 18–21, 79, 90, 173–5
Japan, 19, 78–9, 86
democracy (in East Asia), 18, 70, 202–6
developmental state, 30–4, 37, 50–1, 155, 201 206
see also Asian model
Dibb, Paul, 190–1
Dornbusch, Rudiger, 87, 90

East Asia
  economic development, 11–12, 15, 28–9, 45–70
  economic prospects, 4, 21, 198–9
  political influences on development, 54–5
  security, 189–92
East Asian development model *see* Asian model
East Asian economic crisis
  implications, 8, 17–21, 167, 180–92, 191, 193–207
  origins, 1, 16, 159–79, 208–14
Economist, 29
Estonia, 117
exchange rate speculation, 8
exchange rates, 8, 15–17, 51–2, 77, 95–101, 105–6, 160–7, 170–3, 198
  see also individual countries

Feldstein, Martin, 168
feminism, 201–2
financial liberalisation, 161
financial panic, 164, 170, 177
  and East Asian crisis, 159–62, 167
Fingleton, Eamonn, 34
Fischer, Stanley, 163

Fisher, Irving, 79
flying geese theory, 48–9, 52

Garnaut, Ross, 146
globalisation, 176–7, 195
Great Depression, 175
Greenspan, Alan, 16, 80, 174, 176–7, 184–5, 196

Habibie, B.J., 48, 67, 137, 140, 155–6
Hale, David, 19, 129
Halla Group, 127
Hanbo Iron & Steel Company, 120, 123–5
Hanke, Steven, 151–4, 156
Harmoko, 140
Hasan, Mohamad 'Bob', 157
Hashimoto, Ryutaro, 71–2, 79
Hatch, Walter, 52
high technology international financial system, 16, 176–7, 196
Hill, Hal, 66, 142–3, 156
Hokkaido Takushoku Bank, 81, 83
Hong Kong
  and East Asian crisis, 19, 111–13, 181, 197
  economic development, 61
  economy, 208–14
  exchange rate, 19–20, 111–12
  political system, 203
  share market, 111–12, 117
Horioka, Charles, 41
Howard, John, 186
Hyundai, 127, 130

individualism, 199–202
Indonesia
  Chinese in, 140–1, 143, 147–9
  economic crisis, 116, 137–58, 169
  economic development, 65–7
  economy, 208–14

exchange rate, 142–5, 152–5
inflation, 142, 144–7, 149
military 140–1
political system, 203
pribumi (indigenous Indonesians), 147–9
refugees, 111, 116, 149
response to economic crisis, 157, 191, 197–8
social consequences of crisis, 145, 147–9
industrial policy, 32, 36
see also developmental state
inflation, 86, 173
interest rates *see* monetary policy
International Bank Credit Analyst, 175
International Monetary Fund (IMF), 107, 110, 195
1997 annual meeting, 6
and East Asian crisis, 14, 161–70, 178–9
and Indonesia, 14, 139, 140, 144–7, 149–58
and Thailand, 102–4
and Korea, 125–8, 132

Japan
and East Asia, 9, 11, 12, 14, 15, 47, 53, 77, 87
and East Asian crisis, 1, 10, 20, 26–7
and Korea, 122–3
and Thailand, 95
and US, 26–7
Bank of Japan, 32, 83
deflation, 78–9
economic crisis, 88
economic development, 22–42
economic policy 84–6
economy, 71–93, 96, 174, 208–14
economy (1990s), 34, 71–91
exchange rate, 11, 15–16, 20, 25, 75–7, 88, 97, 129
financial system, 38–40, 78–83, 93

Ministry of Construction, 73
Ministry of Finance, 31, 32, 38–9, 85
Ministry of International Trade and Industry (MITI), 22–5, 30–2, 39, 48
response to economic crisis, 17, 169, 191, 192, 196–7
saving, 11, 40–1
security, 189
society and culture, 41–4, 85, 91–3
Japanese miracle, 9, 33, 74
see also Japanese model
Japanese model, 29–30, 34, 48–9, 56, 89, 193
Johnson, Chalmers, 9, 29–31, 33, 52

Katz, Richard, 37
Kennedy, Paul, 26
Keynes, John Maynard, 207
Khoo, Boo Teik, 45–7
Kia Motor Corporation, 125
Kim Dae-jung, 132–4
Kim Hyun-chul, 125
Kim Jong-il, 171
Kim Jong-pil, 134
Kim Young-sam, 58, 119–21, 123–5, 130–1, 134
Kindleberger, Charles, 90, 166, 168, 177
Kinmont, Alexander, 35, 40
Koll, Jesper, 82
Koo, Richard, 82
Korea
and China, 182
economic development, 55–8, 121–3
economy, 208–14
exchange rate, 56–7, 82, 125–8
financial system, 124–9
political system, 203
politics, 119–21, 132–6

Index

response to economic crisis, 17, 119–36, 191, 197–8
Korean Confederation of Trade Unions, 135
Krugman, Paul, 86, 105, 170–2
Kwan, C.H., 77, 95, 99, 172

Latin America, 117–18
Lau, Lawrence, 172
Lee In-hyung, 129
Lee Kuan Yew, 61, 62, 155
Lehmann, Jean-Pierre, 13
Li Lanqing, 180
Lim, Linda, 63
Lincoln, Edward, 84
Lingle, Christopher, 62–3
Long Youngtu, 181–2

MacArthur, Douglas, 73
McDonald, Hamish, 139
McKibbin, Warwick, 162, 185, 188–9, 214
Mackie, J.A.C. (Jamie), 54–5
McLeod, Ross, 142–5
Mahathir Mohamad, 9
  economic doctrines, 45–7, 106–11, 193
  on economic crisis, 6–8, 45, 169, 196
Malaysia, 53
  economic crisis, 106–11, 169
  economic development, 64–5
  economy, 208–14
  exchange rate, 108–10
  political system, 203
  response to economic crisis, 191, 197
  see also Mahathir Mohamad
markets, role of, 14, 35, 52, 194–6
Maruyama, Masao, 43–4
Mexico, 117–18
Ministry of International Trade and Industry (MITI) see Japan, Ministry of International Trade and Industry

Mitsuzuka, Hiroshi, 81, 84
Mo Jongryon, 135
monetary (interest rate) policy, 18–20, 74–6, 86, 128, 144, 156, 162, 166, 186, 189, 198
Moody's Investors Service, 78, 81, 88, 113, 116, 165
Moon Chung-in, 135
Murphy, R. Taggart, 39

Nakatani, Iwao, 36
Narongchai Akrasanee, 94, 100–1, 105, 114

Ogawa, Alicia, 79
Ohga, Norio, 87
oil shock (1973), 23
Organisation for Economic Cooperation and Development (OECD), 131

Park Chung-hee, 56, 122
Peregrine Investments, 112
Petronas Twin Towers, Kuala Lumpur, 108
Philippines
  and East Asian crisis, 114–15
  economy, 213
  exchange rate, 114
  response to economic crisis, 191
Plaza Accord, 97
Political and Economic Risk Consultancy, 109, 115

Radelet, Steven and Sachs, Jeffrey, 159, 164–7, 170
Reischauer, Edwin, 9
revisionists, 9–10, 26, 34–6, 52, 68
Rohwer, Jim, 43
Rubin, Robert, 88, 156
Rukmana, Hardijanti (Tutut), 157
Russia, 117–18, 187

Sachs, Jeffrey, 163–4
  see also Radelet and Sachs
Sarel, Michael, 68
Sato, Koko, 71–2
Sayle, Murray, 200
Shanghai, 183
Singapore
  and East Asian crisis, 115–16
  economic development, 61–4
  economy, 208–14
  political system, 203
  response to economic crisis, 198
Smith, Heather, 128
Smith, Patrick, 9, 73
Sodedradjad, 151–2
Soeharto, 65–7, 137–48, 150–2
Soros, George, 134, 177–8
  Mahathir on, 45, 47, 108
  on East Asian economic crisis, 6–8, 193, 196
Soviet Union, 171
Stockwin, J.A.A. (Arthur), 202–5
Sukarno, 65, 137
Summers, Lawrence, 84

Taiwan
  and East Asian crisis 115–17, 198
  economic development, 58–61
  economy, 208–14
  exchange rate, 112
  political system, 203
Tasker, Peter, 36, 76
Terry, Edith, 49
Thailand
  Bank of Thailand, 97–8, 100–2, 104
  economic crisis, 94–108
  economic development, 67
  economy, 208–14
  exchange rate, 95, 97–106, 141
  political system, 203
  response to economic crisis, 17, 191, 197–8

Tokuyo City Bank, 81, 83
Tsang, Donald, 113
Tutut see Rukmana, Hardijanti

Ukraine, 117
United States, 134
  and East Asian crisis, 178–9
  and Indonesia, 146, 149–50, 156
  and International Monetary Fund, 103, 167, 179
  and Japan, 73–4, 76, 83–5, 87
  and Korea, 134
  monetary policy, 214
  response to East Asian crisis, 17, 20, 184–6, 192
  security, 189–90
  share markets, 111, 184–6

van Elkan, Rachel, 63
van Langenberg, Michael, 139
Veneroso, Frank, 15

Wade, Robert, 15, 58–9
Walters, Patrick, 148
Warr, Peter, 95
western culture, 199–202
Wiranto, 140
women, role of in East Asia, 201–2
World Bank (International Bank for Reconstruction and Development)
  East Asian crisis, 146, 178
  The East Asian Miracle, 31, 49, 50–1, 56, 59, 60, 68–9
Wyplosz, Charles, 159–62

Xie, Andy, 182

Yamaichi Securities, 81, 83
Yamamura, Kozo, 52
Yao, Y.C., 61